MODERN

POETRY

AFTER

MODERNISM

# MODERN
# POETRY
# AFTER
# MODERNISM

James Longenbach

New York    Oxford  •  Oxford University Press    1997

Oxford University Press

Oxford   New York
Athens   Auckland   Bangkok   Bogota   Bombay   Buenos Aires
Calcutta   Cape Town   Dar es Salaam   Delhi   Florence   Hong Kong
Istanbul   Karachi   Kuala Lumpur   Madras   Madrid   Melbourne
Mexico City   Nairobi   Paris   Singapore   Taipei   Tokyo   Toronto   Warsaw

and associated companies in
Berlin   Ibadan

Published by Oxford University Press, Inc.
198 Madison Avenue, New York, New York 10016

Oxford is a registered trademark of Oxford University Press

Library of Congress Cataloging-in-Publication Data

Longenbach, James.
Modern poetry after modernism / by James Longenbach.
p.   cm.
Includes bibliographical references and index.
ISBN 0-19-510177-4 (cloth); —ISBN 0-19-510178-2 (pbk.)
1. American poetry—20th century—History and criticism—Theory,
etc.   2. Postmodernism (Literature)—United States.   I. Title.
PS325.L66 1997
811'.509113—dc21                                   96-45288

1 3 5 7 9 8 6 4 2
Printed in the United States of America
on acid-free paper

FOR
A. WALTON LITZ

# PREFACE

This book was prompted by my sense that the stories we usually tell about American poetry cannot account for Elizabeth Bishop's career; it grew from my realization that those stories (usually turning on some sense of formal "breakthrough") cannot make good sense of most of Bishop's contemporaries. Like every poet of her generation, Bishop was keenly aware of what was at stake in writing after modernism; but she did not reduce the modern poets' various and contradictory qualities into an easily opposed program. Her career consequently exhibits no "breakthrough" but extends aspects of modernism that other writers suppressed or neglected to see. The poets I've associated with Bishop share her open relationship to their immediate past. They also share her attitude toward poetic form: whether it's called formal or free, open or closed, form is for these poets what constitutes their utterance, not something that needs to be (or could be) broken through.

Whatever their similarities, these poets are also highly idiosyncratic. Each chapter of this book (except for the first) is shaped in response to the distinctive problems of a particular poet's career. And while the chapters are linked by common concerns, anyone wanting to read only about Wilbur or Ashbery will find my treatments of them pretty much self-contained. Anyone wanting a tidy narrative about American poetry after modernism might be disappointed. My goal is not so much to offer a story to replace the "breakthrough" narrative as to explore the different ways in which poets have harnessed their modernist past; I'd like to make it harder to rely on seductively oppositional accounts of twentieth-century literary history. While every generation of writers inevitably seeks to distinguish itself from an earlier one, it seems to me that some versions of our past are more useful—more responsive, more generous—than others.

Inasmuch as this book is about postmodernism in American poetry, it takes the word *postmodern* as literally as possible. When the word is applied to poetry at all, it usually describes a particular school of poetry after modernism; a poet's place in that school is signaled by the use of certain ideologically charged formal strategies. I use the word *postmodern* to describe any poet who writes with a self-conscious sense of coming after modernism; from my perspective, poetic form has no inevitable relationship to any ideological position. Consequently, the cast of characters most often associated with postmodernism is not prominent here. A variety of postmodernisms must be discriminated, since the terms of one will not always account for the development of another: my terms are conceived in response to the circumscribed yet abundant world of American poetry.

I've tried to translate the parameters of my own taste into the widest possible account of that world, one that may honor poets as different as Wilbur and Ashbery. If I haven't strayed from the more-or-less dominant figures of the last fifty years, I've tried to suggest that the mainstream of postmodern poetry is, like that of modern poetry, more strange and equivocal than we might imagine. The poets I've selected seem to me representative in that, however distinctive, they have not been invested heavily in distinctions. Resisting the need to balance enthusiasms with antagonisms, they have welcomed the diversity of their contemporaries and refused to limit the possibilities for poetry to a narrow set of formal strategies or an exclusive vision of their literary past. Most simply put, my goal is to provide a way of appreciating the variety of poetries written in our time—without necessarily requiring us to choose between them.

Writing this book, my greatest debt has been to the poets who responded so generously to my discussions of their work: they became the best critics I could hope for. I want particularly to remember Amy Clampitt, who, shortly before her death, offered several important additions to my argument. I'm also grateful for the help of Robert Boyers, Bonnie Costello, Frederick Crews, Barbara Jordan, Susan Meigs, Adam

Parkes, Christopher Ricks, John Shoptaw, and Willard Spiegelman. Langdon Hammer not only read this book as it grew, page by page, but fueled my interest with his own ongoing study of American poetry. Joanna Scott's imagination sustained me when my own failed.

The Guggenheim Foundation and Worcester College, Oxford, provided time to write, and I'm grateful to David Bradshaw and Richard Smethurst for making my stay in Oxford so memorable. My research assistants, Mary Kelkenberg, Alyssa O'Brien, and Newell Young, never failed to find the material I needed. And the librarians of Amherst College, Vassar College, the Walnut Hill School, the Henry E. Huntington Library, the Rosenbach Museum and Library, the Beinecke Rare Book and Manuscript Library at Yale University, and the Berg Collection of the New York Public Library helped me to locate many uncollected and unpublished texts. Earlier versions of several chapters of the book have appeared in *American Literary History, ELH, Denver Quarterly, The Gettysburg Review, Salmagundi, The Southern Review, Southwest Review,* and *The Future of Modernism,* ed. Hugh Witemeyer (Ann Arbor, 1997).

The dedication records my debt to a critic who, more than any other I've known, embodies the qualities of openness and generosity that I've tried in this book to document and, however fitfully, to emulate.

# CONTENTS

MODERN

POETRY

AFTER

MODERNISM

# WHAT WAS
# POSTMODERN
# POETRY?

*Modern poetry holds in solution contradictory tendencies which, isolated and exaggerated in postmodernism, look startlingly opposed both to each other and to the earlier stages of modernism.* This sentence was almost written by Randall Jarrell. Where Jarrell said *romantic* and *modern*, I've substituted *modern* and *postmodern*, and the resulting sentence not only offers a good way to begin thinking about the vicissitudes of American poetry over the last several decades; it also reminds us that those vicissitudes follow a pattern we've seen before.[1]

The words I've put in Jarrell's mouth are his own. Jarrell was by no means the first person to use the word *postmodern* (it appeared as early as 1926 in discussions of modernist theology); nor was he the earliest poet to feel that literary modernism had slipped into the past: "It is now possible," wrote Laura Riding and Robert Graves in 1928, "to reach a position where the modernist movement itself can be looked at with historical (as opposed to contemporary) sympathy."[2] But by rethinking the vexed relationship of romantic and modern poetry, Jarrell was clearing the ground for the first fully meaningful discussion of poetry written in response to the work of T. S. Eliot, Wallace Stevens, and Marianne Moore: "Who could have believed," he asked in 1942, "that modernism would collapse so fast?"³ Today, more than half a century later, our sense of modernism continues to change, but our characterizations of postmodern poetry too often depend on outmoded notions of modernism. While most readers of modern poetry have long since rejected the narratives supplied by New Critics like Allen Tate or Cleanth Brooks, the same readers often cling to those narratives in order to exaggerate the formal and political idiosyncracy of postmodern poetry.

One version of that exaggeration is evident in this passage from John Ashbery's "The System."

> For many weeks you have been exploring what seemed to be a profitable way of doing. You discovered that there was a fork in the road, so first you followed what seemed to be the less promising, or at any rate the more obvious, of the two branches until you felt that you had a good idea of where it led. Then you returned to investigate the more tangled way, and for a time its intricacies seemed to promise a more complex and therefore a more practical goal for you, one that could be picked up in any number of ways so that all its faces or applications could be thoroughly scrutinized. And in so doing you began to realize that the two branches were joined together again, farther ahead; that this place of joining was indeed the end, and that it was the very place you set out from, whose intolerable mixture of reality and fantasy had started you on the road which has now come full circle.

Having recognized these sentences as a rewriting of Robert Frost's "The Road Not Taken," should we then say that Frost believes that "all the difference" depends on our ability to choose between two different paths, while Ashbery shows such a choice to be specious, revealing difference to be a condition of our existence rather than the result of conscious decisions? That's the story Marjorie Perloff tells about these two poets, but it depends on our reading Frost as a poet of greeting-card wisdom rather than the poet who, in "The Road Not Taken," is like Ashbery undermining easy ideas of difference and suggesting that we live in some kind of indeterminacy.⁴ The speaker of Frost's poem wants to believe that the choice of one path over another has made all the difference, but his equivocations reveal that the paths make no difference at all.

> Then took the other, as just as fair,
> And having perhaps the better claim,
> Because it was grassy and wanted wear;
> Though as for that the passing there
> Had worn them really about the same.

It's tempting to think of Ashbery's prose as an advance on Frost's tetrameters, but once we recognize the equivocations of "The Road Not

Taken" ("as just as fair," "perhaps the better," "really about the same"), then Ashbery's "System" seems more like a repetition of Frost's skepticism than a turn away from it.

Those of us who *tell* the stories of postmodern poetry are usually more invested in polemical distinctions than those of us who *live* them. Yet the most common story was supplied at least in part by the poet whose career it justifies. Reduced to its barest outline, the story goes like this: after writing several books of highly praised New Critical well-wrought urns (objective and impersonal), Robert Lowell understood that poetry could be fragmentary, subjective, personal, and the result was *Life Studies*, a watershed in twentieth-century poetry. *Life Studies* itself tells this story; the volume begins with formal poems that recall the high-church values of Lowell's earlier work, moving on to the free verse anxieties of poems about his family and his mental collapses. Lowell sometimes spoke of this movement as a "breakthrough back into life," as if free verse were not one kind of form among many but a movement beyond the merely literary.[5] Psychic and political health, it seems, could be achieved by breaking the pentameter.

This "breakthrough" narrative offers a narrow and inadequate reading even of Lowell's career. But in the "Age of Lowell," as Irvin Ehrenpreis dubbed it, readers found a similar aesthetic "breakthrough" (often accompanied by a psychological "breakdown") in the careers of many of Lowell's contemporaries, especially John Berryman and Theodore Roethke: a poet's status was often measured by the strength of what one reviewer called, apropos of Roethke, "the famous 'breakthrough' that it is the custom to talk about."[6] The story of Lowell's life in poetry became, as he said in his late poem "For John Berryman," the story of a generation.

> Really we had the same life,
> the generic one
> our generation offered.

Berryman might have approved of these lines, for in his later years he sometimes agreed with Lowell's sense of the limitations of Eliot's modernism. Berryman said this about the structure of *Homage to Mistress Bradstreet*: "let's have narrative, and at least one dominant personality, and no fragmentation! In short, let us have something spectacularly NOT *The Waste Land*." And this about the structure of *The Dream Songs*: "The reason I call it one poem is the result of my strong disagreement with Eliot's line—the impersonality of poetry."[7]

More is at stake here than one generation's need to distinguish itself from an earlier one. Inasmuch as there is a common theory of post-modern American poetry, the "breakthrough" narrative underwrites it, ostensibly explaining the careers not only of Lowell and Berryman but of W. S. Merwin, Frank O'Hara, Adrienne Rich, and many more recent poets. In *From Modern to Contemporary* James Breslin employs the story of Lowell's career—emphasizing its implicit equation of modernism with formalism, mere craft, and stultifying hierarchy—to account for the "breakthrough" of American poetry at large: "At this moment of crisis, poetry once again became disruptive—critical of its culture, of its immediate past, of itself; by way of repudiating orthodox modernism, American poetry once again became modern, 'of the present.' "[8] Modernism emerges from this narrative as a movement whose poems are easily characterized as traditional, impersonal, and hierarchical. And though the narrative has been useful, our continuing faith in it depends (to put it somewhat simply) on a reading of *The Waste Land* as a unified and impersonal poem—something Cleanth Brooks could muster fifty years ago but which is difficult to sustain, given that our knowledge of Eliot's career has increased along with our suspicion of values like unity and impersonality.

Now that Lowell's poetry has lost some of its prestige, the "breakthrough" narrative is no longer invoked quite so explicitly as it was two decades ago; nevertheless, its assumptions are perpetuated by many poets and critics who, whatever their differences, agree that a great deal of cultural weight depends on the choice of poetic form. More often than not, apparently opposed formal means are enlisted in defense of identical social ends: while some readers maintain that a rhymed and metered poem "is political in the sense that it is separating itself from the people," others insist that "by removing meter and rhyme" from poetry, poets are "alienating the audience."[9] An easy confluence of formal and social vision is assumed, and almost any new development in American poetry is heralded at the expense of a previous "breakthrough," now seen to be either too timid or too severe.

In contrast, readers who take the longest view of contemporary poetry have little use for the oversimplifications characteristic of the "breakthrough" narrative (though it is telling that, until recently, Harold Bloom and Helen Vendler have had little to say about Eliot at all). Robert Pinsky's *The Situation of Poetry*, published in 1976, powerfully undermined the logic of the "breakthrough" by stressing the rhetoricity of all poetic forms, however "open" or "closed" we imagine them to be. And more recently, in one of the subtlest accounts of contemporary American poetry, Vernon Shetley has argued that our most interesting poets "tried to find some kind of middle way between the alternatives of a poetry descended from Eliot" and "the oppositional poetics of a figure like [Allen] Ginsberg."[10]

From my perspective, the "middle way" was found not between

Eliot and Ginsberg (however emblematically these names are employed) but within an Eliotic inheritance that poets found more varied and accommodating than most readers recognized; even the New Criticism offered Ashbery support in unpredictable ways. So while it's true that Thomas Hardy, Stevens, or H.D. have often served as alternate models, it is important to recognize that Ginsberg's poetry is in some ways a logical extension of Eliot's contradictory body of work. Those poets who were in the most literal sense postmodern (poets who, whatever their formal choices, were deeply aware of writing after the full flush of modernist achievement) did not stake their originality on a narrow reading of their forebears.

It was not until the publication of *The Waste Land* manuscript that most of Eliot's critics began to see that the poem was, in Eliot's own words, not so much an austere "criticism of the contemporary world" as the anguished "relief of a personal and wholly insignificant grouse against life."[11] But prescient readers had seen this side of Eliot long before the manuscripts revealed it. When Wallace Stevens read *The Waste Land* he ventured that "if it is the supreme cry of despair it is Eliot's and not his generation's."[12] Randall Jarrell, who planned for years to write a book on Eliot's "psychological roots," agreed.

> Won't the future say to us in helpless astonishment: "But did you actually believe that all those things about objective correlatives, classicism, the tradition, applied to *his* poetry? Surely you must have seen that he was one of the most subjective and daemonic poets who ever lived, the victim and helpless beneficiary of his own inexorable compulsions, obsessions? From a psychoanalytical point of view he was far and away the most interesting poet of your century. But for you, of course, after the first few years, his poetry existed undersea, thousands of feet below that deluge of exegesis, explication, source listing, scholarship, and criticism that overwhelmed it."[13]

As Jarrell points out, poets of his generation had to contend not only with Eliot's own critical pronouncements; some of the New Critics exaggerated and codified the poetics of tradition and impersonality, disguising aspects of Eliot's poetry that Stevens could sense early on. In 1948 Berryman reviewed a large collection of what were by then canonical readings of Eliot by I. A. Richards, F. R. Leavis, F. O. Matthiessen, Allen Tate, and Cleanth Brooks. "The book contains most of the best known studies of Mr. Eliot's work," said Berryman, "and will be useful." He had one serious complaint: "Eliot is found 'unified' and 'impersonal' everywhere, unutterably 'traditional,' and so on, all his favorite commendations. . . . Perhaps we have not got it yet. Perhaps in the end this poetry which the commentators are so eager to prove impersonal will prove to be personal, and will also appear then more terrible and more pitiful even than it does now."[14]

Berryman was right, of course. When he wrote these sentences, he was already at work on *Homage to Mistress Bradstreet,* and the effort to produce a poem with a dominant personality seems in this context an extension of Eliot's sensibility rather than a rejection of it. Berryman's later statements rejecting "Eliot's line" consequently seem more cagey than sincere, directed not so much at Eliot himself as at a critical establishment that smoothed his work into a "doctrine." The story of Berryman's career should explain that he was able to write *The Dream Songs* not only by resisting commonplace notions of Eliotic modernism but also by building on aspects of Eliot that most garden-variety literary critics did not want to notice.

But if the "breakthrough" narrative can account for Berryman's career only partially, it cannot account at all for the careers (to name only a few) of Elizabeth Bishop, Richard Wilbur, or John Ashbery. Because the narrative is often cast in the terms of masculine fortitude, it has helped to disguise the importance of many female poets. And male poets like Wilbur, who continues to work in traditional meters and forms, have often appeared "feminized" to readers who accept the terms of the narrative uncritically. Such poets have also been assumed, solely on the evidence of their formal choices, to be politically conservative. "The sociopolitical complacency and conservatism of . . . Eisenhower's eight-year administration," says one recent critic of postmodern poetry, "finds its match in a poetics overawed by tradition and ruled by its sense of decorum."[15] Common as this assumption is, it will make no sense of Wilbur, whose associations with the Communist Party were investigated by the FBI; nor will it make much sense of Ashbery, who remains a practicing Episcopalian. Wilbur himself has rightly rejected the attribution "of a kind of intrinsic sanity and goodness and even moral quality to received forms. . . . There's nothing essentially good about a meter in itself."[16] To believe otherwise is to transform an arbitrary, historically conditioned coincidence (in its most vulgar form, free verse and free thinking) into a kind of transcendental certainty.

The association of personal or social liberation with formal transgression (and the association of any ordering principle, even rhyme, with tyranny) is a good example of what Jürgen Habermas has called the "false negation of culture": everyday life "could hardly be saved from cultural impoverishment through breaking open a single cultural sphere—art."[17] As Habermas suggests in "Modernity—An Incomplete Project," responding to a variety of postmodern theorists, no conception of aesthetic modernism will offer terms that account adequately for the social project of modernity at large. Consequently, our sense of what constitutes a postmodern literature cannot be limited (as Fredric Jameson once put it) to "a particular style" of writing.[18] The poems of both John Ashbery and Richard Wilbur are shaped by a keen awareness of what is at stake in writing after Eliot and Stevens; their very different styles embody equally legitimate responses to modernism. And inasmuch as Ashbery and Wilbur are both deeply skeptical of the attribution of social power to any particular poetic form, the two poets have a great deal in common.

Elizabeth Bishop shared their skepticism. With the Lowell who in 1957 told William Carlos Williams, "it's great to have no hurdle of rhyme and scansion between yourself and what you want to say most forcibly,"[19] Bishop could not agree, because she understood that all forms of poetry, as linguistic confections, offer one or another screen through which the world is experienced. But a lingering distrust of conventional form continues to skew our sense of her development, despite the fact that she has become the most admired American poet of her generation. Many of Bishop's readers have attempted to increase her prestige by misrepresenting her subtle and gradual development as a breakthrough to freer forms, franker confessions, and more forceful politics. This is to read Bishop through a dated sense of modernism—even as that sense of modernism is in other contexts superseded. In contrast, William Meredith has hinted at Bishop's real importance by suggesting that "she will yet civilize and beguile us from our silly schools. The Olsons will lie down with the Wilburs and the Diane Wakoskis dance quadrilles with the J. V. Cunninghams."[20] Because of her personal knowledge of Eliot (among other things), Bishop understood his work as if she had read *The Waste Land* manuscript, and her sense of her own relationship to modernism was consequently not so clearly or comfortably antagonistic.

Lowell often said that it was Williams who catalyzed his conversion to free verse in *Life Studies*; other times, thinking of "Skunk Hour," he gave the honor to Bishop. Readers like Breslin have tended to focus on Williams because it's easier to contrast his values with the New Criticism, telling the story of Lowell's career as a linear trajectory rather than as an attractively circuitous muddle. In my reading, Bishop was the crucial influence precisely because it was not possible for Lowell—as it is not possible for us today—to align her work clearly with one camp or another. "You can see," Lowell once said, "that Bishop is a sort of bridge between Tate's formalism and Williams' informal art."[21] In *For the Union Dead* (more than in *Life Studies*), Lowell began to write poems with a less assertive kind of rhetoric, poems he found more amenable to the vicissitudes of personal experience. Bishop herself learned to write such poems by reading, very carefully, the modernist poetry that many of her contemporaries thought of as closed and impersonal.

By no means are all notions of postmodernism identical with antimodernism, whatever the currency of oppositional narratives in discussions of American poetry. While Jameson does maintain that postmodernism occurs when modernist works of art become "a set of dead classics," he also argues—more productively—that works embodying "the most classical high modernist aesthetic values" often seem "capable of a thoroughgoing rewriting into the postmodern text." Unwilling to establish a postmodern canon in clearly oppositional terms, Jameson extends this benefit of the doubt not only to more easily recuperated moderns (Roussel, Stein, or Duchamp) but to "mainstream moderns" such as Flaubert, Stevens, and Joyce. Yet when confronted by the poet who seems to me the most crucial representative of the mainstream, even this act of generosity is curtailed: "are all the classics of yesteryear rewritable in this fashion? . . . is T. S. Eliot recuperable?"[22] Within the world of American poetry, Eliot has been recuperated many times over. Randall Jarrell's sense of a future for poetry became possible when he understood that what passed for Eliotic notions of modernism were far from inevitable; those notions could not even account adequately for Eliot himself.

In 1934 Wallace Stevens wrote an introduction to Williams's *Collected Poems* that Jarrell read closely. "There are so many things to say about [Williams]," said Stevens. "The first is that he is a romantic poet. This will horrify him."[23] Stevens's point was not only polemical, for (as his slightly defensive "Sailing After Lunch" reveals) he felt himself deeply to be a romantic poet. He did hope to shake up other people besides Williams, however, and in a review of Marianne Moore's *Selected Poems* he was willing to say that even Eliot was a romantic. Since Eliot had written the introduction to Moore's poems, surrounding her work with imagist and neoclassical precedents, Stevens's argument was especially provocative. After reading the review in manuscript, Moore told Stevens that his allusion to Eliot would "do him good."[24]

Having read Stevens on both Williams and Moore, Jarrell saw fissures in what had previously seemed to him the monolithic world of modern poetry—especially as he had been initiated into it by his New Critical teachers, Warren and Tate. In an introduction to his first collection of poems, *The Rage for the Lost Penny* (1940), and two years later in an essay called "The End of the Line," Jarrell was able to say definitively that " 'Modern' poetry is, essentially, an extension of romanticism; it is what romantic poetry wishes or finds it necessary to become." When this sentence was published in the early forties, its argument was unheard of, except by devoted readers of Stevens; critical works that would popularize the argument (like Frank Kermode's *Romantic Image*) lay decades in the future. But Jarrell's purpose was less to characterize modernism than, in revealing it as the end of the romantic line, to speculate about what might come next: "How," he asked, "can poems be written that are more violent, more disorganized, more obscure, more—supply your own adjective—than those that have already been written?"[25]

For a brief moment in the late thirties, W. H. Auden seemed to Jarrell to make a successful move beyond modernist violence, disorganization, and obscurity: "Auden at the beginning was oracular (obscure, original), bad at organization, neglectful of logic, full of astonishing or magical language, intent on his own world and his own forms; he has changed continuously toward organization, plainness, accessibility, objectivity, social responsibility."[25] Jarrell tried to embody these values (both formal and political) in his own first poems—

> Love, in its separate being,
> Gropes for the stranger, the handling swarm,
> Sits like a child by every road
> With begging hands, string-dwindled arms

—but almost immediately he thought that this movement in the right direction had gone too far: Dylan Thomas's rejection of plainness and accessibility soon suggested that Auden's poetry represented one more reaction to modern values rather than a potent turn away from them.

While it was clear to Jarrell that modernism had passed, what was to take its place was not so clear. And though he sensed very cannily the affiliations of romantic and modern poetry, he was understandably less adept at sensing the similarly compromised relationship of modernism and whatever was to follow it. "During the course of [my] article," wrote Jarrell in his introduction to *The Rage for the Lost Penny*, "the reader may have thought curiously, 'Does he really suppose he writes the sort of poetry that replaces modernism?'"[27] Jarrell declined to answer the question directly, but when John Crowe Ransom reviewed the book, he quoted extensively from Jarrell's characterization of modernism, conjecturing that his precocious student "forbids us to say yet that he is a post-modernist" but "probably he will be."[28]

Ransom himself was unwilling to suggest what a "post-modernist" poet might look like; he would rely heavily on Jarrell's essay once again when he offered a tentative glimpse of the future in the final pages of *The New Criticism* (1941). Jarrell would offer some more meaningful conjectures in his 1947 review of Lowell's *Lord Weary's Castle*.

> Mr. Lowell's poetry is a unique fusion of modernist and traditional poetry, and there exist side by side in it certain effects that

one would have thought mutually exclusive; but it is essentially a post- or anti-modernist poetry, and as such is certain to be influential.[29]

Jarrell is unsure here if the right word would be *anti-modernist* or *post-modernist*, unsure if those two words mean different things. His use of the word nonetheless caught on quickly; a year later Berryman would remark that "Randall Jarrell . . . has described Lowell's poetry as 'postmodernist'; and one certainly has a sense that some period is drawing to a close."[30] But Jarrell's confusion seems to me functional, or at least honest, in that Jarrell has given up his earlier conception of a postmodern practice, located in Auden and in his own early poems, that would supersede the long history of romantic and modern poetry. Lowell's poems represent "a unique fusion of modernist and traditional poetry," and that fusion now seems to Jarrell properly postmodern.

But consider the poetry Jarrell was talking about—poetry that sounds, as Jarrell put it, like a man "grinding his teeth together till his shut eyes ache."

> A brackish reach of shoal off Madaket,—
> The sea was still breaking violently and night
> Had steamed into our North Atlantic Fleet,
> When the drowned sailor clutched the drag-net. Light
> Flashed from his matted head and marble feet.

Given our now commonplace stories about Lowell's career, these gnarled lines from "The Quaker Graveyard in Nantucket" sound like the kind of poetry Lowell had to overthrow in order to reach the really new achievement of *Life Studies*. To many readers, the poem epitomizes New Critical or modernist practice and seems anything but post- or anti-modern.

Why did it seem that way to Jarrell in 1947? Explaining what was distinctive about the poems of *Lord Weary's Castle*, he said that their organization "resembles that of a great deal of traditional English poetry—especially when compared to . . . semi-imagist modern organization."[31] This sentence is more specifically descriptive of Lowell's career than Jarrell reveals. Lowell's famous conversion from the poetry of *Lord Weary's Castle* to the poetry of *Life Studies* was not the first "breakthrough" in his career—as Randall Jarrell knew well. In the late fifties, when Lowell sent poems to William Carlos Williams, his midlife mentor, he said, "At forty I've written my first unmeasured verse."[32] That was a fib. When he first came to Harvard in 1935, Lowell was writing the sort of traditionally formalist poems that, so far as he knew, constituted poetry. But he met a young man named James Laughlin, fresh from a long visit to Rapallo, who was publishing an annual called *New*

*Directions* and writing what Lowell called "deliberately flat descriptive and anecdotal poems" based on the practice of Williams.[33] This contact initiated Lowell's first conversion: he became, following Laughlin, what seemed to Jarrell a modernist poet. His second conversion, following Tate and resulting in the poems of *Lord Weary's Castle*, transformed Lowell into what consequently seemed to be a postmodern poet: he had worked through what Jarrell called the "semi-imagist modern organization" of poetry to a "unique fusion of modernist and traditional poetry." For Jarrell, this postmodern poetry does not *oppose* modern poetry outright but *fuses* its sensibility with a formal tradition that modernism was thought to supersede. From Jarrell's point of view, consequently, Lowell's third conversion, resulting in the poems of *Life Studies*, could not represent a watershed in either Lowell's career or the history of American poetry: it represents a fork in a road that Lowell had passed many times before. Choosing one path or the other didn't make all the difference, since each led to the very place Lowell had set out from.

That fork would be negotiated many times after Lowell, and it was negotiated many times before him too. Ezra Pound proclaimed, late in his life, that "to break the pentameter, that was the first heave." But when we read his early career in detail, it's clear that Pound turned to free verse not as an alternative to formal verse (this distinction would have seemed bizarre to Pound) but as one more rhetorical possibility among the multitude of metrical and rhythmic experiments he was conducting. Soon afterwards, when free verse became an orthodoxy rather than a possibility, Pound broke rank: as he recalled many years later, he and Eliot "decided that the dilutation of *vers libre*, Amygism, Lee Masterism, general floppiness had gone too far and that some countercurrent must be set going. . . . Rhyme and regular strophes."[34] The results were the crisply rhymed quatrain poems of Pound's *Hugh Selwyn Mauberley* and Eliot's *Ara Vos Prec*, which did not influence Williams (as the imagist Pound had) but did shore up the anti-Romanticism of Ransom and Tate.

In his introduction to Lowell's *Land of Unlikeness*, published in 1944, Tate proclaimed that "T. S. Eliot's recent prediction that we should soon see a return to formal and even intricate metres and stanzas was coming true, before he made it, in the verse of Robert Lowell." Eliot had made that prediction in his 1942 essay "The Music of Poetry," but Tate needed to ignore earlier precedents in order to make *Land of Unlikeness* seem like a pivotal achievement: Lowell's turn to traditional meters repeated the earlier turns of Hart Crane's *White Buildings*, Auden's *Look, Stranger!*, Pound's *Mauberley*, and Eliot's own *Ara Vos Prec*. The poetic practices that seemed to Jarrell modern and postmodern—and that often continue to seem so today—represent not mutually exclusive, but complementary alternatives that grew out of the far from monolithic practice of modern poetry.

The precedent set by Hart Crane was particularly vexing to Tate, and, in telling ways, Crane continues to vex us today. Eighteen years before he wrote the introduction to *Land of Unlikeness*, Tate wrote the introduction to Hart Crane's *White Buildings*: in retrospect, those eighteen years amount to a much shorter period of time than the four years separating *White Buildings* from *The Waste Land*. Crane is arguably the first American poet to come of age with a strong sense of a modernist achievement behind him (rather than feeling, as even the terminally belated Williams did, that he was Eliot's contemporary), and Crane's way of reacting to modernism established a pattern on which American poets continue to spin variations. Although a fully meaningful discussion of postmodernism in American poetry begins with Jarrell, the postmodern impulse has existed for almost as long as there has been a modernist achievement that poets could look back on.

The story of Crane's career is well known, but it is a messier story—a less neatly oppositional story—than is usually acknowledged. Like Lowell, Crane became a disappointment to Allen Tate; both poets seemed at first to write poems compatible with Tate's critical principles, and both poets later appeared to desert those principles, Lowell in *Life Studies* and Crane in *The Bridge*. Like Berryman, Crane sometimes said that his own work was designed as a correction of Eliot's; his way of reading *The Waste Land* seems alternately confrontational and responsive. But the poet he corrected was the Eliot codified by his friends Winters and Tate: before *The Sacred Wood* gave his friends their rules of taste, Crane came to know the poet Jarrell thought of as one of the most daemonic who ever lived—a poet who seems more similar to the author of *The Bridge* than not.

In a 1922 letter, Crane responded to Tate's anxiety over Eliot's influence by copying down this passage from "Reflections on Contemporary Poetry," one of Eliot's uncollected essays.

> Admiration leads most often to imitation; we can seldom remain long unconscious of our imitating another, and the awareness of our debt naturally leads us to hatred of the object imitated. If we stand toward a writer in this other relation of which I speak we do not imitate him, and though we are quite as

The quotation breaks off here because the remainder of the letter has been lost. Eliot's essay continues,

> likely to be accused of it, we are quite unperturbed by the charge. This relation is a feeling of profound kinship, or rather of a pe-

culiar personal intimacy, with another, probably a dead author. It may overcome us suddenly, on first or after long acquaintance; it is certainly a crisis; and when a young writer is seized with his first passion of this sort he may be changed, metamorphosed almost, within a few weeks even, from a bundle of second-hand sentiments into a person. . . .

We may not be great lovers; but if we had a genuine affair with a real poet of any degree we have acquired a monitor to avert us when we are not in love. . . . We do not imitate, we are changed; and our work is the work of the changed man; we have not borrowed, we have been quickened, and we become bearers of a tradition.[35]

Eliot had a great deal to say about influence in "Tradition and the Individual Talent," the centerpiece of *The Sacred Wood*, but instead of the official pronouncement, Crane remembered an essay (never reprinted) that had appeared in the *Egoist* three years before he sat down to write his conciliatory letter to Tate. Recently, "Reflections on Contemporary Poetry" has become as important to Eliot's critics (even Harold Bloom has cited it) as "Tradition and the Individual Talent" was to Tate. But if Tate ever read the passage Crane sent him, he immediately suppressed it. In order to keep his vision of Eliot whole, Tate needed to understand the formal and emotional chaos of *The Waste Land* as a self-conscious dramatization of the failure of the antiromantic values Eliot articulated in *The Sacred Wood* and the programmatic quatrain poems of *Ara Vos Prec*. An Eliot who spoke of influence as a homoerotic "love affair" reft by "crisis" and "passion" (rather than an ordered assessment of existing monuments) might really have believed in the beauty and power of "the awful daring of a moment's surrender / Which an age of prudence can never retract."

The same Eliot was especially attractive to Crane. He often said that "For the Marriage of Faustus and Helen" was a response to *The Waste Land*, but his poem was nearly completed when Eliot's long poem appeared in the *Dial* in 1922. One detail was inserted after Crane read *The Waste Land*.

> And yet, suppose some evening I forgot
> The fare and transfer, yet got by that way
> Without recall,—lost yet poised in traffic.

These lines present the turn in "Faustus and Helen" from the claustrophobic space of the mind to the world beyond, and they are meant to recall Eliot's Phlebas the Phoenician, who "forgot . . . the profit and loss" and suffered a sea-change. In contrast to Tate, who read *The Waste Land* as the negative example of Eliot's true social vision, Crane read the "Death by Water" lyric as an augury of imminent rebirth and redemption—the kind of metamorphosis or quickening that Eliot described in "Reflections on Contemporary Poetry." Crane would later make a similar allusion for the same purpose in the "Van Winkle" portion of *The Bridge*: "And Rip forgot the office hours / and he forgot the pay." At this point in the long poem, the poetic quester leaves the private world of sleep and dreams to begin his journey to and fro in the earth. Read through Tate's perspective, the ecstasies of "For the Marriage of Faustus and Helen" and *The Bridge* would appear to resist Eliot's so-called classicism; but Crane's response to *The Waste Land* was already contained within an Eliot more divided and strange than Tate's codifications of *The Sacred Wood* could allow. Tate's and Winters's eventual dissatisfaction with *The Bridge* was a kind of displaced critique of the romantic Eliot they could not afford to recognize.

Despite its enthusiastic admirers, *The Bridge* stands in the no man's land between enemy camps that are staked out in the world of American poetry to this day, and it has never found a comfortable place in the annals of modern poetry. Even as critics and poets of the last twenty years have rescued Crane from critical judgments dominated by a straw-man Eliot, some of Tate's blindness continues to limit their readings. Since the fall of the New Criticism, as Eliot's stock has declined and Crane's risen, Crane's champions have stressed the revisionary power of his correction of Eliot; Whitman and Blake become the heroes in a contest against Dante and Donne. But this story remains plausible (paradoxically enough) only if its narrators continue to accept the most dogmatically New Critical notions of the author of *The Waste Land*, refusing to see how much of Eliot's achievement was fueled by his admiration for a literature outside the canon defined by Winters or Tate. *The Bridge* follows *The Waste Land* in the same way that John Ashbery's "The System" responds to "The Road Not Taken": the poems seem antagonistic only if we continue to accept a strategically oversimplified reading of our modernist past.

*Life Studies*, which Tate asked Lowell not to publish, includes a poem spoken in Hart Crane's voice: Lowell wanted to associate his breakthrough with what Tate led him to think of as Crane's rejection of Eliot. "Who asks for me, the Shelley of my age," wrote Lowell, masquerading as Crane, "must lay his heart out for my bed and board." The implication of these lines is that Lowell's self-transformation in *Life Studies* has been equally catastrophic. But as Langdon Hammer has discovered, "Words for Hart Crane" began its life as "(An) Englishman Abroad (1950)," a poem virtually identical to the final version except that it nowhere refers to Crane: "Crane's name and example were later fitted, a little roughly, into a formula Lowell had on hand."[36] The formula was the "breakthrough" narrative, which fits Crane's poetry as roughly as it fits Lowell's. Like Crane before him, Lowell was productively inconsistent in his attitude towards Eliotic values. "I seesaw back and forth between something highly metrical and something free," said Lowell in an unguarded moment; "there isn't any one way to write."[37] A "seesaw" is a much more suggestive metaphor for Lowell's development than a "breakthrough," one that allows us to appreciate the wide range of Lowell's accomplishment, much as we have come to see Crane's or even Eliot's.

Today, Lowell more often appears as a minor, catalyzing figure in critical narratives about Bishop's career, much as Bishop once appeared as a footnote to Lowell's formal breakthrough. While this shift is partly due to an increased recognition of Bishop's real power, it is also a by-product of the inevitable turn, following Lowell's death, against a poet who helped to create the taste by which he was judged. But if readers who came of age at the height of Lowell's popularity continue to belittle him, younger poets continue to read him productively. As Robert Hass has suggested, dismissals of Lowell's power too often seem "to be based on the sociology of Kenyon College or the fact of meter or Lowell's early models, on everything but a reading of the poems."[38] For Hass, the New Critical ascendancy or the fact of meter are no longer fighting matters. Judgments such as his suggest that Lowell will soon resemble the Eliot whom, with Crane's help, we can see today: a poet whose reputation was overwhelming, even stifling, during his lifetime—but a poet who remains vital because other writers could see aspects of him that the reputation obscured.

This Lowell will become clearer to us if we jettison the "breakthrough" narrative and its attendant mystifications of modernism, politics, and poetic form. We may also need to abandon the notion that *Life Studies* is the crucial achievement in Lowell's career. Like *Lord Weary's Castle*, which derives much of its power from its repudiation of Lowell's Puritan past, *Life Studies* establishes its authority (as I've suggested) by telling the story of Lowell's rejection of an earlier style and self. Sternly confrontational, the book has lost some of its power because the battles in which it engages no longer seem quite so meaningful. As Bishop recognized most clearly when she wrote to Lowell about his use of Elizabeth Hardwick's anguished letters in *The Dolphin* ("*art just isn't worth that much*"),[39] Lowell had a tendency to stake his poetic claim at the expense of almost anything: this is what can make his poems seem simultaneously appalling and seductive.

In his review of Bishop's *North & South*, Randall Jarrell made the following comment about Bishop's values; appearing just a few months before his review of *Lord Weary's Castle*, in which he worried about

Lowell's "denunciatory prophetic tone," the comment seems to address Lowell's values as well.

> She is morally so attractive, in poems like "The Fish" or "Roosters," because she understands so well that the wickedness and confusion of the age can explain and extenuate other people's wickedness and confusion, but not, for you, your own; that morality, for the individual, is usually a small, personal, statistical, but heartbreaking or heart-warming affair of omissions and commissions the greatest of which will seem infinitesimal, ludicrously beneath notice, to those who govern, rationalize, and deplore.[40]

I think Jarrell had Lowell in mind here, for throughout his career Lowell sometimes was a poet who governs and deplores—a poet who does feel that the wickedness and confusion of the age can explain his own. Lowell told Bishop that when he sent *Life Studies* to Philip Rahv, editor of *Partisan Review*, Rahv said, " 'Diss is da break-through for Cal [Lowell] and for poetry. The one real advance since Eliot.' " Lowell went on to give Bishop the credit: "really I've just broken through to where you've always been."[41] But when Lowell adapted Bishop's loosened-up formal strategies in the breakthrough poem "Skunk Hour," he did not necessarily pick up Bishop's values. As Lowell came to recognize, "I thought that civilisation was going to break down, and instead *I* did."[42] Apocalyptic fervor fills both *Lord Weary's Castle* and *Life Studies*, and it's a trait one finds nowhere in Elizabeth Bishop—except in her jacket blurb for *Life Studies*. (On the jacket of *A Cage of Spines*, in contrast, she praised May Swenson for "a directness and optimism that are unusual in these days of formulated despair.") This is why Lowell's poems could seem so particularly astonishing in the "tranquillized *Fifties*," as he dubbed the decade; this is also why the poems may seem less relevant—unfairly so—today: *Life Studies* was too easily accommodated by readers who, like Rahv, had championed a prophetic Eliot.

The Lowell who will continue to astonish is the poet who seduces without appalling—the poet for whom art is not worth that much, the poet who does not stake his authority on aggressive gestures of confrontation, whether stylistic or thematic. Seamus Heaney, who has learned a great deal from Lowell, writes perceptively of the "ruling passion for sounding victorious" that drives both *Lord Weary's Castle* and *Life Studies*, however antithetically the two books may have been conceived. The Lowell who matters to Heaney is the poet of a "less assertive voice," the poet who "relaxed the method of decisive confrontation which he had pursued in *Life Studies*."[43] This poet is audible most consistently in *Day by Day*, Lowell's autumnal last book; but it did not take Lowell a lifetime to become this poet. The less assertive voice is

heard in many of the poems of *For the Union Dead*, the book that followed *Life Studies* (and languished in the shadow of Lowell's "breakthrough").

> Our end drifts nearer,
> the moon lifts,
> radiant with terror.
> The state
> is a diver under a glass bell.

> A father's no shield
> for his child.
> We are like a lot of wild
> spiders crying together,
> but without tears.

> Nature holds up a mirror.
> One swallow makes a summer.
> It's easy to tick
> off the minutes,
> but the clockhands stick.

> Back and forth!
> Back and forth, back and forth—
> my one point of rest
> is the orange and black
> oriole's swinging nest!

These lines from "Fall 1961" are immediately recognizable as Lowell's; but even though they treat one of Lowell's signature topics—a
Cold War sense of impending doom—their tone is unemphatic, the
voice more domestic than prophetic. The poem does not rationalize or
deplore; it establishes its authority through a focused attention on common things (the ticking clock, the swinging nest) and received wisdom
("Nature holds up a mirror. / One swallow makes a summer"). Perhaps
most important, the poem's relationship to its own form feels unpolemical: the gentle syntax is achieved within (not in spite of) the formal
requirements of the poem; the unstressed rhymes are not forced to embody the poet's sense of what constitutes freedom and oppression outside the world of poetry. Given the quiet way in which Lowell faces
wickedness and confusion in this poem, it seems appropriate that one
of its most compelling images is adapted from Elizabeth Bishop's response to the music of Anton Webern: "It's like a lot of spiders crying
together but without tears."[44] "Fall 1961" does not sound like Bishop,

but neither do we feel that the poem compels us to choose unnecessarily—that its power is bought at the expense of anything else.

As we look toward the future, a critical narrative that forces us to choose between Lowell and Bishop (or between Eliot and Crane) will only provide ammunition for the next inevitable backlash. So while it's true that, like most readers, I prefer certain poets to others, my goal is to offer an account of American poetry after modernism (beginning with Crane's example) that allows us to choose from among a variety of poetic practices, not between them. There is a long tradition in romantic poetry of associating the desire for originality with anxiety and competition; but there is an equally long tradition of associating it with openness and generosity. "The only means of strengthening one's intellect," said Keats, "is to make up one's mind about nothing—to let the mind be a thoroughfare for all thoughts."[45] Lowell and Berryman were famously jealous of each other's achievement, but even Berryman could say, apropos of Lowell, that "there is no competition either on Parnassus or on the hard way up there. Darley, that is, with *Nepenthe* and a lyric or so, is as good as Keats."[46] This is not a critic's idealism but the working poet's real generosity, born of a humble sense of how difficult it is to write good poems, much less the great ones.

It is sometimes difficult to separate generosity from a lack of sharpened critical tools; anyone can enjoy a good fight over the canon, as long as the weapons are sharp enough to be interesting in themselves. For too long, however, such battles have held our attention at the expense of American poetry. Even if we date the postmodern impulse to Jarrell's early essays (rather than to *The Bridge*), the impulse has a longer history than modernism had when Harry Levin asked the question *what was modernism?* in 1960. But my reasons for dwelling on Crane, Jarrell, or Bishop are not only historical. That is, while I think that Crane's relationship to Eliot has been oversimplified, I also think that the future of American poetry depends on a more finely tuned understanding of that relationship. At the same time, I don't think that any particular imperative—that poetry must become more difficult, more accessible, more formal, more disjunctive, more self-conscious—is ever very useful. Questioning recent manifestations of antimodernism, Theodore Weiss (born a year before Lowell) suggests, "surely one may complain about critical positions and poetic practices that, whatever their reasons, tend to shrink the world of poetry, to limit its possibilities."[47] The positions that are currently available do shrink the world of poetry. They force us to choose between competing ideas of what poetry might be, and each of those ideas forces us to understand modernism as a diminished thing.

Our ideas about postmodernism are only as good as our ideas about modernism. By reconsidering the terms of the "breakthrough" narrative, I think we can see even more clearly than Jarrell could fifty years ago that our postmodernism is usually not an antimodernism, however deep our need for polemical distinctions has been—or remains. In 1991 the Poetry Society of America sponsored a forum called "Free Verse vs. Formalism: Robert Bly and Brad Leithauser." From the perspective of the final decade of the century, these distinctions have begun to look wildly dated, and it's time to begin asking the question, *what was postmodern poetry?* A tentative answer might be found in this sentence, which was almost written by Randall Jarrell: *Postmodern poetry was, essentially, an extension of modernism; it was what modern poetry wished or found it necessary to become.*

# ELIZABETH BISHOP'S
# BRAMBLE BUSHES

Elizabeth Bishop's first meeting with Marianne Moore, outside the third-floor reading room of the New York Public Library, has become a crucial episode in stories told about Bishop's career. Missing from those stories is an account of a meeting that took place a year earlier, this one with a modernist poet more threatening and more crucial to Bishop's sense of what it meant to be a writer. In the spring of 1933, T. S. Eliot came to Vassar College to attend the premiere production of his fragmentary drama *Sweeney Agonistes*. He also read his poetry to Vassar students and submitted to an interview for the *Vassar Miscellany News*: Elizabeth Bishop conducted the interview. The following week, this report appeared in the *Miscellany News*.

> Before reading selections from *The Waste Land*, Mr. Eliot declined to explain it, saying that he had read explanations of it which were much better than his own intention. Critics have called it a "criticism of the contemporary world," but "to me," he confessed, "it was just a piece of rhythmical grumbling."[1]

This remark by Eliot rings bells today because it appeared as the epigraph to the facsimile edition of *The Waste Land* manuscript (with a more dubious provenance than this newspaper report provides—recorded by Henry Ware Eliot, Jr., who heard it quoted by Theodore Spencer). In the last twenty years this remark has become crucial to readings of Eliot's poem in the way that chatter about "mythical method" once was; but before 1971 the remark—and its implications about Eliot's status as culture czar—was virtually unknown. Imagine, then, what it must have been like for a young poet to hear Eliot describe *The Waste Land* in these terms in 1933. Decades before it became fashionable to do so, Bishop would argue (as Mary McCarthy remembered) that Eliot's poem is " 'about impotence.' Not symbolic impotence—it's about the thing."[2]

Bishop's reading of Eliot was of course determined by more than this brief encounter, but the meeting is emblematic of her way of reading Eliot. Soon after interviewing Eliot, Bishop wrote an essay called "Dimensions for a Novel." In this early stage of her career Bishop was as devoted to the writing of fiction as she was to poetry: her very first professional publications were short stories, and she described herself in the contributors' column of *The Magazine* as "writing a novel about family life in a Nova Scotia village." Her plan for this novel, like Randall Jarrell's prose of the same period, reveals a strong desire to produce something different from her modernist forebears. As much as Bishop admired the work of Joyce, Mann, Proust, and Woolf (she discussed them all), she thought that their moment had passed. But as she sketched out a theory for a kind of narrative that might supplant theirs, she grounded this self-conscious foray into a postmodern practice in the work of T. S. Eliot. Not Eliot as Allen Tate read him: Bishop came face to face with the more strange and malleable poet Hart Crane discovered in "Reflections on Contemporary Poetry."

Bishop began "Dimensions for a Novel" by quoting the well-known passage from "Tradition and the Individual Talent" about the "existing monuments" of literary history forming an "ideal order" that is altered by the introduction of the "really new" work of art. "Whoever has approved this idea of order," Eliot concluded, " . . . will not find it preposterous that the past should be altered by the present as much as the present is directed by the past."[3] This passage has accumulated a complicated critical history, for it supports contradictory readings. The more dogmatic of the New Critics tended to ignore that final sentence and focus on words like "monuments" and "order," preferring the Eliot who wrote finely metered poems and stressed the values of impersonality and objectivity. More recently, Eliot's readers have emphasized the final sentence, fortified by their knowledge of Eliot's investment in post-Hegelian skepticism and his resulting awareness of the contingency of anything like impersonality.

Bishop read "Tradition and the Individual Talent" in the same way (as a theory of hermeneutic indeterminacy), and she reoriented Eliot's focus from the continual remaking of historical narratives to the continual remaking of fictional narratives.

> A constant process of adjustment is going on about the past— every ingredient dropped into it from the present must affect the whole.
>      Now what Mr. Eliot says about the sequence of works of art seems to me to be equally true of the sequence of events or even of pages or paragraphs in a novel. I have mentioned what I call the "march" of the novel, implying movement and a linear sequence to the writing; but I know of no novel which deliberately makes use of this constant readjustment among the members of any sequence.

Though modern novelists complicate the time structure of their work, Bishop explained, that complication nevertheless takes place within a well-made novelistic structure that "keeps its front." Searching for a narrative that would read more like Beckett's "The Unnamable" than Joyce's *Portrait*, Bishop suggested that a novel should not only show the "perpetually changing integration of what has been written with what is being written"; in addition, "the *recognition* itself of what is being written must be kept fluid." She confessed that were she to diagram the narrative structure of the kind of novel she had in mind, it would look, even if greatly oversimplified, "something like a bramble bush."[4] For Bishop, Eliot's prose ultimately justified narrative structures nothing like a well-wrought urn.

Little of the novel for which Bishop's essay provided the "dimensions" survives, but several of Bishop's early, uncollected stories attempt the kind of narrative experiments she had in mind. In "Chimney Sweepers" and "Mr. Pope's Garden" she constructs fictional narratives from factual materials, appending scholarly footnotes whose irony it is difficult to gauge. In "Seven-Days Monologue" she comes closer to realizing her "bramble bush" with a sequence of journal entries that confound any clear sense of temporal progression and thwart any sense of narrative closure. In one of the entries Bishop offers a parable that epitomizes her stuctural aims.

> Like two dim forests edging together the Now and the Then stood, almost silent. What strange animals crept to the verge of each and stared at one another from their own territories? What rough or velvet coats, and fearful eyes, bright claws and teeth, did each side see? Their shadows wove together and their sunlight and moonlight were the same, but they never approached each other, never mated.[5]

"Seven-Days Monologue" possesses more narrative coherence than this passage might suggest: even as Bishop wanted her work to embody her Eliotic sense of the indeterminacy of understanding and perception, she didn't want her bramble bushes to remain untrimmed by the shears of Horatian clarity. Bishop understood from the start that bramble bushes could never grow "naturally" because they were inevitably shaped by whatever rhetorical tools she possessed. In writing poems (which quickly became the focus of her creative energies) she came to see that her bramble bushes—poems that seemed in motion, poems able to accommodate a jumble of observations—did not necessarily require the rejection of what she once called poetry's "ancient, honorable rules."[6]

Among the poets she loved best, Gerard Manley Hopkins helped Bishop to see that poetic structures could be bent but never broken through. As David Kalstone has suggested, Bishop admired Hopkins not for his obvious effects (the quick alliterations and gnarled syntax) but for the kind of rhythmic movement that, as Hopkins himself put it, combined "opposite and, one wd. have thought, incompatible excellences, markedness of rhythm . . . and naturalness of expression."[7] Discussing the motion of Hopkins's poems in her 1934 essay on the poet, Bishop offered this parable, equating the poet and her poem with a marksman and his target: "the poet is set on bringing down onto the paper his poem, which occurs to him not as a sudden fixed apparition of a poem, but as a moving, changing idea or series of ideas. . . . [T]he target is a moving target and the marksman is also moving." This is a reworking, in subtler terms, of Bishop's thoughts about narrative bramble bushes: not only is the stuff of the poem in motion, so is the process by which that stuff is apprehended and then given the illusion of closure and coherence. Bishop admired Hopkins because he resisted that illusion: "Hopkins, I believe, has chosen to stop his poems, set them to paper, at the point in their development where they are still incomplete, still close to the first kernel of truth or apprehension which gave rise to them. . . . In this manner the boundaries of the poem are set free, and the whole thing is loosened up."[8]

Marianne Moore's poems, with their combination of intricate design and prose rhythm, reinforced some of the lessons Bishop learned from Hopkins. But Bishop's own poems were loosened up in a way that Moore's were not: while Moore's poems transform description into a structural principle, Bishop's turn the process of describing into a structural principle. To adopt a phrase Bishop quoted from the critic Morris Croll in her Hopkins essay, Moore's poems offer the mind's achievement of thought while Bishop's offer "not a thought, but a mind thinking."[9] Jarrell once described Moore's poems as "visual and instantaneous rather than auditory and temporal, a state rather than a process," and the terms he rejects (auditory, temporal, a process) would fit Bishop's poems well.[10] As Bishop herself put it in the Hopkins essay, she tried to set poems to paper "at the point in their development where they are still incomplete."

Early on, Bishop's effort to "set free" the "boundaries" of her poems is more subtle than in later poems such as "At the Fishhouses," since the effort did not necessarily involve a rejection of those things that constitute the boundaries of poems. In 1935 Bishop's first professionally published poem was "The Imaginary Iceberg."

> We'd rather have the iceberg than the ship,
> although it meant the end of travel.
> Although it stood stock-still like cloudy rock
> and all the sea were moving marble.

In this quatrain, rhymes have mutated into alternating stressed and unstressed endings, and as the poem progresses, the pattern of this opening quatrain disintegrates further so that we might not even notice that the poem consists of three identically shaped stanzas, each ending with a couplet.

Even as the formal pattern of "The Imaginary Iceberg" is loosened up, the poem itself seems to emphasize enclosure and completion rather than openness and looseness: "This iceberg cuts its facets from within," a self-sustaining artifact that "a sailor'd give his eyes for." But Bishop's irony is keen, for the problem with this well-wrought iceberg is that it forces us to hand over our powers of perception; it is "imaginary" rather than "imagined," and that is the problem. Like several of Bishop's earliest poems ("The Weed" and "The Monument" come to mind), "The Imaginary Iceberg" is a fable that, while enacting Bishop's values of openness and looseness on the minute level of poetic structure, demonstrates thematically the dangers of enclosure and completion.

In her famous poem "The Fish," in contrast, Bishop was able to demonstrate the value of openness and discovery within the poem's unfolding of its thematic content. She provides at the beginning of "The Fish" no sense of its conclusion; instead, the poem seems to discover its direction only as we read it, and (as in Bishop's parable) both the target and the hunter are in motion. The fish and the fisherman become apprehensible to us through the sequence of similes characterizing the fish. (Metaphors, suggesting firmer equivalencies, are avoided.)

> Here and there
> his brown skin hung in strips
> like ancient wallpaper,

and its pattern of darker brown
was like wallpaper:
shapes like full-blown roses
stained and lost though age.

This fish is not "imaginary" (Bishop emphasizes its brute otherness by dwelling on its sharp gills and sea-lice) but it is, unlike the iceberg, "imagined": that is, it makes sense—tentatively—only as values are attributed to it. By its very otherness the fish seems to teach the speaker how to imagine and therefore appreciate her world. The epiphany in the poem's final lines, when everything is "rainbow, rainbow, rainbow," becomes possible when the speaker turns from the fish and sees a rainbow in the oil spread out in the ugly rented boat. Having begun by setting down the poem when still "incomplete" (to borrow the terms of her essays), Bishop ends by demonstrating "not a thought but a mind thinking."

Marianne Moore herself recognized that Bishop's essays on Hopkins and modern fiction provided a foundation on which Bishop's poems would stand for many years to come; when Bishop was planning her first book, Moore suggested that she publish a combination of poetry and prose, including her early stories and essays: they "support . . . and necessitate one another," she urged.[11] Bishop's career demonstrates not so much a linear development as a continual unfolding of the possibilities inherent in positions she articulated early on. And those possibilities continued to unfold, dramatically so, in more adventurous poems like "Over 2,000 Illustrations and a Complete Concordance" and "At the Fishhouses," published a decade after the essays (though begun much earlier).

In contrast to "The Fish," "Over 2,000 Illustrations" rejects a "linear sequence" for what Bishop called (extending Eliot's discussion of tradition) a "perpetually changing integration of what has been written with what is being written." Yet within the poem her attitude toward this kind of associational structure—and the mode of comprehension it implies—is initially ambivalent. "Thus should have been our travels," the poem begins, comparing the uncertainty of travel with the clarity of the engravings in the family Bible. The lines the burin made are like "God's spreading fingerprint," and the sense of order this metaphor conjures up is stultifying: the illustrations are "familiar," "obvious,"— "they all resolve themselves." The stories they tell are not only predictable but sinister, and worse, they perpetuate the values of a well-closed mind: "Often the squatting Arab, / or group of Arabs, plotting, probably, / against our Christian empire."

By the end of this first movement of the poem, we sense that the initial attraction to these engravings has been dispelled by the act of

describing them. With no transition, the second movement of the poem
launches on an apparently random catalogue of the travels dismissed
in the poem's opening line.

> Entering the Narrows at St. Johns
> the touching bleat of goats reached to the ship.
> We glimpsed them, reddish, leaping up the cliffs
> among the fog-soaked weeds and butter-and-eggs.
> And at St. Peter's the wind blew and the sun shone madly.
> Rapidly, purposefully, the Collegians marched in lines,
> crisscrossing the great square with black, like ants.
> In Mexico the dead man lay
> in a blue arcade; the dead volcanoes
> glistened like Easter lilies.

Not only thematically (as in "The Fish") but structurally, these lines
reject the order of "God's fingerprint"; St. Peter's is windblown, and its
officials run like ants. These lines seem to run like ants as well, tumbling
over one another with little sense of progression; but a tenuous order
emerges when we notice throughout the passage an increasingly threatening sense of doom, culminating in these lines: "It was somewhere
near there / I saw what frightened me most of all: / A holy grave, not
looking particularly holy." Looking back over this movement of the
poem, we can now see it was from the beginning a catalogue of frightening things—things as unsettling as the Tomb, Pit, and Sepulcher of
the engravings.

Bishop is not, by collapsing the opposition of the biblical order of
the illustrations and the existential disorder of travel, implying that she
would rather have the Bible than the ship—even though the end of the
poem might seem to suggest that she does.

> Everything only connected by "and" and "and."
> Open the book. (The gilt rubs off the edges
> of the pages and pollinates the fingertips.)
> Open the heavy book. Why couldn't we have seen
> this old Nativity while we were at it?
> —the dark ajar, the rocks breaking with light,
> an undisturbed, unbreathing flame,
> colorless, sparkless, freely fed on straw,
> and, lulled within, a family with pets,
> —and looked and looked our infant sight away.

Returning to the book, Bishop realizes that order and randomness are
not inherent in any form of experience (neither the illustrations nor the
travels) but in the attitudes we bring to experience. As the Bible crum-
bles, the gilt rubbing from the pages and pollinating not only her fin-

gertips but her imagination, she is able to reinterpret a Nativity scene (an idealized location of our origins) as something inconsequential, even mundane, and yet miraculous—not for its traditional connotations but for its mundanity; the implication is that she could have similarly remade any of the scenes described. At the end of the poem, the certainty of "God's fingerprint" has been replaced by the hope that we have "looked and looked our infant sight away." The end casts that revisionary glance over the beginning of the poem—and over a traditional image of our beginnings. To say, borrowing again the words of Bishop's discussion of Eliot, that "Over 2,000 Illustrations" reveals the "perpetually changing integration of what has been written with what is being written" is to recognize that the writing of this poem addresses not only itself but the history of Western culture.

The final lines of Bishop's "At the Fishhouses" (published a year before "Over 2,000 Illustrations" in 1947) articulate the notion of historical understanding on which her poems, early and late, come to rest. Bishop speaks here of a sea so cold that, should you dip your hand in it, "your bones would begin to ache and your hand would burn."

> It is like what we imagine knowledge to be:
> dark, salt, clear, moving, utterly free,
> drawn from the cold hard mouth
> of the world, derived from the rocky breasts
> forever, flowing and drawn, and since
> our knowledge is historical, flowing, and flown.

These lines offer a charged metaphor for the origins of knowledge, the rocky breasts, an image Bishop often associates with the Nova Scotia landscape where she lost her mother. At the same time, the lines caution that, like all metaphors, this one is made and therefore provisional—doubly so: "It is *like* what we *imagine* knowledge to be."

The realization that "knowledge is historical, flowing, and flown" raises not only questions of poetic structure but questions of value. In "At the Fishhouses," Bishop links the Nova Scotia landscape with the female body but reminds us at the same time that the equation is historically contingent. In "Brazil, January 1, 1502," Bishop reveals what is at stake in forgetting the provisionality of that metaphor. The poem's title invokes the date on which Portuguese explorers named what they supposed, in error, to be the mouth of a great river—"Rio de Janeiro" or "River of January." The poem's epigraph, "embroidered nature . . . tapestried landscape," comes from a passage in *Landscape into Art* in which Kenneth Clark describes medieval depictions of the Hortus Conclusus, a garden enclosing the Virgin. The poem itself begins with the most neutral description of the landscape possible ("purple, yellow, two yellows, pink") but moves on to explain how the explorers' error was compounded by the imposition of European religious and sexual values on the Brazilian landscape. Charged metaphors accumulate quickly: a group of lizards "is Sin"; the moss unfolds in "hell-green flames"; and the smaller lizard, the "female one," is most threatening of all: "her wicked tail straight up and over, / red as a red-hot wire."

Not until the third movement of the poem is it possible to charge the Portuguese with responsibility for these metaphors. In 1502 they found this landscape "not unfamiliar":

> no lovers' walks, no bowers,
> no cherries to be picked, no lute music,
> but corresponding, nevertheless,
> to an old dream of wealth and luxury
> already out of style when they left home—
> wealth, plus a brand-new pleasure.
> Directly after Mass, humming perhaps
> L'Homme armé or some such tune,
> they ripped away into the hanging fabric,
> each out to catch an Indian for himself—
> those maddening little women who kept calling,
> calling to each other (or had the birds waked up?)
> and retreating, always retreating, behind it.

These final lines of the poem make explicit the oppressions implicit in the acts of describing (the metaphors) used to characterize the Brazilian landscape. But the poem is more than an unveiling of Portuguese colonialism; it is also a recognition of the possibility of Bishop's—or anyone's—complicity in the continuing imposition of those values. Like the other poems I've examined, "Brazil, January 1, 1502" unfolds coyly: Bishop strategically delays her characterization of Portuguese imperialism until the end of the poem, and only retrospectively does it seem responsible for the sexist metaphors. "Januaries, Nature greets our eyes / exactly as she must have greeted theirs," begins the poem. When we first read the lines, we're not sure who "they" are, and we might not take much notice of the traditional association of nature with femininity. Returning to these lines, we not only see the danger of that association, but we're forced to wonder who is making it. Bishop is keenly aware of the values imposed by sexual metaphors, but she suggests that awareness alone may not stop the perpetuation of the values; the metaphors accumulate a life of their own. Knowledge is certainly historical, flowing, and flown in "Brazil, January 1, 1502," but so, for better and for worse, is the knower. The date on which Bishop herself arrived in Brazil is appended to "Arrival at Santos," the poem which precedes "Brazil, January 1, 1502" in *Questions of Travel*: January 1952.

If the prognosis for change in "Brazil, January 1, 1502" consequently seems dim, the poem should be compared with "Santarém," one of Bishop's final—and finest—efforts. "Santarém" recalls Bishop's trip down the Amazon to where it meets the Tapajos, but the narrative is wayward, a string of loosely connected observations, and the poem once again dramatizes the self-revising process of a mind thinking. Its opening line admits the possibility of error—"Of course I may be remembering it all wrong"—and the poem often shows the mind resisting its own mistakes: twice Bishop calls the cathedral a church and corrects herself, suggesting that the mind is stubborn, its will to wander difficult to control.

In this way the mind mirrors the village of Santarém, where the two rivers converge: everything Bishop saw there was in motion, in flux, and the vagaries of thought raise this uncertain place to an even greater power of mutability. In "Brazil, January 1, 1502" the landscape had become a tapestry, a tissue of other people's descriptions, well before Bishop experienced it; in "Santarém" the landscape is not a static work of art but is like knowledge itself, flowing and flown, and Bishop shows the landscape resisting any human effort to contain it.

> Suddenly there'd been houses, people, and lots of mongrel
> riverboats skittering back and forth
> under a sky of gorgeous, under-lit clouds,
> with everything gilded, burnished along one side,
> and everything bright, cheerful, casual—or so it looked.
> I liked the place; I liked the idea of the place.
> Two rivers. Hadn't two rivers sprung
> from the Garden of Eden? No, that was four
> and they'd diverged. Here only two
> and coming together. Even if one were tempted
> to literary interpretations
> such as: life/death, right/wrong, male/female
> —such notions would have resolved, dissolved, straight off
> in that watery, dazzling dialectic.

Bishop calls the riverboats "mongrel," but the word could describe everything she recalls. Mixed of a variety of contrary qualities, Santarém resists all binary oppositions, all neatly resolving narratives. But since the poem itself is also in process, Bishop dramatizes first her desire to shape this place into a familiar narrative ("Hadn't two rivers sprung / from the Garden of Eden?") and then her rejection of the narrative's powerful surge toward closure.

Eden seems to come to mind because Santarém seemed so idyllic: "everything bright, cheerful, casual—or so it looked," says Bishop, hinting that some more sinister aspects of the place may not yet be apparent.

Halfway through "Santarém," Bishop begins the poem all over again, and those aspects begin to unfold.

> Two rivers full of crazy shipping—people
> all apparently changing their minds, embarking,
> disembarking, rowing clumsy dories.
> (After the Civil War some Southern families
> came here; here they could still own slaves.
> They left occasional blue eyes, English names,
> and *oars*. No other place, no one
> on all the Amazon's four thousand miles
> does anything but paddle.)

The implication of those "mongrel" riverboats has become clearer. This place is no Eden but is in fact the same Brazilian landscape we encounter in "Brazil, January 1, 1502," a landscape built from a history of oppression—a landscape that Western invaders wanted to imagine as Eden. But in these lines Bishop suggests that the place and its people are stronger than the displaced Southerners. While some residue of their presence remains (names, blue eyes, even the useful oars) they have been incorporated into the "dazzling dialectic" of this place, diffused and disarmed. But not completely. The cathedral, evidence of even earlier invaders, is still standing, though precariously: having been struck by lightning, "One tower had / a widening zigzag crack all the way down."

I think "Santarém" is one of Bishop's most daring poems because, unlike even "Over 2,000 Illustrations" or "Brazil, January 1, 1502," it does not end at all conclusively. Nothing in its nearly random agglutination of observations prepares us for this final anecdote—unless it is the *blue* of Southern eyes, the *stucco* walls of Santarém's houses, and the *electricity* of lightning.

> In the blue pharmacy the pharmacist
> had hung an empty wasps' nest from a shelf:
> small, exquisite, clean matte white,
> and hard as stucco. I admired it
> so much he gave it to me.
> Then—my ship's whistle blew. I couldn't stay.
> Back on board, a fellow-passenger, Mr. Swan,
> Dutch, the retiring head of Philips Electric,
> really a very nice old man,
> who wanted to see the Amazon before he died,
> asked, "What's that ugly thing?"

In another poem, these final lines might seem crushingly ironic. Bishop teases us with the possibility of a stable irony (Mr. Swan doesn't appreciate the beauty that Elizabeth Bishop and the reader can see), but she also leaves us with the uncomfortable notion that the poem, taken in its entirety, must be more complex than that. Linked to the rest of the poem metonymically, this final anecdote does not provide a metaphor that encompasses all of "Santarém," even though its prominent position at the end of the poem suggests that it might. The anecdote of the wasps' nest merely offers one memory among several others, and its irony cannot account for the poem at large: it offers just the kind of "literary" interpretation ("right/wrong") that the poem rejects. Similarly, if the wasps' nest itself functions as an emblem for what we value and retain from any place—an emblem for poetry itself—it is also an emblem of how much of the world poetry leaves out or leaves behind. "Santarém" both includes the anecdote of the wasps' nest and sloughs it off, unable to assimilate it into a complete pattern of meaning, just as the Brazilian landscape diffuses any effort, physical or ideological, to tame its wayward energies.

The Bishop who insists on the historicity of the structures of knowledge in this poem is not far, on the one hand, from the John Ashbery who admires her poems above all others, and not far, on the other hand, from the much younger Bishop who tried to describe, in the wake of modernism, new ways of writing novels and poems—not by rejecting T. S. Eliot's ideas of history but by adapting them to her own use.

To say this is to leave one question unaddressed, however: though we can see that certain aspects of "Tradition and the Individual Talent" support the sense of history in "Over 2,000 Illustrations," "Brazil, January 1, 1502," or "Santarém," it is not easy to say that Eliot would agree with the revisionary attitude toward Western culture which, in Bishop's poems, that sense of history encourages. It would be even more difficult to say this about the Eliot whom Bishop interviewed in 1933—the Eliot who had just delivered the notoriously closed-minded Page-Barbour Lectures at the University of Virginia, extending his earlier sense of tradition in a direction quite different from Bishop's.

Reading American poetry, I've rejected a differentiation of the modern and the postmodern that depends on the artificial segregation of certain formal properties: equally unsatisfactory is a differentiation that depends on an artificial segregation of values. While it might be tempting to associate what we often think of as the "openness" of postmodern poetry with varieties of ideological "openness," my reading of Bishop's career suggests that there is no particular relationship between these formal and ideological characteristics. Bishop could build a poetic practice out of her reading of Eliot without adopting Eliot's values.

This ability to reshape rather than reject Eliot is the dynamic (beginning with Crane) on which postmodernism in American poetry is often based. But in Bishop's particular case the dynamic was shaped by the social turmoil of the 1930s. In that decade, while Eliot was championed by New Critics but scorned by leftists, Bishop stood among a precarious group of writers and intellectuals who wanted both to retain their political values and revere Eliot. Her values have not always seemed clear because readers too often assume that a formal "breakthrough" must accompany any radical politics in poetry: Elizabeth Bishop's social conscience requires a different story.

# ELIZABETH BISHOP'S SOCIAL CONSCIENCE

In "Contradictions: Tracking Poems," the long sequence that makes up the second half of *Your Native Land, Your Life*, Adrienne Rich meditates on Elizabeth Bishop's late villanelle, "One Art."

> acts of parting     trying to let go
> without giving up     yes Elizabeth     a city here
> a village there     a sister, comrade, cat
> and more     no art to this but anger.

"The art of losing isn't hard to master," Bishop said, and Rich's response to the line cuts two ways. On the one hand, she admires Bishop's artistry, feeling that she herself has not mastered the art—"only badly-done exercises." On the other hand, Rich is uncomfortable with Bishop's reticence, preferring the anger of the badly done to the artistry of a villanelle.

Although Bishop has always been championed by male poets—from Jarrell and Lowell to Ashbery and Strand—she has (until recently) presented a difficult example to female poets, especially those of Rich's generation. In an essay on Bishop written around the same time as "Contradictions," Rich explained that for a long time she "felt drawn, but also repelled" by Bishop's poetry. "Miss" Bishop—that is, Bishop as she was "selected and certified" by Lowell—was part of the problem: "Elizabeth Bishop's name was spoken, her books reviewed with deep respect. But attention was paid to her triumphs, her perfections, not to her struggles for self-definition and her sense of difference. In this way, her reputation made her less, rather than more, available to me."[1] Here, as in "Contradictions," Rich wants less art and more anger, and I sense that she is talking about her earlier self while addressing Bishop. In the 1950s the precocious Rich was also selected and certified by the literary establishment, and Bishop seemed to Rich the poet she could too easily become: the poet who was considered, in Robert Lowell's phrase, the author of "the best poems . . . written by a woman in this century."[2]

Bishop herself despised that kind of praise, and she suffered under the reputation of "Miss" Bishop. "Most of my writing life I've been lucky about reviews," she admitted to George Starbuck. "But at the very end they often say 'The best poetry by a woman in this decade, or year, or month.' Well, what's that worth?" Bishop's feminism rarely seemed this pronounced or undivided. In the same interview she dismissed the "tract poetry" of feminist writers like Robin Morgan, and she insisted that she never made any distinction between male and female poets. But she also made this provocative remark: "I was in college in the days—it was the Depression, the end of the Depression—when a great many people were communist, or would-be communist. . . . I never gave feminism much thought, until . . ."[3]

Unfortunately, George Starbuck interrupted at this point. But the historical context that Bishop emphasizes for her early career—the 1930s—is pertinent to an understanding of her relationship to feminism. Living in Brazil, Bishop claimed that she was "much more interested in social problems and politics now" than she had been in the thirties.[4] She even went so far as to attempt a poem about the suicide of Getúlio Vargas, the elected president and former dictator of Brazil. But Bishop never completed "Suicide of a Moderate Dictator," her most overtly political poem; its progress was hampered by her long-standing distaste for what she called "tract poetry." Although Bishop considered herself "a 'Radical,' of course," she nevertheless wondered, apropos of Marianne Moore's sense of the "tentativeness" of her poetry, if the problem were her unwillingness to delineate a coherent political position within the poems.[5] The stumbling block for Bishop, early and late, was not her values as such but her discomfort, nurtured in the thirties, with the conventions of political poetry.

Bishop's values, especially her feminism, entered her poems in other ways. Characterizing her more recent rapprochement with Bishop, Rich remarks that "poems examining intimate relationships" are replaced in

Bishop's work by "poems examining relationships between people who are, for reasons of inequality, distanced: rich and poor, landowner and tenant, white woman and Black woman, invader and native."[6] I would alter this insight to say that poems emphasizing social inequality do not take the place of poems emphasizing sexuality; rather, for Bishop, the consideration of gender and sexuality grew to be inseparable from the consideration of nationality or race. Missing in Bishop's poetry is almost the complete domain of what she thought of as political poetry; but from the begining of her career, Bishop was "more interested in social problems" than, in retrospect, she would allow.

Until 1934, Bishop was an undergraduate at Vassar College. She lived in New York City for the next few years, traveling widely, and then settled in Key West, Florida, just before the Second World War broke out. Her lifestyle, supported by a small trust fund and by occasional employment, was neither lavish nor uncomfortable, but many years later she would recall her experience of the "Marxist thirties."

> I was very aware of the Depression—some of my family were much affected by it. After all, anybody who went to New York and rode the Elevated could see that things were wrong. But I had lived with poor people and knew something of poverty at firsthand. About this time I took a walking-trip in Newfoundland and I saw much worse poverty there. I was all for being a socialist till I heard Norman Thomas [the Socialist Party presidential candidate in 1932] speak; but he was *so* dull. Then I tried anarchism, briefly.[7]

Bishop was, to be sure, someone who "rode the Elevated" and looked down on the social conditions of the Depression. And she was also someone who distrusted the easy proclamation of ideological associations and shifts—even in herself ("Then I tried anarchism, briefly"). But Bishop was aware of the conditions of the rural poor in Newfoundland and Key West, as well as in her native Nova Scotia. Even at Vassar she experienced the intellectual and political alternatives of the 1930s. Mary McCarthy, with whom Bishop established the alternative magazine *Con Spirito*, recalled the political climate of Vassar when she and Bishop were students there: "Most of our radicals were Socialists [rather than Communists], and throughout that election year they campaigned for Norman Thomas, holding parades and rallies. . . . Then our trustee, Franklin Roosevelt, was elected President. . . . With the impetus of the New Deal and memories of the breadlines behind us, even we aesthetes began reading about Sacco and Vanzetti and Mooney."[8] Like McCarthy, Bishop was more or less an "aesthete," but she was also reading about

Sacco and Vanzetti. "Politically I considered myself a socialist," she remembered, "but I disliked 'social conscious' writing. I stood up for T. S. Eliot when everybody else was talking about James T. Farrell."[9]

Bishop may have stood apart, but she did not stand alone. Her sensibility finds its mirror during the thirties in *Partisan Review*, whose editors were, like Bishop, trying to maintain a left-wing concern with social conditions without diluting the literary values they had learned from modernism. While Granville Hicks of the *New Masses* maintained that the function of art is to "lead the proletarian reader to recognize his role in the class struggle," William Phillips and Philip Rahv said this in the opening editorial of *Partisan Review*: "We shall resist every attempt to cripple our literature by narrow-minded, sectarian theories and practices."[10]

Bishop would eventually publish many poems and stories in *Partisan Review*, but even her earliest work reveals her complicated relationship to the political and intellectual climate of the thirties. Her story "Then Came the Poor" describes a wealthy family's flight from communist rebels who have successfully overthrown the government: "My whole family might have been getting ready for a wonderful picnic or party," says the narrator, a disaffected son, who watches his parents and siblings attempt to pack their clothing, port, and even the dining-room chandelier in the car. The narrator decides to stay behind, and he wakes to find his house crawling with "reds." When they prepare a banquet on the lawn and invite the narrator to join them he feels "at home" for the first time.[11]

This conclusion suggests that only when the narrator overthrows his class origins may he feel "at home" in his own house. But there remains another aspect to the narrator's transgression. When he is subsumed into the mob, he rejects not only the upper-class privilege of his family but also its heterosexual structure. The crowd draws lots for rooms in the mansion, and the narrator offers to live with a man named Jacob Kaffir. "I caught Jacob's eye and smiled as hard as I could," he explains, and the story ends with Jacob accepting the proposition: " 'We'll have fun, huh?' he said, waving an empty bottle at me, and he gave me a wink I could almost hear." The sexual undertones of this passage become stronger when we recall a scene the narrator witnesses when he re-enters his house after the mob has overtaken it.

> From father's bathroom came howls of laughter, splashings, and slappings. I looked in and discovered two naked men jumping in and out of the shower and bath (all the water on full force), throwing powder and bathsalts at each other, and spitting shining spouts of water out the window into the sunshine and onto their amused friends below.

This is the one passage in which the narrator drops his ironic tone and describes what he sees with something like wonder. Meeting Jacob Kaffir, the narrator is almost as amazed by the man's moustache, red fez, and skin the color of "a well-used penny": his proposition transgresses not only sexual but racial boundaries as well.

Throughout "Then Came the Poor" these transgressions are encased within the more obvious drama of the transgression of class boundaries. At the same time, the story displays Bishop's divided attitude toward the idea of a "social conscious" writing. "Then Came the Poor" is a wicked parody of the wealthy sensibility Bishop knew well from her Boston grandparents, but it also pokes fun at the idea of a single-mindedly proletarian literature. While the story welcomes the revolution, it nevertheless "stands up for Eliot." Before the narrator's family flees, it receives this telegram: "REDS WIN DAY SULLIVAN AND KROWSKI SHOT THREE THOUSAND HEADED EAST VACATE OR OFFER NO RESISTANCE ELIOT MAY HOLD." This joke—Eliot may hold—would have been clear to Mary McCarthy, if not to everyone. And today, the joke shows how Bishop's retrospective statement about her interest in social problems is and is not true: while "Then Came the Poor" does poke fun at the typical idea of "social conscious" writing (the narrator even remarks that his life has become "a silly story told by a propagandist"), the story is nevertheless deeply socially conscious in other ways.

It was easier for the young Bishop to walk this thin line in her stories than in her poems. In 1937 she sent a poem called "War in Ethiopia" (now lost) to Horace Gregory, thinking that the anthology he was editing might be "all 'social consciousness.'" But Bishop was uncomfortable with her poem, adding that she was not sure if her "attempts at this kind of thing are much good." She didn't much admire other poets' attempts (Louis MacNeice's work seemed to her "shortsighted" and "ignorant"), but she did admire *Owl's Clover*, Wallace Stevens's sequence of poems about the role of poetic and political power in a time of economic depression. Whatever its flaws, Bishop told Marianne Moore, *Owl's Clover* was a wonderful "display of ideas at work—making poetry, the poetry making them, etc. That, it seems to me, is the way a poet should think, and it should be a lesson to his thicker-witted opponents and critics, who read or write all their ideas in bad prose and give nothing in the way of poetry except exhortation or bits of melancholy description."[12] Stevens's sternly dialectical poem showed Bishop a way of harnessing her natural "tentativeness" (as Moore called it) in poems that grappled with the social questions of the thirties while avoiding the generic constraints of political poetry.

Bishop was also guided by Moore's review of *Owl's Clover*; but while

Moore felt that *Owl's Clover* was critical of the artistic attitudes it portrayed, Bishop thought it defended them (a disagreement that repeats a tension central to Stevens's poem):

> I am afraid my own idea of *Owl's Clover* is much more simple and "popular." I took it as a defense of his own position, and the statue—dear me—I felt, and still cannot help feeling, is ART—sometimes the particular creation, sometimes an historical synthesis, sometimes his own work—but always his own conception of such art. In the first section I thought he was confessing the "failure" of such art (I don't like to use these words but they seem to be the only ones) to reach the lives of the unhappiest people, and the possibility of a change—of something new arising from the unhappiness, etc.[13]

Bishop extended these thoughts in her notebook, following the entry with a pen and ink sketch of the artifact she would describe in "The Monument." This poem offers a work of art that unlike Stevens's statue can reach its audience, though not without some necessary difficulty. Like several of the poems of *Owl's Clover*, "The Monument" oscillates between two voices, one sympathetic and the other hostile to the abstract and ambiguous monument.

> "Why did you bring me here to see it?
> A temple of crates in cramped and crated scenery,
> what can it prove?
> I am tired of breathing this eroded air,
> this dryness in which the monument is cracking."
>
> It is an artifact
> of wood. Wood holds together better
> than sea or cloud or sand could by itself,
> much better than real sea or sand or cloud.
> It chose that way to grow and not to move.

This defense of a "useless" artifact is a quintessential document of the thirties, the decade in which the kind of modernist abstraction exemplified by Bishop's monument first came under attack. Once again, Bishop is standing up for Eliot. Yet Bishop's monument differs from other artistic icons (Keats's urn, Yeats's golden bird, or even Stevens's humble jar in Tennessee) in that it is made of wood, organic and decaying. Though it is more lasting than sea or sand, it does not offer a refuge from reality. The monument is flawed, a little ridiculous, and undeniably human-made; its "crudest scroll-work says 'commemorate,'" suggesting that it is a monument to the potential grandeur of human folly and failure. Unlike "A Miracle for Breakfast" (which

Bishop would later recall as a " 'social conscious' poem"[14]), "The Monument" is not so obviously marked as a poem of the thirties; but it asks more rigorous questions about the relevance of art and imagination to (in the words of Bishop's letter about *Owl's Clover*) "the lives of the unhappiest people."

In contrast to "Then Came the Poor," "The Monument" doesn't show how the terms of gender and race may inflect those questions. But those terms became more consistently prominent in the poems Bishop began to write in Key West during the Second World War. In part, the reasons for this shift are cultural: the war emphasized differences between the social roles occupied by men and women, and, at the same time, helped to obscure the prominent class differences of the Depression by offering an enemy common to all Americans. So while "Roosters" is well-known as Bishop's war poem (Bishop said she was thinking "of those aerial views of dismal little towns in Finland and Norway, when the Germans took over"[15]), it is more precisely the poem's linkage of national and sexual aggression that marks it as a product of the Second World War. "Roosters" breaks into two halves, the first suggesting that the national aggression of war is essentially masculine.

> Cries galore
> come from the water-closet door,
> from the dropping-plastered henhouse floor,
>
> where in the blue blur
> their rustling wives admire,
> the roosters brace their cruel feet and glare
>
> with stupid eyes
> while from their beaks there rise
> the uncontrolled, traditional cries.

After the roosters have fought to the death and the body is flung on the ash-heap "with his dead wives," the poem considers a second way to understand a rooster's significance. Rather than invoking masculine aggression (and feminine passivity as its complement), their crowing now recalls St. Peter, who was reminded of his denial by a rooster: " 'Deny deny deny' / is not all the roosters cry." By introducing the New Testament significance of roosters in the second movement of the poem, Bishop isn't suggesting that the roosters' cries are not emblematic of masculine aggression; rather, she suggests that this association is far from essential or unchangeable. Bishop asks her roosters, "what are you projecting?" but her poem makes us aware of what we project onto roosters: as emblems, the birds mean what we make them mean, and we are not doomed to war because of roosters or masculinity as such. At the end of the poem, when the sun rises "faithful as enemy, or friend," Bishop emphasizes the multiple significances of anything to which we grant meaning.

The significance of Key West society, the subject of several other poems, didn't always seem so equivocal. While Bishop lived there, Key West suffered an economic depression severe even for the time. Because of political turmoil in Cuba, and later because of the world war, there was a large military presence; racial tensions ran high. In "Cootchie," a poem exploring the stunted intimacy that grew between two women divided by race and by class, the very landscape seems racially divided: when Cootchie dies, the skies are "egg-white for the funeral / and the faces sable"; her body "lies in marl, / black into white she went / below the surface of the coral reef." But in "Faustina" (named, like "Cootchie," for someone Bishop actually knew in Key West), these social divisions no longer seem so inevitable. This poem once again describes a relationship between two women that is also a relationship between servant and mistress, black and white. Everything in the old woman's room is "white" (her hair, the sheets, the clothes hung on chairs, even the bowl of farina Faustina brings to her), but the significance of this color seems far more equivocal than it does in "Cootchie."

> She bends above the other.
> Her sinister kind face
> presents a cruel black
> coincident conundrum.
>         Oh, is it

> freedom at last, a lifelong
> dream of time and silence,
> dream of protection and rest?
> Or is it the very worst,
> the unimaginable nightmare
> that never before dared last
>         more than a second?

To Faustina, the old woman's white face is both actually and figuratively "the other." To the old woman, Faustina's face seems simultaneously sinister and kind—simultaneously an image of kindness and companionship (a "dream of protection and rest") and an image of sinister distrust ("the unimaginable nightmare"). And the questions Bishop asks are unanswerable: "There is no way of telling. / The eyes say only either." Like Bishop's roosters, Faustina may be read in multiple ways:

in terms of gender she is a companion, in terms of class a dependent, and in terms of race a potentially vindictive inferior.[16]

After settling in Brazil in 1951, Bishop saw even more clearly that these terms may be understood only in relation to one another. In *Brazil*, the book she wrote for the Life World Library, Bishop explained that "Brazilians have great pride in their fine record in race relations. Their attitude can best be described by saying that the upper-class Brazilian is usually proud of his racial tolerance, while the lower-class Brazilian is not aware of his—he just practices it."[17] Because of the way her editors mangled her text, Bishop later dismissed this book, but some of her poems do present Brazil as the same kind of paradise of tolerated difference that this passage describes. In "Under the Window: Ouro Prêto" Bishop describes the happy congregation of women around an ancient drinking fountain; she also celebrates her own relationship with a woman, for it was from Lilli Correia de Araújo's bedroom window that Bishop observed this scene.

> The conversations are simple: about food,
> or, "When my mother combs my hair it hurts."
> "Women." "*Women!*" Women in red dresses
>
> and plastic sandals, carrying their almost
> invisible babies—muffled to the eyes
> in all the heat—unwrap them, lower them,
>
> and give them drinks of water lovingly
> from dirty hands, here where there used to be
> a fountain, here where all the world still stops.

A simple iron pipe has replaced the old, elaborate fountain (it's "in the museum"), but the water still draws these women together, past and present: "all have agreed for several centuries" that the water is "cold as ice." Soon the women are joined by an old man, a boy carrying laundry on his head, and two truck drivers; the gathering becomes sexually and racially mixed. The women's conversation crosses with the talk of men ("She's been in labor now two days." "Transistors / cost too much"), and the poem ends with an image of the truck's oil seeping into the fountain's standing water. But Bishop transforms this contamination into an emblem, beautiful and natural, for the mingling of differences: the water "flashes or looks upward brokenly, / like bits of mirror—no, more blue than that: / like tatters of the *Morpho* butterfly." The poem's final image invokes both morphology and Morpheus, the god of dreams, who has presided throughout this vision glimpsed below the bedroom window.

Morpheus may be the more important reference, for in some moods Bishop wanted desperately to see Brazil as a kind of haven; she was self-conscious about recreating there an image of her lost Nova Scotian childhood. But Bishop often resisted this nostalgia too. While she praised Brazilian race relations in *Brazil*, she also recognized that prejudice continued to structure Brazilian society: "the 'poor' whites, Negroes and mulattoes" at "the bottom of the scale" are "treated with a combination of warmth and intimacy on the one hand, and an autocratic manner on the other." Women continued to exist somewhere below the bottom: "The double standard could scarcely be more taken for granted. ... In this man's world, women are classified as 'the mother of my children' or 'the bearer of my name.' "[18] Other poems about Brazil reflect this awareness: "Going to the Bakery" almost seems like a rewriting of "Under the Window" in more sordid terms. Here the people gathering near a bakery (a childish whore who dances feverishly, a black beggar with a phoney wound on his side) emphasize the divisions of Brazilian culture. The baker himself is "sickly," and the "gooey tarts are red and sore"; the "loaves of bread / lie like yellow-fever victims / laid out in a crowded ward." There is no conversation here; the people congregate around the bakery but they do not meet. The poem does end with an effort at communication with the beggar—"I give him seven cents in *my* / terrific money, say 'Good night' / from force of habit"—but the exchange merely emphasizes cultural and racial difference. Throughout "Going to the Bakery" the speaker has stood apart from the scene's sordidness; in these final lines, Bishop recognizes her complicity (the complicity of the American tourist) in the perpetuation of Brazil's divided culture.

Some of Bishop's poems avoid that recognition; her note to "Manuelzinho" specifies that "a friend of the writer is speaking"—as if Bishop were afraid that the poem's exasperation with a servant would be mistaken for her own. In comparison, "Going to the Bakery" seems both more honest and more interesting. Richer still is "Brazil, January 1, 1502," in which (as I've already suggested) Bishop harnesses the confusion between herself and her subject to suggest that no matter how self-conscious she might be about social injustice, she nevertheless remains implicated in its perpetuation. It would be wrong, as Barbara Page has pointed out, to maintain that Bishop aligns herself in this poem with "aggressive masculinity and with intending rapists."[19] But it would not quite be right to suggest that Bishop, always conscious of her status as an outsider, aligns herself clearly with the retreating Indian women: while as an exposer of racism and sexism she sympathizes with these women, she nevertheless recognizes that her own discovery of Brazilian culture may be shaped by the social codes of the conquistadors. As in

"Roosters," Bishop suggests that no particular values are essential to any place or people; but in "Brazil, January 1, 1502" that realization seems far less liberating.

It initially seems even less liberating in "In the Waiting Room," a poem that shows how the very idea of selfhood is predicated on racial and sexual codes. Throughout this late poem there is a strong sense of the world's violence, natural and contrived: outside of the dentist's waiting room is the hard Massachusetts winter and the First World War. Bishop's date for the experience of the poem (February 5, 1918) points to an additional, more threatening aspect to the world outside. In Bishop's native Nova Scotia, on December 6, 1917, a munitions ship laden with eight million tons of dynamite collided with another vessel and exploded. This was the world's most powerful man-made explosion prior to the bombings of Hiroshima and Nagasaki, and many thousands of people were killed or injured. Over half of Halifax was flattened. Since Bishop had been taken by her grandparents to live in Massachusetts only weeks before, it must have seemed to her as if her lost Nova Scotia was destroyed.

This event does not appear in the poem (though Bishop's drafts show that she originally gave much more space to the image of the exploding volcano); but our knowledge of it helps us to see why Bishop would have thought of the "outside" world as such an extraordinarily threatening place. And I think it's important to feel the strength of that threat, because the poem's greater horror turns on the realization that there is no "inside" world safe from this exterior violence—not the warmth of the waiting room, not the security of the individual consciousness. While Aunt Consuelo sees the dentist, the child reads the *National Geographic*, and though its images are meant to showcase a Western mastery of "primitive" culture, the child finds each image more threatening than the one before it:

> black, naked women with necks
> wound round and round with wire
> like the necks of light bulbs.
> Their breasts were horrifying.

It is at this point that the child hears an exclamation of pain "from inside," and though she recognizes her aunt's voice (inside the dentist's office), the child herself could be speaking (the sound coming "from inside" of her): in either case, the child recognizes another person's voice as her own, just as she recognizes her own destiny in the racial and sexual otherness of the African women. Any sense of a world "inside," clearly differentiated from other cultures and people, collapses.

> But I felt: you are an *I*,
> you are an *Elizabeth*,
> you are one of *them*.
> *Why* should you be one, too?

The child is learning that whatever sense of selfhood she possesses is a precarious social construction—that she has in fact never been "inside," separated from the violence of war, the trauma of adult sexuality, or what she had been taught to think of as the cultural practices of "primitive" peoples. Bishop's repeated use of the word "inside" emphasizes this point: if, at the beginning of the poem, Aunt Consuelo is "inside" the dentist's office, then the child has been "outside" from the start; if the "inside" of a volcano is full of ash and fire, then it is not different from the violent world "outside." An erupting volcano is itself an image of the breakdown of the barrier between inside and outside, and, as Bonnie Costello has shown, Bishop's early drafts reveal that she equated the unstable interior spaces of the volcano, the waiting room, and the self: "Had a family voice misled me / into a crater of ashes / among Ten Thousand Smokes?"[20]

In the final lines of the poem, the waiting room has understandably become "too hot": it is no longer a safe haven but a place of discomfort. But the child's recognition of a world "outside" is finally not a threat but a welcome certainty.

> The War was on. Outside,
> in Worcester, Massachusetts,
> were night and slush and cold,
> and it was still the fifth
> of February, 1918.

The experience "In the Waiting Room" commemorates is initially traumatic, but the poem ends calmly, recognizing that the racially and sexually charged image of "those awful hanging breasts" does not pose a threat to selfhood but offers the very terms in which the self, however fragile, is constituted: this is simply the nature of selfhood. To see, with Bishop, that the self's contingency is also its strength is to suggest that what begins as a poem of dissolution ends, at least potentially, as a poem of empowerment.

"In the Waiting Room" is well known as perhaps Bishop's most explicitly personal poem; some readers, bolstered by Bishop's unpublished poems, have wanted to see it as a kind of "breakthrough." The poem's representation of sexuality seems less unique once we recognize the complicated ways in which sexuality and race enter much of Bishop's work, beginning with "Then Came the Poor." While Bishop's career is not static, it is not marked by an abrupt turn in the way that Rich's career is. Bishop did not begin writing with an attenuated conception of poetry as impersonal, apolitical, or closed, and she never had to make exaggerated gestures toward the personal and the open in order to express her values.

I think that Bishop's formal idiosyncrasy (her desire to bend traditional poetic forms without breaking them) accounts for the fact that some of Bishop's admirers lament the lack of greater frankness in the poems. In Lowell's mind, male poets were better equipped to overthrow poetic convention and achieve the formal "breakthrough": "Few women write major poetry."[21] But women poets of Rich's generation sometimes politicized the breakthrough as well: after her own conversion to free verse, Rich considered traditional poetic forms to be "asbestos gloves"—something that might be necessary to a poet early on but which must ultimately be discarded for the "barehanded" treatment of more immediate experience.[22] Rich and Lowell would not have agreed on what the value of experience was, but each of them implied that poetic form can be an impediment to the proper values—something that needs to be "broken through." Rebelling against the "tranquillized *Fifties*," they made free verse seem as if it had something to do with other kinds of freedom.

In contrast, Bishop was comfortable (as "In the Waiting Room" suggests) with the idea that poems cannot break through their linguistic fabric, just as the self cannot be separated from the social codes from which it's made. In their less polemical moments, Lowell and Rich were comfortable with this idea too; Rich elsewhere acknowledges the necessity of struggling within language, even as "the words / get thick with unmeaning."[23] But the common reduction of political valence to poetic form has made Bishop (who understood that all poetry offers some kind of rhetorical screen) seem apolitical. The judgment has more to do with her formal qualities as such than with the values expressed by her poems.

During the fifties, Bishop was of course living in a country that unlike the United States seemed anything but tranquil. In an essay about Rio de Janeiro, she made these comments about the "compensations" of living in such a politically and economically volatile place.

> Recently a large advertisement showed a young Negro cook, overcome by her pleasure in having a new gas stove, leaning across it toward her white mistress, who leaned over from her side of the stove as they kissed each other on the cheek.
>
> Granted that the situation is not utopian, socially speaking, and that the advertisement is silly—but could it have appeared on billboards, or in the newspapers, in Atlanta, Ga., or even in New

York? In Rio, it went absolutely unremarked on, one way or the other.[24]

Bishop made herself vulnerable here, for despite her admission that the billboard is not "utopian," she was attacked by a Brazilian journalist for her outsider's view of racial tolerance. But I think that what Bishop admired in this image was much closer to her experience than the journalist could see. While Bishop does emphasize Rio's relative freedom from prejudices that permeated Atlanta during the civil rights movement, she is describing a transgression of the social boundaries of gender and class as well as race: the three transgressions seem indistinguishable. Perhaps even more than any of the poems I've examined, this passage seems to me closest to Bishop's sensibility: more idealistic than "Going to the Bakery" (but not as utopian as "Under the Window"), it offers an image of the freedoms Bishop yearned for and too rarely found—freedoms that were ultimately, as "One Art" explains with painful reticence, lost to her.

# RANDALL JARRELL'S SEMIFEMININE MIND

As a boy, Randall Jarrell posed for the statue of Ganymede, loved by Zeus, adorning the replica of the Parthenon in Nashville's Centennial Park. Jarrell's adult friends were bemused by this anecdote, for it seemed almost too appropriate to their idea of Jarrell's sensibility: over and over again their memoirs return, more or less uncomfortably, to Jarrell's lack of manly virtues. Berryman remembered that Jarrell once had a hangover brought on by a poisoned canapé: "He's the only poet that I've ever known in the universe who simply did not drink." Robert Watson (Jarrell's colleague at Greensboro) remembered that neither did Jarrell smoke, use profanity, or enjoy jokes about sex. To Robert Lowell, consequently, Jarrell never quite seemed one of the boys: "one felt, beside him, too corrupt and companionable."[1]

Jarrell himself would not have denied these characterizations; teaching at Princeton, he complained openly about the "improper subjects" that marred conversations with his male colleagues. But Jarrell wasn't simply a prude. He took considerable delight in his transgressions of typically masculine behavior. Robert Fitzgerald remembered him as "one of the few men I have known who chortled. He really did. 'Baby doll!' he would cry, and his voice simply rose and broke in joy."[2] These exclamations were spontaneous, but they were not unself-conscious, at least after Jarrell had known Berryman, Lowell, and Fitzgerald for many years. A man who writes his publisher that he's coming into New York on the "choo-choo" is making practiced fun of professional solemnity. So is the newly bearded poet who says this to Robert Penn Warren, his old teacher: "When I look in the mirror it's just as if the fairies had stolen me away."[3] There's not only something appropriate but something lovely in the fact that Jarrell's first encounter with high art was posing as Ganymede.

But if Jarrell's friends were sometimes uncomfortable with this sensibility, his detractors were unsympathetic. The *New York Times* reviewer of *The Lost World* was downright mean, calling Jarrell's poems—among other things—corny, cute, folksy, infantile, pathetic, self-indulgent, sentimental, and tear-jerking. Jarrell was understandably upset by this notice (friends speculated that it contributed to the depression preceding his death), but he couldn't have been surprised, since these adjectives had been used for years to describe his poems (only not so many at once). Part of what Jarrell's male readers were complaining about was his repeated use of female speakers. And his female readers weren't fully convinced by these voices either: Elizabeth Bishop complained about "his *understanding* and sort-of-over-sympathizing with the lot of women."[4] As a more recent critic of both Jarrell's and Berryman's representations of female consciousness has said, "it is finally a narrow view of the feminine that he gives voice to."[5]

Unlike Berryman, however, Jarrell was not so much interested in prescribing a voice for women as developing a socially respectable way of coming to terms with his own divided sensibility. As a critic, Jarrell was certainly comfortable with the professional man's world of hard-nosed reviewing (this may account, at least in part, for the common opinion that Jarrell's criticism is superior to his poetry). But the aggressive stance of his essays often seems defensive—a strategy that bolsters his ostensibly masculine credentials while allowing him to occupy a more marginalized position in his poems. Bishop once remarked to Lowell that Jarrell's women "seem to be like none I—or you—know,"[6] and she was right: the female speakers of Jarrell's poems are closer to a man who doesn't drink or participate in locker-room banter but who likes to read fairy tales and shout "Baby doll!"

Even if a compelling explanation of Jarrell's female personae could be mounted, the question of Jarrell's style (which also seemed feminine to many readers) would still remain. Close friends found Jarrell's poems formally wayward or—Allen Tate's word—limp. But just as Jarrell knew what he was doing when he cried "Peachy!" in the Princeton faculty club, he understood the implications of avoiding certain modernist tenets of good writing. As Langdon Hammer has suggested in an important reevaluation of Jarrell, the "manifest excesses" of his poetry are "evidence of his dissatisfaction with the boundaries within which he was obliged to work."[7] Early in his career, Jarrell set out to write poems that would not always be well read through the lens of Tate's version of modernism. The results were poems that to an eye trained to look for irony seemed sentimental—poems that to Allen Tate seemed feminine.

Jarrell was able to capitalize on this impression. "I like your poetry better than anybody's since the Frost-Stevens-Eliot-Moore generation," he told Elizabeth Bishop, "so I looked with awed wonder at some phrases feeling to me a little like some of my phrases, in your poems; I felt as if, so to speak, some of my wash-cloths were part of a Modigliani collage, or as if my cat had got into a Vuillard."[8] Bishop was the contemporary poet to whom Jarrell felt closest. Despite her sense of the limitations of his female personae, Jarrell found not only his words but his life uncannily reflected in her poems. And while Jarrell's own poems don't often resemble Bishop's, they do exemplify Bishop's stylistic ideal of "a mind thinking" rather than a finished thought. Jarrell associated that ideal, as Bishop did not, with certain notions of femininity. But unlike Bishop, whom Tate or Lowell never expected to write "like a man," Jarrell had to defend his stylistic choices. Just as a woman's voice allowed him to dramatize himself more openly, it also allowed him to publish poems that rubbed against the kind of modernism he learned from Tate, Ransom, and Warren. For Jarrell, the dramatization of a feminine sensibility became inseparable from the exploration of what might be possible in American poetry at the end of the line.

During his freshman year at Vanderbilt (1932–33), Jarrell was assigned to classes with both John Crowe Ransom and Robert Penn Warren. Four years later, he and the slightly younger Lowell migrated to Kenyon College, continuing their studies with Ransom and Tate. Before he completed his M.A., Jarrell's poems appeared in the *American Review* (edited by Tate), the *Kenyon Review* (edited by Ransom), and the *Southern Review* (edited by Warren). But almost from the start Jarrell's teachers recognized that they had an uneasy disciple on their hands. "I like to talk shop, and aesthetics more or less is," said Jarrell, "politics and freeing the slaves not much."[9] Jarrell's politics kept him distant from Agrarian aesthetics as well. His early Marxism, fueled by Auden, gave him a more supple sense of poetry's historicity ("A poem, today, is both an aesthetic object and a commodity"), and his keen sense of the complexity of Tate's classicism allowed him to learn openly from his romantic and Victorian predecessors: "the best modern criticism of poetry is extremely anti-romantic, and the change in theory covers up the lack of any essential change in practice."[10]

While he questioned his teachers, Jarrell didn't want his opinions to eclipse theirs entirely. He never lost respect for the rigor of Tate's formalism. And he always insisted that Tate and Blackmur (as well as Kenneth Burke and Edmund Wilson) wrote the best criticism of his time. But Jarrell's loyalty was never confused with dogmatism. When Margaret Marshall asked him to take her place as literary editor of the *Nation*, Jarrell thought himself worthy of the job precisely because he wasn't associated with "any particular variety of literary opinion." Thinking of the *Kenyon* and *Southern* reviews, he explained that several of his friends were editors: "their dogmatic convictions and idiosyncrasies and general sectarian leanings hurt their work a lot."[11]

Jarrell meant to criticize the editorial decisions of Ransom and Warren, but he might as well have been discussing Warren's poems—though not Ransom's, with which Jarrell did feel some affinity: "To expect Tate's and Warren's poems to be much influenced by Ransom's is like expecting two nightmares to be influenced by a daydream."[12] Two nightmares: what bothered Jarrell most about Warren and Tate was their delight in violence and evil—a sensibility that Jarrell knew was deeply romantic, despite any gestures toward antiromantic classicism. Tate's poems about the Second World War especially troubled Jarrell: "violence is to him, perhaps unconsciously, an intrinsic good," he told Lowell. His criticism of Warren's 1944 *Selected Poems* suggested the political dangers of this aesthetic position: "[T]he only excuse you can find for doing nothing is to say that the world is essentially evil and incurable, that anything you did would only be a silly palliation to hide from yourself the final evil of existence; and so you believe in Original Sin, and dislike progress, science, and humanitarianism, and go in for religion and the Middle Ages, and so-on."[13] Ultimately, for Jarrell, this fascination with evil allowed Warren to avoid responsibility for the world's condition, however engaged with the social problems of the American South Warren's poems may have been.

Jarrell would sometimes be accused of maintaining too rosy an outlook on the modern world; but it was the dominance of Warren's sense of modernity's essential horror (present, Jarrell said, in the work of "thousands of others") that eventually made Jarrell's position seem sentimental. To save Jarrell from this fate, some of his admirers have tried to grant him the prestige associated with Lowell's or Berryman's public agonies, insisting that Jarrell's death was a suicide. Helen Vendler has more sensibly wondered if Jarrell, after being separated from his beloved paternal grandparents, became a chronically depressed child:

"One could read the life . . . as a desperate one, heroic in its struggle against emptiness, as though a drowning man were to come up for air a hundred times rather than thrice."[14] Like most people, Jarrell was not unacquainted with suffering; but his lifelong effort to portray "difficult ordinary happiness" (a phrase he admired in Adrienne Rich's poetry) was fueled by his sense of the danger, so carefully avoided by Bishop, of idealizing human suffering.

Even when Jarrell was a student, he developed remarkably prescient terms to describe his distance from Tate's sensibility. In a 1939 letter he explained why he didn't feel any "abyss" of modern uncertainty opening up beneath him: "I think all in all I've got a poetic and semifeminine mind, I don't put any real faith in abstractions or systems; I never had any certainties, religious or metaphysical, to lose, so I don't feel their lack."[15] Here Jarrell is relying, as Bishop would later point out, on a sexist idea of femininity (one that equates it with amorphous physicality and uncertainty), but he is freely offering to Tate the terms in which his own poems would be discussed for many years to come. The difference is that Tate would never use the word "feminine" in anything but a derogatory sense; Jarrell, in contrast, welcomes the appellation.

*The Rage for the Lost Penny*, Jarrell's first collection of poems, appeared in 1940 as part of a New Directions gathering of *Five Young American Poets*. When Tate offered the first of several uncomfortable criticisms of the "limpness" of the poems, Jarrell responded that the effect was intentional: "it's an occupational risk, a defect of quality. In other words, I'd rather seem limp and prosaic than false and rhetorical."[16] "A Story," which opens with these lines, was probably the object of Tate's censure.

> Even from the train the hill looked empty.
> When I unpacked I heard my mother say:
> "Remember to change your stockings every day—
> Socks, I mean." I went on walking past their
> Buildings gloomy with no lights or boys
> Into the country where the roads were lost.

This is the only poem from *The Rage for the Lost Penny* that Jarrell would include in his *Selected Poems* (half of "For an Emigrant" was also included, though heavily revised). And it is the only poem in which we can feel the presence of Jarrell's later fascination with the fragile state of childhood domesticity.

If "A Story" consequently seemed limp and prosaic, it was in contrast to far more rhetorical lines like these, from "The Machine-Gun."

> Our times lie in the welded hands,
> Our fortune in the rubber face—

> On the gunner's tripod, black with oil,
> Spits and gapes the pythoness.    ‚

Some of Jarrell's earliest poems do veer closely to his teachers' apocalyptic sensibility (associated here, not coincidentally, with a threatening vision of femininity—the gaping pythoness): it was this side of the early Jarrell of which Tate approved. Even as late as 1985 Warren would say that some of Jarrell's best poems were written while Jarrell was still a student. But the attitude of those poems was learned behavior for Jarrell (his contemporaneous letters don't show it at all). Reading Tate's or Warren's recollections of Jarrell, one has the impression that they saw him as they saw Hart Crane: the prodigiously talented young poet who never equaled his earliest successes, in part because of his suspicious sexuality.

The year after *The Rage for the Lost Penny* appeared, Edmund Wilson accepted a half dozen of Jarrell's poems for the *New Republic*: once again Tate expressed discomfort with some of their lines. The subsequently well-known "90 North" compares a childhood fantasy of discovering the North Pole with the adult realization of the meaninglessness of discovery. For the adult, there is nowhere to go but backwards; all steps are to the South. For the child, every night offers a new discovery.

> In the child's bed
> After the night's voyage, in that warm world
> Where people work and suffer for the end
> That crowns the pain—in that Cloud-Cuckoo-Land
>
> I reached my North and it had meaning.

Tate wanted Jarrell to cut the first four of these lines, presumably because he once again found them limp and sentimental in contrast to the adult's confrontation with meaninglessness. The poem ends with lines much closer to Tate's sensibility ("Pain comes from the darkness / And we call it wisdom. It is pain"). But as William Pritchard has pointed out, "90 North" differs from Jarrell's earlier apocalyptic poems in that it "enacts its discovery of the world as pain *within* the poem, instead of laying it on from outside." Jarrell's childhood fantasy is essential to the process; he conceded to Tate that "the stanza may be bad" but assured him that "it's impossible just to remove it."[17]

I doubt that Jarrell thought the stanza was bad, however, since its idealization of childhood once again foreshadows the preoccupations of his fully mature poems. But I suspect that Tate's continuing criticism helped to persuade Jarrell to cast his dramatizations of the "semifeminine" mind in a different form: "The Christmas Roses," published in the *New Republic* a few months after "90 North," is the first poem Jarrell wrote in a woman's voice. Compared to other poems Jarrell wrote at the same time, there's nothing about the content of "The Christmas Roses" that particularly demands a female speaker; a dying woman speaks to her former lover from a hospital bed. But in "The Christmas Roses" Jarrell's idea of femininity is crucially different from his vision of the gaping pythoness; it is much closer to his poems of childhood vulnerability. While Jarrell wrote poems about childhood from the very start of his career, his adoption of female personae came somewhat later: it was a strategy that allowed Jarrell to dramatize his own sensibility more fully. Mary Jarrell would call these poems "semi-self portraits." And she would remember that on at least one other occasion Jarrell wrote a poem in his own voice before changing it to a woman's: in "The Face" he simply replaced the word "handsome" with "beautiful" and added an epigraph from Strauss's *Rosenkavalier*, associating the poem with the Marschallin's lament over her aging face.[18]

Jarrell must have suspected that Tate (or almost anyone else) wouldn't know how to read the overwrought final lines of "The Christmas Roses."

> Come to me! Come to me! . . . How can I die without you?
> Touch me and I won't die, I'll look at you
> And I won't die, I'll look at you, I'll look at you.

These lines came to Jarrell naturally (like his cries of "Baby doll!"), but he was canny as well as sincere, aware that he "was writing in an age in which the most natural feeling of tenderness, happiness, or sorrow was likely to be called sentimental." Jarrell made this comment apropos of Ransom, who, he went on to say, "needed a self-protective rhetoric as the most brutal or violent of poets did not." Jarrell's "Christmas Roses" needed protection as well. He told the more violent Tate that the poem "is supposed to be *said* (like a speech from a play) with expression, emotion, and long pauses. It of course needs a girl to do it. I can do it pretty well for myself, to anybody I get embarrassed."[19] This explanation of "The Christmas Roses" is especially revealing of Jarrell's general predicament: given that he found his own sensibility "semifeminine" in contrast to Tate's glorification of the abyss, all of Jarrell's poems needed, as it were, a girl to do them. And since Jarrell was embarrassed by the sound of his own girlish voice, he enlisted female personae to speak for him. It was around the time he wrote "The Christmas Roses" that Jarrell also wrote his own epitaph in "To Be Dead," a poem that remained unpublished until after his death: " 'Woman,' men say of him, and women, 'Man.' "

It was also at this time that Jarrell was drafting "The End of the Line," his declaration of independence from the antiromantic modernism he had absorbed at Vanderbilt and Kenyon. The contiguity of these efforts suggests that Jarrell was trying self-consciously to write poems that wouldn't reflect Agrarian values—poems that were at least in this limited sense "postmodern." I mentioned in chapter 1 that for a brief time Auden offered an important example to Jarrell; by 1946 Lowell seemed to Jarrell the legitimately postmodern poet. And while Jarrell did try to write like Auden, he was not influenced by *Lord Weary's Castle*, even as he helped to canonize it as the decade's most important book of poems. Much modern poetry seemed to Jarrell primarily negative in impulse: it "rejects a great deal, accepts a little, and is embarrassed by that little."[20] Writing poems like "The Christmas Roses," Jarrell wanted to risk even more embarrassment by including a wider range of human emotion. Lowell wasn't embarrassed enough, and Jarrell helped to make his friend's poems more encompassing, more forgiving.

Corresponding about the manuscript of *Lord Weary's Castle*, the agnostic Jarrell found Lowell's explanations of Christianity "humane and sympathetic" but was dismayed that there was "almost no indication of this attractive Christian attitude" in the fire-breathing poems. Lowell's early poems too often seemed to Jarrell (to borrow the phrase he used to criticize his own work) "false and rhetorical" in their savoring of evil and damnation.[21] Jarrell consequently helped Lowell to change the ending of "After the Surprising Conversions" from this—

> The multitude, once unconcerned with doubt,
> Once neither callous, curious, nor devout,
> Starts at broad noon, as though some peddler whined
> At it in its familiar twang: "My friend,
> Come, come, my generous friend, cut your throat. Now;
> 'Tis a good opportunity. Now! Now!"

—to this, the version Lowell would publish in *Lord Weary's Castle*:

> The multitude, once unconcerned with doubt,
> Once neither callous, curious nor devout,
> Jumped at broad noon, as though some peddler groaned
> At it in its familiar twang, "My friend,
> Cut your own throat. Cut your own throat. Now! Now!"
> September twenty-second, Sir, the bough
> Cracks with the unpicked apples, and at dawn
> The small-mouth bass breaks water, gorged with spawn.

As Bruce Michaelson has shown, all that Jarrell did to provoke this revision (much like Pound, editing *The Waste Land*) was to criticize the diction, rhythm, and metrics of the earlier version.[22] His motive was to soften Lowell's tendency to emulate his teachers' delight in violence: having altered the earlier lines, casting the speech in the past tense, Lowell realized that the poem could end with an image of natural continuity rather than apocalyptic horror. Its last three lines comprise one of the earliest manifestations of what Seamus Heaney has called Lowell's "less assertive voice," the voice that would distinguish many of the poems of *For the Union Dead*.[23]

An even more revealing response to Lowell came in "The End of the Rainbow," first published in 1954 and later included in *The Woman at the Washington Zoo*. *Lord Weary's Castle* ends with "Where the Rainbow Ends," Lowell's apocalyptic vision of Puritan Boston: "I saw the sky descending, black and white, / Not blue, on Boston." Jarrell's much longer poem traces the thoughts of a female painter (named "Content") who has moved from Massachusetts to Southern California. She hasn't been able to abandon her heritage completely; among her possessions are pieces of Pilgrim Rock, a copy of Emerson's *Compensation*, and a miniature of her great-great-great-grandfather, "pressed to death in Salem / For a wizard." Content is aging, lonely, and obsessed with the ghosts of her past. Like Lowell, she almost sees the sky descending, "black and white":

> She looks around her:
> Many waves are breaking on many shores,
> The wind turns over, absently,
> The leaves of a hundred thousand trees.
> How many colors, squeezed from how many tubes
> In patient iteration, have made up the world
> She draws closer, like a patchwork quilt,
> To warm her, all the warm, long, summer day!
> The local colors fade:
> She hangs here on the verge of seeing
> In black and white,
> And turns with an accustomed gesture
> To the easel, saying:
> "Without my paintings I would be—
> > why, whatever *would* I be?"

This turn from potential nightmare to the saving routine of daily life is quintessential Jarrell: not paintings, not even the act of painting, but the act of turning to the easel saves her, and the gesture is so much a part of her daily life that she can't imagine her existence without it. Her realization is almost empty of meaning ("whatever *would* I be?"), but it is crucial to the continuity of her life.

The realization also underwrites the poem's structure. "The End of the Rainbow" is typical of Jarrell's mature work in that it follows the turns and digressions of meditation, avoiding a clear sense of an ending or even of accumulated significance. And though the meditation is a woman's, Jarrell invites us to see "The End of the Rainbow" as a record of his own thoughts.

> If you look at a picture the wrong way
> You see yourself instead.
>                                   —The wrong way?

Content looks at the glass covering her painting and sees herself in her own work. This is not the "wrong" way to view the painting or to read the poem: Jarrell suggests that he may similarly be found in what he has made. "The End of the Rainbow" focuses on a woman because Jarrell associated its healthy acquiescence with femininity, just as he associated Lowell's apocalyptic tendencies with masculinity. Explaining what troubled him about the heroine of "The Mills of the Kavanaughs," Jarrell said, "You feel, 'Yes, Robert Lowell would act like this if he were a girl'; but whoever saw a girl like Robert Lowell?"[24]

At the same time that he was reading *Lord Weary's Castle*, Jarrell saw himself in the poems of a particular woman. In this passage from his review of Elizabeth Bishop's *North & South* (which appeared shortly before the review of *Lord Weary's Castle*), Jarrell seems to be describing the ideals of his own poems.

> Instead of crying, with justice, "This is a world in which no one can get along," Miss Bishop's poems show that it is barely but perfectly possible—has been, that is, for her. Her work is unusually personal and honest in its wit, perception, and sensitivity—and in its restrictions too; all her poems have written underneath, *I have seen it*. She is morally so attractive, in poems like "The Fish" or "Roosters," because she understands so well that the wickedness and confusion of the age can explain and extenuate other people's wickedness and confusion, but not, for you, your own; that morality, for the individual, is usually a small, personal, statistical, but heartbreaking or heart-warming affair of omissions and commissions the greatest of which will seem infinitesimal, ludicrously beneath notice, to those who govern, rationalize, and deplore.

For Jarrell, Bishop's poems offered a powerful corrective to the idealization of violence he found in Warren, Tate, Lowell, and "thousands of others." "It is odd how pleasant and sympathetic her poems are," he continued, "in these days when many a poet had rather walk down children like Mr. Hyde than weep over them like Swinburne, and when many a poem is gruesome occupational therapy for a poet who stays legally innocuous by means of it."[25] In his own poems, Jarrell preferred to weep, even if he gave readers like Tate the chance of finding his poems sentimental. Bishop herself never weeps, but she never rails against the world's evil, exempting herself from responsibility to that world—keeping herself "legally innocuous."

The other words Jarrell uses to praise Bishop's work (sympathetic, personal, honest, sensitive, moral, heartbreaking) describe qualities Jarrell sought in his own. "Your poems seem really about real life," he told Bishop with calculated naiveté, "and to have as much of what's nice and beautiful and loving about the world as the world lets them have." Jarrell used these grand terms (life, beautiful, loving) intentionally; they allowed him to describe the mysterious ways in which the formal qualities of Bishop's poems, in contrast to Moore's, made them seem like a part of human life, rather than an artistic record of it: "I've quite got to like your poems better than Marianne Moore's as much as I do like hers—but life beats art, so to speak, and sense beats eccentricity, and the way things really are beats the most beautiful unreal visions, half-truths, one can fix up by leaving out and indulging oneself."[26] Jarrell admired exactly what Bishop tried hardest to capture in her poems: the process of thinking, rather than the completed thought—a formal structure that eschewed the contours of the well-wrought urn for a more wayward and self-questioning kind of poetry. "We think of the structure of poetry too much in static terms," said Jarrell in a lecture he delivered at Princeton in 1942: "But the poem is completely temporal, about as static as an explosion."[27]

It would not be exactly right to say that Bishop was a crucial influence on Jarrell's poems; by the late forties his sensibility was fully formed. But as his letters to Bishop suggest, Jarrell thought that his mind was uncannily similar to hers: "It's a feeling I never have with anybody else," he told her, " . . . It's as if you were a color I see so easily I hardly have to look."[28] Bishop's work provided him with a compelling example of his own aesthetic goals (one that he could write about more gracefully than he could write about himself), and in his review of *North & South* Jarrell easily enlists Bishop in his effort to undermine his teachers' values. In this regard, Bishop was especially useful to Jarrell because her poems did not overthrow those values completely. During the 1940s and 50s Jarrell would write appreciations of poets (Williams and Whitman most prominently) whose sensibility was far more capacious than Bishop's. Just as he never tried to write like Lowell, however, he never tried to write like Williams either. Poems like "A Game at Salzburg," "The End of the Rainbow," or "The Night Before the Night Before Christmas" are loosened up in the way that Bishop's "bramble bushes" are; they retain an amount of formal clarity even as they trace the temporal process of a mind thinking.

Like Bishop's career, consequently, Jarrell's reveals a gradual development rather than a "breakthrough" to unprecedented formal or autobiographical openness. The early books offer suggestions of Jarrell's mature sensibility, and in *The Seven-League Crutches*, published in 1951, Jarrell perfected the formal strategies that would sustain his work until the end of his life. Reviewing the volume, Lowell praised "A Game at Salzburg" in terms that recall Bishop's way of talking about her own poems: it "has the broken, chanced motion of someone thinking out loud."[29] Jarrell had taught in the Salzburg Seminar in American Civilization in the summer of 1948, and the poem is set in the Schloss Leopoldskron, where Jarrell lived. The setting provides the only link between the three "games" the poem describes. First, Jarrell plays a game of tennis with a German man. Next, he meets a three-year-old girl who initiates a game well known to German children: she says to Jarrell, *"Hier bin i'"* [Here I am], and Jarrell, aware of the rules, replies *"Da bist du"* [There you are]. Throughout these two games, arbitrary and pleasant in themselves, there are hints of some darker significance. The tennis partner had been a prisoner of war in Colorado; and while Jarrell sits on the veranda with the little girl, "a darkness falls, / Rain falls." The poem's third game takes place when the storm has passed.

> But the sun comes out, and the sky
> Is for an instant the first rain-washed blue
> Of becoming: and my look falls
> Through falling leaves, through the statues'
> Broken, encircling arms
> To the lives of the withered grass,
> To the drops the sun drinks up like dew.

> In anguish, in expectant acceptance
> The world whispers: *Hier bin i'*.

"A Game at Salzburg" is a definitively postwar poem: Jarrell remains conscious of the Second World War but explores the odd ways in which the world absorbs its own destructiveness, moving forward. Though he wants to accept the loveliness of the world, there can be no answer to the world's "Here I am": his acceptance is fragile, hesitant, like the associative structure of the poem itself.

A month after he published *The Seven-League Crutches*, Jarrell wondered about the "monotonous violence and extremity" of "The Mills of the Kavanaughs," likening it to "a piece of music that consisted of nothing but climaxes."[30] In contrast, Jarrell's "Night before the Night before Christmas," the longest poem in *The Seven-League Crutches*, seems like a piece of music with no climaxes at all: it embodies a process of almost constant variation or metamorphosis. Like "A Game at Salzburg," though on a much larger scale, "The Night before the Night before Christmas" traces the thoughts of a "wandering mind." But its prosody is looser. And the poem is even more characteristically Jarrell's in that its protagonist is a fourteen-year-old girl. She is (like Jarrell himself) a child of the thirties, and her mind is full of Marx and Engels, John Strachey's *The Coming Struggle for Power*, and Bertolt Brecht's "In Praise of Learning." Throughout the night, the girl's mind wanders between the "real" world these books describe and a dream-world populated by her mother and pet squirrel, both of whom have recently died.[31]

Even as she wraps Christmas presents, the girl cannot accept religious consolation ("how could this world be / If he's all-powerful, all-good?"), but she does believe that Marxist education might save her family. In her dreams, Engels becomes an angel; her squirrel might not have died, she muses, half asleep, "if he were educated." Ultimately, however, her dreams won't protect her from her own life, from "the abyss that is her home." In her final dream, she imagines that she and her brother (who is sick and may be dying as well) are Hansel and Gretel and then John and Wendy from *Peter Pan*.

> Staring, staring
> At the gray squirrel dead in the snow,
> She and her brother float up from the snow—
> The last crumbs of their tears
> Are caught by the birds that are falling
> To strew their leaves on the snow
> That is covering, that has covered
> The play-mound under the snow. . . .
> The leaves are the snow, the birds are the snow,
> The boy and girl in the leaves of their grave
> Are the wings of the bird of the snow.
> But her wings are mixed in her head with the Way
> That streams from their shoulders, stars like snow:
> They spread, at last, their great starry wings
> And her brother sings, "I am dying."
>
> "No: it's not so, not so—
> Not *really*,"
> She thinks; but she says, "You are dying."
> He says, "I didn't know."
>
> And she cries: "I don't know, I don't know, I don't know!"
>
> They are flying.

These lines offer a condensed version of the poem's almost constant process of metamorphosis; their force is centripetal, pushing the poem in several directions at once. Instead of saying "I am flying" as the children do in *Peter Pan*, the girl's brother says "I am dying." Her dreams had been her only refuge from her mother's death, but death has intruded even there. She makes room for it, however, imagining death as one of childhood's delightful adventures: the word "flying" initially allowed the word "dying" into the dream, but now the acts of flying and dying merge in a fantasy of omnipotence. Yet the dream ends, as it must, and the poem itself ends with these lines.

> She feels, in her hand, her brother's hand.
> She is crying.

Given his friends' earlier responses to his poems, Jarrell must have known he was courting all the usual objections to his "semifeminine" sensibility. Bishop's example had helped him to write "The Night before the Night before Christmas," but Bishop herself was uncomfortable with the poem. She told Jarrell that she liked it, but she also wondered if it were loose, overly long, and possibly self-indulgent. Jarrell replied cheerfully that "Rilke certainly is monstrously self-indulgent a lot of the time."[32] Years earlier, he had told Tate that limpness was an "occupational risk," and Jarrell responded similarly to Bishop's charge of self-indulgence. "The Night before the Night before Christmas" represents his most ambitious effort to write against the grain of certain prejudices his teachers distilled from their strategically limited reading of modernism. And if the poem resists any effort to read it closely; if it violates Poundian strictures against Victorian sentiment; if it fits comfortably neither with the poems of Williams nor the poems of Tate; if it even seems mannered or self-indulgent in its preoccupation with children and fairy tales, then the poem has succeeded in the terms Jarrell valued most. Lowell seemed to recognize this when he wrote that "The Night before the Night before Christmas" was the "best, most mannered, the most unforgettable, and the most irritating poem" in *The Seven-League Crutches*.[33]

Like Lowell, Bishop did admire Jarrell's poems, whatever her misgivings; she seemed genuinely dismayed when her second book won the Pulitzer instead of Jarrell's *Selected Poems*, and she praised Jarrell for avoiding (as she did herself) the "anguish-school that Cal [Lowell] seems innocently to have inspired."[34] But given Jarrell's consistent admiration for Bishop, it isn't simply ironic that Bishop was particularly troubled by *The Seven-League Crutches*. Writing about "A Girl in a Library," another poem from this volume, Langdon Hammer wonders if Jarrell's decision to address the girl "begins to look like a way of preserving male authority by making it appear benevolent."[35] This charge might be brought against others of Jarrell's poems: their desire to speak to, for, and about women could be a way of appropriating (and thereby delimiting) the terms of femininity. After Jarrell's death, Mary Jarrell recalled that "The Lost Children" (spoken by a woman) grew from her account of one of her own dreams; the most famous lines in the poem ("I *know* those children. I know all about them. / Where are they?") were actually written by Jarrell's wife. What may initially seem like an act of appropriation and mastery on Jarrell's part is something more complicated, however, since Mary Jarrell recognized that her words echo lines that Jarrell himself had already written in "Thinking of the Lost World." To her, "The Lost Children" was as much about Jarrell's "happy-sad recollections of lost boyhood" as it was about "a woman's happy-sad remembrances of lost motherhood." Similarly, she felt that "The Night before the Night before Christmas" was the first of Jarrell's "lengthy semiautobiographical poems that culminated in the three-part *Lost World*."[36] There are some poems (Hammer is right to single out "A Girl in a Library") in which Jarrell asserts male authority in the guise of sympathy for women; but other poems (like "The Night before the Night") suggest that Jarrell sometimes occupied within our culture a legitimately and productively feminized position.

The importance of granting this possibility is suggested by the *New York Times* review of *The Lost World*. Dismissing most of the volume, Joseph Bennett wrote that there were four successful poems. Two of them ("Woman" and "In Nature There Is Neither Right nor Left nor Wrong") are unique in *The Lost World* for their sexism: "Men are what they do, women are what they are," says the tough-talking female narrator of "In Nature." In contrast to these poems, "The Lost World" and "Thinking of the Lost World" are not spoken by women; nor do they concern women's experiences. Having spent many years impersonating a woman's voice, Jarrell seems to drop the mask, speaking openly of his love of childhood, fairy tales, and pets. Tellingly, Bennett found these poems to be infected by "an indulgent and sentimental Mamaism."[37] Jarrell had done something worse than pretend to be a woman: he had pretended to be himself.

Thematically, structurally, and prosodically, "The Lost World" and its pendant "Thinking of the Lost World" seem in retrospect to be the work Jarrell was always pushing toward. "Thinking of the Lost World" strikes a note that is not uncommon in Jarrell's poetry; in "The End of the Rainbow" or in "The Lost Children" there is a similar sense of emptiness transfigured into something palpable and dear. What is different about "Thinking of the Lost World" is that Jarrell openly associates these feelings not with women but with his own idiosyncratic

sensibility. Judith Butler has argued that the act of female impersonation, even when it draws on highly conventional styles of femininity,
"implicitly reveals the imitative structure of gender itself—as well as its
contingency."[38] "Thinking of the Lost World" may in this sense be the
logical conclusion of Jarrell's lifelong act of impersonation, since its effort of self-definition is no less dependent on masquerade—on the necessity of dramatizing an identity, rather than taking it for granted.

At the end of "Thinking of the Lost World," the bearded Jarrell
drives past a boy who calls out "Hi, Santa Claus." Jarrell waves, willing
to play along, but startled by the awareness that he's now as old as his
grandparents once were. He looks at his hand on the steering wheel,
and the hand becomes his grandmother's, brown and spotted: "Where's
my own hand?" To answer this question, Jarrell confronts a vision of
himself as a child. He knows that the child has nothing to give him. But
as in Stevens's "Snow Man" (and looking back to *King Lear*), "nothing"
becomes a powerful presence. As Jarrell drives inexorably forward, into
the future, nostalgia is revealed as a fool's game—a game of pretense
and disguise that Jarrell plays lovingly, over and over again.

> I seem to see
> A shape in tennis shoes and khaki riding-pants
> Standing there empty-handed; I reach out to it
> Empty-handed, my hand comes back empty,
> And yet my emptiness is traded for its emptiness,
> I have found that Lost World in the Lost and Found
> Columns whose gray illegible advertisements
> My soul has memorized world after world:
> LOST—NOTHING. STRAYED FROM NOWHERE. NO REWARD.
> I hold in my own hands, in happiness,
> Nothing: the nothing for which there's no reward.

# RICHARD WILBUR'S
# SMALL WORLD

Poem after poem is gracefully and competently done, there is
good taste and intelligence throughout, there is variety of theme
and an interesting, largely mythological, field of allusion. . . . But
on the whole the poet's many evident talents only add to one's
sense of frustration at the tameness and not-quiteness of his poetry; if this be the new decorum, I suggest we scoot back to modernism.[1]

Back to modernism: in the aftermath of the turmoil Pound and Eliot
injected into the American literary scene, Richard Wilbur's poetry has
sometimes seemed a little too calm, and this statement is similar to
many responses his poetry received throughout the 1940s and 50s.
Randall Jarrell was sympathetic but skeptical: he wrote to Elizabeth
Bishop, "who'd have thought that the era of the poet in the Grey Flannel
Suit was coming?"[2] But poets like Robert Bly weren't sympathetic at all.
Writing in *kayak*, Bly quoted Wilbur's "Mind," and said, "as a fist, *kayak*
is raised against stuff like this, crystallized flower formations from the
jolly intellectual dandies."[3]

The battle lines of American poetry after modernism seem clear enough here (the bardic Bly and the fastidious Wilbur) and other poets have been quick to jump to Wilbur's defense. Anthony Hecht once praised Wilbur for standing apart from "this poetic era of arrogant solipsism and limp narcissism—when great, shaggy herds of poets write only about themselves."[4] That's one way to respond to Bly's fist: with another fist. Wilbur's response, "A Postcard for Bob Bly," took a different form: "Granted that it's a figurative fist," Wilbur admitted, "That critics punch as harmlessly as kittens"; nevertheless, "when you incite to riot / Against your friend, he is not pleasured by it."[5] Refusing to raise a fist, Wilbur reminds Bly that he retains a stockpile of ammunition. Bly and Wilbur were both at Harvard in the late 1940s, and Wilbur surely remembered (even if Bly didn't) the shaggy bard's earlier incarnation as New Critical aesthete. As the editor of the *Harvard Advocate*, Bly gave this slap on the wrist to Kenneth Rexroth.

> Perhaps it is unfortunate that Rexroth should have been let loose on the Romantics; there is, I think, a difference between the desire to express personal emotion by increased direct reference to the world of nature, and the desire to overthrow all external discipline of morals of government.[6]

The symmetries are perfect here. The early Bly offers an opinion of which the later Hecht might have approved. Wilbur stands in the middle of the fray, seemingly aware that an unnuanced extreme can too easily fold into its opposite.

Which is not to say that Wilbur is a poet without opinions. The quotation with which I began is in fact not a criticism of Wilbur (though it sounds like one) but Wilbur's own criticism of John Heath-Stubbs, offered in 1950. Even at this early point in his career, Wilbur had little patience for the values that are usually ascribed to him (mere grace, taste, craft, or elegance), and though it's tempting to say that Wilbur is criticizing himself in the mirror of Heath-Stubbs, I think it's safer to say that Wilbur is that rare thing: a seriously misunderstood poet. Because the style of his poetry is so distinctive, so easily opposed to the later Bly, readers assume that Wilbur is deeply invested in distinctions. The poetry itself shows otherwise. Wilbur has gleefully gone "back to modernism" to learn from Moore, Stevens, Eliot, Frost, and Williams; at the same time, he has moved past it precisely because of his openness to modernism's variety of poetic practices.

Wilbur's respect for Williams offers one potent example of this openness. In the same review in which he found Heath-Stubbs's poetry tepid, Wilbur called the form of Williams's poetry "perfect" (though he confessed that he couldn't say exactly why it was so). A few years earlier, Wilbur wrote a response to talks given by Williams and Louise Bogan at the now legendary Bard College poetry conference, organized by Theodore Weiss. Wilbur disagreed with Williams, who argued for the historical necessity of free verse, and agreed with Bogan, who maintained—brilliantly—that the last hundred years had witnessed not a steady opening up of poetic form but an "alternate and gradual loosening and tightening of form."[7] But Wilbur was adamant that "in criticizing Dr. Williams' criticism" he was "not out to attack free verse." Especially not Williams's free verse. Wilbur's prime contention was that "poets can't afford to forget that there is a reality of things which survives all orders great and small," and his examples of this "heartfelt subservience to the external" included Williams's "ashcans, wastepaper and red wheelbarrows," along with Marianne Moore's poems, Cézanne's paintings, and James Agee's *Let Us Now Praise Famous Men*.[8] Wilbur's own work, culminating in the poems of *Things of This World*, also displays a radical loyalty to the physical world, even though the poems don't sound at all like Williams.

In an essay on Wilbur's poetry of "being," Nathan Scott rehearses the great divide between New Critical and Black Mountain poets, suggesting that "in the case of Wilbur at least, we may notice in one important particular this divide being surmounted, in the degree to which he appears to be seeking a kind of metaphysical ground not unlike that at which, say, a poet like Robert Duncan aims."[9] But even if the metaphysics are similar, the verse sounds different. Like Elizabeth Bishop, from whom he first learned "the joy of putting a poem together,"[10] Wilbur never felt the need to overthrow or break through traditional poetic forms in order to bring his poetry closer to the physical world. No matter how fully engaged with the realities, natural and political, of his time, consequently, Wilbur's style made him seem "irresponsible." That is Wilbur's own word, but one could add (given the ways in which formal extravagance has been associated arbitrarily with certain values) elitist, insincere, and reactionary.

Wilbur is none of these things. The external world that elicits his loyalty includes laundry dazzled by sunlight; but it also includes the Vietnam War. And though the laundry may seem more prominent, the political upheavals of the last fifty years have been the ballast of Wilbur's poetry. Writing "Little Gidding," T. S. Eliot worried that the poem required "some acute personal reminiscence (never to be explicated, of course, but to give power from well below the surface)."[11] In Wilbur's poetry, the material that lies below the surface of the poem, giving it power, tends to be public and historical rather than private and personal. On the surface, Wilbur may not often seem like a political poet, but his inspiration has come consistently from the public events of his time.

Unlike Elizabeth Bishop, Wilbur has written more than a few explicitly political poems ("Mined Country," "Speech for the Repeal of the
McCarran Act," "A Miltonic Sonnet for Mr. Johnson," or "A Fable," to
name only a few). Wilbur tends to engage the mainstream of American
liberal politics in a way that Bishop (whose poems follow an equally
powerful path) does not. Like Bishop, however, Wilbur is uncomfortable
with what he has called the "speechifying" of much political poetry,
preferring to recognize the ways in which "any full poetry is bound to
have an implicit political dimension."[12] Wilbur's poems have many
other important qualities, but their "political dimension" interests me
especially, given the ways in which the poems have been misread as
mere formal confections, pretty but irresponsible. In fact, Wilbur's
poems take their extravagant shapes precisely because of his respect
for the magnitude of the world, both lovely and horrific, outside the
poet's mind.

The McCarran Internal Security Act, enacted by Congress in 1950, required members of the Communist party to register with the attorney
general; other organizations had to supply lists of their members.
Wilbur's "Speech for the Repeal of the McCarran Act" was published
only a few months later, and it grew from a long-standing opposition
to government censorship and coercion. In 1938 the House of Representatives formed its special committee to investigate un-American activities. Wilbur's comment on its chairman, Martin Dies, appeared in the
Amherst *Touchstone*.

> He'd banish all the aliens
> If you gave him half a chance.
> The ample seat of Mr. Dies'
> Extremely ample pants
> Is filled with all the bitingest
> Of patriotic ants.[13]

These lines are taken from one of the first poems Wilbur published, a
clever undergraduate poem that is also politically astute. When one of
Wilbur's classmates wrote to the *Amherst Student*, objecting to Wilbur's
views in patriotic terms, Wilbur's response was abrupt: "the primary
threat to our democracy, as has been said often but not often enough,
is that Red-baiters, Jew-baiters and professional patriots will impair our
civil liberties in their haste to suppress those whom they believe
threaten those liberties."[14]

Wilbur became the editor of the *Student* and again and again wrote
editorials defending the preservation of civil liberties. Characteristically
undogmatic, Wilbur once remarked that "the question is not one con-

cerning the merits of Communism"; his satire on Martin Dies was published beside another on "Labor's William Green."[15] But Wilbur also
published his own interview (signed "Lenin") with Earl Browder, sec-
retary of the American Communist Party, and it was with Browder that
Wilbur's sympathies lay. Many years later, Wilbur would remember his
own brush with intolerance after he was drafted in 1942.

> Reporting for duty at Fort Dix, I was assigned to cryptographic
> training, and thereafter sent on to a secret cryptanalytic camp in
> the woods of Virginia, where (as I later discovered) my progress
> into cryptanalysis was cut short by adverse security reports from
> the CIC and FBI. It was quite true that I held leftist views and
> had radical friends, and that I had been so stupid as to keep a
> volume of Marx in my footlocker; but then as now I had an un-
> complicated love of my country, and I was naively amazed to
> learn that my service record was stamped "Suspected of Disloy-
> alty."[16]

Perhaps it was this experience that made Wilbur hold onto his reverence
for civil liberties in the fifties, when many members of his generation
succumbed to a more urgent postwar sense of alarm over national security.

Wilbur had opposed the war, often writing in the *Student* about the
dangers of dogmatic, unspecific patriotism. His position was not popular. "You're all afraid for your skins," shouted one professor to a
group of anti-interventionist students; another told Wilbur that "if we
refuse to fight, we refuse to do our duty; there is, after all, a Christian
way of fighting, a way of fighting with as much decency and good
sportsmanship as possible." But Wilbur took far more heat when he
suggested that it was wrong even to expect the certainty of conviction
from people of his generation: "What is taken for idealism in Youth is
inexperience and verbosity, and our enthusiasm is the product of good
health and bad judgment." When the editor of the *Williams Record* wrote
to protest this editorial, Wilbur responded by holding up the value of
hesitancy and doubt in a time of easily adopted convictions: "An education ought to disillusion, then reconstruct. Its disease and its glory is
indecision. A man who is barely beginning his education, should be
thoroughly maladjusted in the world of ideas. If hesitation and suspense
of judgment strike him as 'cowardly,' it is evident that he is more interested in conditioning than free education."[17]

There's a touch of grandstanding here (the young Wilbur is enjoying
his notoriety) but the position was neither jejune nor unique; more experienced journalists (like Kenneth Burke) were paying for it as Wilbur
wrote. And while the older Wilbur has understandably downplayed the

interest of these early writings, his early impatience with dogmatism became the seedbed for his later nonoppositional thinking—the kind of thinking that allows him to learn from Williams even as he disagrees with him. Objecting to Wilbur's response to Williams and Bogan, James Breslin says that "Wilbur is so sensible, so balanced, has such 'complexity of attitude' on the question of form that he is left with no ground to stand on."[18] But the early political writings, in which Wilbur learned how to maintain such an attitude, show that doubt and hesitation offered him a solid foundation.

"The poetic position is seldom on the fence," lamented Wilbur in one of his few college editorials about poetry rather than politics: "Any grail will do. . . . The war is a natural, and the most stimulating side of the fence is the crusader's, of course." Just as Wilbur wondered about the ability of youth to cope with complicated political questions, he worried about the capacity of poetry too: "what are the natural limitations of emotional poetry?" But when the United States entered the war, Wilbur recognized sensibly that while his poems could continue to sit on the fence, he could not: "now that we are fighting, what is needed is unanimity and determined action." Even this level of conviction was not firm enough for Wilbur's critics, however; he quoted these sentences from the Pearl Harbor editorial of the *Williams Record* in order to justify his own eschewal of passionate conviction: "We fight Nazis and Nipponese together, to crush a revolutionary nihilism that has sought to corrupt the world. We fight them with our steel and our blood and our lives, until we build the union of free peoples everywhere that alone can guarantee the life we cherish."[19]

Without ever adopting this sort of rhetoric, Wilbur served with the 36th Infantry Division in Italy and Southern France and along the Siegfried Line in Germany. (The army overlooked his disloyalty, installing Wilbur as the division's cryptographer, when his predecessor suffered a mental breakdown.) Wilbur had considered a career in journalism, but it was during the war (as he subsequently explained in "On My Own Work") that Wilbur wrote his first serious poems: "My first poems were written in answer to the inner and outer disorders of the Second World War and they helped me, as poems should, to take ahold of raw events and convert them, provisionally, into experience."[20] His first professionally published poem, "Italy: Maine" (signed by Pvt. Richard P. Wilbur), remains uncollected but, from today's perspective, the poem seems closer to Wilbur's mature voice than several of the poems that made it into *The Beautiful Changes*, his first book.

> Whose song is for swarm and surfeit, let him win
> This passive land, moist-green and sun-stunned.

I'll go after
Spike grass, crab apple, gargoyle tamarack
And the last crazy jack pine climbing Cadillac's back.[21]

These final lines of "Italy: Maine" sound a note that will be richly harmonized throughout Wilbur's later poems: a devotion to the unmasterable and apparently insignificant details of the natural world, lovingly catalogued. But the lines are especially useful because they help to show how this aspect of Wilbur's sensibility was formed. In one of his Amherst columns Wilbur offered a list of trivial events (a hen laying a triple-yolk egg; the Song Writers' Protective Association voting 372 to 24 to censure "She Had to Go and Lose It at the Astor"; a member of the House of Representatives objecting so loudly to the Wages and Hours bill that his opponent's hearing was restored) that transpired along with the first battles of the World War: "A daily reading of these items in this war year should be a tonic to us all, a reassurance that everything is not dramatic, world-shaking and momentous, for these little stories are about the people whose lives are the true history of this year 1940 and of all years."[22]

Visible here, as in "Italy: Maine," is the Wilbur who would more than a decade later complain that "there is at present no want of apocalyptic emotionalism or of connoisseurial detachment among us, but the poem of modest and genuine feeling does not seem to come readily."[23] Wilbur was trying to write those poems himself, and he would eventually offer a kind of credo for them in "A Wood," published in *Walking to Sleep*: "Some would distinguish nothing here but oaks, / Proud heads conversant with the power and glory," the poem begins. Wilbur wants to notice the dogwood—"overshadowed, small / But not inclined to droop." And given that the sun is, practically speaking, equally distant from dogwood and oak, he concludes that "no one style, I think, is recommended." Wilbur has always understood that his own style may cause him to be underestimated, no matter how timely his utterance. As James Dickey put it early on, "Wilbur's is not essentially a tragic mind, and the lack of this one quality will probably keep him, in the estimates of literary historians and other fossils, from being called a 'major poet': one having made large Miltonic or Poundian flights."[24]

Once again the wartime context reveals the real power of Wilbur's position. After "Italy: Maine," Wilbur's next publication was a group of poems that appeared in *Foreground*, along with a harrowing prose account of wartime deprivation and displacement. "The Day After the War" culminates in this passage:

When all you can remember is the getting up in the morning,
the lineup, the bored cruelties of the guards, the tasteless soup

and sawdust bread, the goaded dragging hurrying line to the field, the road, the tunnel, the mine, the lathe, the sawmill, the powder-plant; and the grey shadows on the ceiling all night when it was too cold to sleep

When you have lost all identity, all relation, all significance of speech, all notion of belonging anywhere in the world, when you have experienced *nothing* as a real entity, touching, filling, numbing and abolishing you

Then the passing of a truck will fill your whole head with the clatter of bouncing planking, and the sight of leaves silvered on the undersides by road-dust will please you to smiling, and the sight of a child suckling will make you want to fall to your knees, and the explosion of a thrush will make you laugh in your throat, and the rain falling on you and coursing down your face and plastering your shirt to your skin, running down your stomach and your legs and filling your shoes will make you grin like a fool.[25]

As a student, Wilbur understood the value of little things; as a new private, just shipped off to Italy, he yearned for the particularity of Maine's landscape. Wilbur's experience as a soldier taught him intimately that the details of the most insignificant thing may, in a particular place and time, hold more power than the grandest Miltonic or Poundian flight.

Most of the poems published with "The Day After the War" were war poems ("Place Pigalle," "Potato," "Mined Country"), and among them, "Potato" values what is "too common to cherish or steal." But it is in "Cigales," published a few months later, that the power of particular things is explored most deeply. This poem, eventually chosen as the opening poem in *The Beautiful Changes* (and later retitled "Cicadas"), contains lines that the deep-imagist Bly might have written—"Even the leaves / have thick tongues"—but builds on Marianne Moore's probing of the animal world's moral value. Wilbur's focus is the cicada, and the way it resists any human effort to locate significance in its song: "Such a plain thing / morals could not surround."

> This thin uncomprehended song it is
> springs healing questions into binding air.
> Fabre, by firing all the municipal cannon
> under a piping tree, found out
> cicadas cannot hear.

Wilbur had wondered, given most poetry's inability to sit on the fence, if it were possible to write an isolationist poem. "Cigales" is such a poem, for despite Wilbur's rejection of any human meaning for this insect, its song functions as an emblem for poetry—especially poetry written in a time of war. Wilbur suggests that the poet sings as the cicada sings, deaf to the cannon's roar. And yet, like the self-made song of Stevens's "The Idea of Order at Key West," the cicada's song nevertheless becomes involved with the world it cannot sense. "Cigales" rejects the terms of most war poetry (terms implying, as Wilbur would later put it, that a poem is " 'serious' and 'significant' because it mentions the atomic bomb"[26]) and turns from the momentous to the commonplace and the particular. Yet Wilbur's position in *The Beautiful Changes* is not consistent enough to be dogmatic: while other poems in the volume (notably "Objects" and "A Dutch Courtyard") extend his praise for minutiae, the poems immediately following "Cigales" include much grander images of war ("On the Eyes of an SS Officer"), suggesting that it is difficult—an achievement rather than a retreat—to keep the poem focused on little things.

Given the importance of Moore's example for Wilbur, it is interesting to note that his way of responding to the Second World War was closer to Moore's than Elizabeth Bishop's was. When Moore read Bishop's "Roosters" she was shocked by what seemed to her the violence of its rhymes and the coarseness of its images, going so far as to rewrite the poem. She might have approved of "Cigales," however, for, like Wilbur's, Moore's preoccupation with the commonplace was in part a response to the pressure of wartime vulgarity. Moore's "Reinforcements," first published during the First World War and later collected in her 1921 *Poems*, begins with these stanzas.

The vestibule to experience is not to
    be exalted into epic grandeur. These men are going
to their work with this idea, advancing like a school of fish through

still water—waiting to change the course or dismiss
    the idea of movement, till forced to. The words of the Greeks
ring in our ears, but they are vain in comparison with a sight like this.

Moore wants her title to invoke the idea of military reinforcements, but the poem also addresses the ways in which the language of poetry—the usual terms of war poetry—might become a "reinforcement" of war. Faced with the vastness of war, the words of the Greeks ring in her ears, but she is unwilling to exalt the experience with epic grandeur. Moore's later response to the war was to write self-consciously "little" poems rather than ambitious (and, for Moore, masculine) poems that answer an epic challenge. Analyzing Moore's response to Bishop's "Roosters," Betsy Erkkila shows that Moore's "moral, decorous, and ladylike aesthetic posture" was, at least in the early years of Moore's career, a finely honed weapon.[27] But by the time Bishop wrote "Roosters," Bishop was not interested in appearing ladylike, no matter what benefits might be derived from it. By extending Moore's aesthetic, in contrast, Wilbur became a poet who was (like Jarrell) sometimes perceived as "ladylike," especially in a poetic climate that valued the transgression of all decorums.

Wilbur was undaunted by this perception; the poems of his second volume extend Moore's method even as they cease to respond to warfare. *Ceremony* is clearly a postwar book, and its poems engage a different world. In "Driftwood" Wilbur meditates on the particular qualities of a length of wood, considering how it once knew a "rapt, gradual growing" before it was "milled into / Oar and plank" and then released into "the great generality of waters." Human significance begins to accumulate: the living tree knew its "own nature only," and even after it was subjected to the generalizing ocean, it did not "dissolve" but rather became "involved" with "the gnarled swerve and tangle of tides." At the end of the poem Wilbur (mindful of the lesson of "Cigales") addresses his own effort to understand driftwood as an emblem of integrity.

> In a time of continual dry abdications
> And of damp complicities,
> They are fit to be taken for signs, these emblems.

Although Wilbur might seem to offer driftwood as a timeless sign, these lines insist that driftwood is fit to be taken for a sign in a particular time—"a time of continual dry abdications / And of damp complicities." Wilbur is describing the initial years of the Cold War, as his note on "Driftwood" makes even clearer: "the poem began when a friend tried to argue me into a revolutionary political party on the grounds that there are at present two choices only, Communism or Fascism." Like Wallace Stevens, Wilbur distrusted political affiliations so singleminded that they were easily adopted and just as easily dropped. His early drafts for the poem show that he began by describing generally this time of damp complicities before he focused on the emblematic qualities of driftwood: "On a day of an age when allegiance is always too heavy or light / I singular walk to myself on the glass banks of the sea."[28] As Wilbur recognized, he was assigning meaning to this landscape (and thinking perhaps too consciously of Whitman and Stevens), rather than deducing meaning, and he turned his eye to the particular qualities of driftwood as a better way of earning his convictions.

Wilbur may have been worried that in the process the political content of "Driftwood" was obscured: he first published the completed poem beside "We," which clearly locates the time of dry affiliations in the postwar years. Once an ally, Russia quickly replaced Germany as the enemy against which a fragile sense of American identity could be shaped.

> How good to have the Russians to abhor:
> It lets us dance the nation on our knee
> Who haven't been quite certain since the war
> Precisely what we meant by saying *we*.[29]

Wilbur never collected this poem. While it has some of the attractive verve of the political verse he wrote in college, it doesn't stand up against a mature poem like "Driftwood." I think Wilbur came to see that his particular strength did not lie in this kind of political poem— or in the kind of political poem that "Driftwood" appeared to be in its initial drafts. Ultimately, the final version of "Driftwood" didn't need "We" to bolster its examination of damp complicities: the struggles of the Cold War lay behind its metaphors in the way that Eliot wanted personal experience to lie beneath "Little Gidding."

Published along with "Driftwood" and "We" in 1948 was "To an American Poet Just Dead," a more clearly topical poem that did make it into *Ceremony*. "It is out in the comfy suburbs I read you are dead," says Wilbur to the American poet Phelps Putnam, who won't be mourned by sprinklers, deep-freeze units, or Studebakers: "The suburbs deepen in their sleep of death." Characteristically, Wilbur won't ignore the contradictions of his position; he admits that he himself lives in the suburbs. But over and over again throughout his poems of the 1950s Wilbur chastises the complacency embodied here in the word "suburbs" or (more surreptitiously) in the word "peace." In "From the Lookout Rock" he surveys a world without any kind of vital contention, concluding that "for this was not the peace we prayed." In "Grasse: The Olive Trees" he surveys a landscape where "luxury's the common lot"; but this condition is not pleasing to Wilbur, and he's relieved to notice that "the olive contradicts." These anxious, famished branches seem like "clouds of doubt against the earth's array," and Wilbur concludes that they teach "the South it is not paradise." Neither of these poems refers openly to political complacencies, but, as in "Driftwood," Wilbur's metaphors stand on his awareness of the history of his time.

This distrust of suburbs, luxury, and paradise is especially interesting to me because Wilbur is often thought of as a poet who values these things above anything else: "The Poetry of Suburbia" was the title of Horace Gregory's review of *Things of This World*. This is one of the ways in which, as I began by saying, Wilbur is deeply misunderstood: the plain content of his poems is often overlooked because of associations readers bring to his formal dexterity. Even more suspicious than the use of meter and rhyme is the fact that Wilbur's style hasn't changed much over the years. In "Poetry and Happiness" Wilbur applauded Robert Lowell's transformation in *Life Studies*, saying that these poems represented a "withering into the truth" (Yeats's phrase) that at some point occurs "in the life of every poet," though not necessarily so dramatically.[30] But in the world after *Life Studies*, free verse seemed essential to such a withering, and Wilbur's formalism seemed like the sign of complacency, luxury, suburbia—everything Wilbur abhors.

Wilbur never needed to buck against the traditions of poetic form because he accepted the idea that any human utterance is by nature indirect: wanting to cleave as closely to the external world as possible, he resists any mystical sense of the poet's ability to transcend the boundaries of language or thought. In an uncollected essay on landscape, Wilbur says he was "not out to deny the distance" between himself and the natural world: "fusing [the landscape] with my thoughts and feelings and interpreting it through my human senses, it does not trouble me that my words do not essentialize it."[31] Far from troubling him, the artificiality of language seems to Wilbur an unavoidable aspect of experience: in the essay responding to Williams and Bogan, Wilbur is adamant that a "heartfelt subservience to the external" could be sustained only through a recognition (Wilbur compares the poet's formal ingenuity with a rain-dancer's) of "the difficulty—the impossibility—of achieving a direct expressive relationship with the rain, or with any other real thing."[32] Like Marianne Moore or the Williams of *Spring and All* before him, Wilbur feels that only an extravagantly artificial art may, by respecting the alterity of the genuine, approach it. ("What is more precise than precision?" asked Moore: "Illusion.") This healthy skepticism, not the formal artifice of his poetry, is what ultimately separates Wilbur from poets like Duncan, whose allegiance to the physical world he otherwise shares.

That allegiance, apparent in earlier poems like "Cigales" and "Driftwood," became the keynote of Wilbur's third book, published in 1956. *Things of This World* received both the Pulitzer Prize and the National Book Award, and the volume still stands, along with *Walking to Sleep*, as one of Wilbur's finest achievements. "Love Calls Us to the Things of This World" or "A Baroque Wall-Fountain in the Villa Sciarra" are as full of the joy of language as they are of the joy of the physical world: especially in the latter poem, language becomes a physical presence, the syntax so intricate, yet so plainly apprehensible, that it begs to be turned over in the mouth. The quieter "Love Calls Us to the Things of This World" is, famously, a poem of immanence: angels exist because, for a moment, the mind imagines them in laundry hanging on the line. But this argument against a world-denouncing spirituality is only half of the poem's purpose. A more violent, urgent world is registered in Wilbur's diction: words like *rape* and *hunks* slip into his elegant vocabulary, and their prominence has sometimes troubled the poem's admirers. Wilbur's point is that a devotion to laundry alone—to the world's sensual pleasures, physical and linguistic—may be as world-denying as the most ascetic spirituality. While the soul cries, "let there be nothing on earth but laundry," the language of the poem has suggested that this desire is unrealistic even before the poem's final lines (spoken by the soul as it descends into the awakening body) make Wilbur's position clear.

> "Bring them down from their ruddy gallows;
> Let there be clean linen for the backs of thieves;
> Let lovers go fresh and sweet to be undone,
> And the heaviest nuns walk in a pure floating
> Of dark habits,
> > keeping their difficult balance."

The balance here is not only between the physical and spiritual, but between a state of mind that dallies with physical pleasures and a necessary awakening to a sterner, even more challenging ground.

I wouldn't argue that "Love Calls Us to the Things of This World" has much of (in Wilbur's phrase) "an implicit political dimension." But I do think that the poem became possible because of Wilbur's earlier meditations on wartime loss and postwar deprivation. Similarly, the final poem in *Things of This World*, "For the New Railway Station in Rome," grew from Wilbur's impatience with Cold War doom and gloom—an intellectual climate in which one disapproving reviewer of *Things* asked, "how can he be so damnably good-natured in an abominable world?" Like Jarrell, Wilbur sides with Robert Frost, who responded to postwar apocalypticism by pointing out that every generation stakes its own claim for historical ultimacy: "I say they claimed the honor for their ages. They claimed it rather for themselves. It is immodest of a man to think of himself as going down before the worst forces ever mobilized by God."[33]

"For the New Railway Station" begins with a litany of the doomsayers' favorite images (Rome, hurt pillars, rubble, dust, the forum) before it upends a cliché: "there's something new / To see in Rome."

> See, from the travertine
> Face of the office block, the roof of the booking-hall
> Sails out into the air beside the ruined
> Servian Wall,
>
> Echoing in its light
> And cantilevered swoop of reinforced concrete

>    The broken profile of these stones, defeating
>        That defeat.

At this point the shards begin to speak as eloquently as Keats's urn. But Wilbur's well-wrought stanzas (as masterful as those of "A Baroque Wall-Fountain in the Villa Sciarra") do not trace the contours of an ancient urn or fountain. Appearing after Wilbur's paean to Roman antiquity in *Things of This World*, "For the New Railway Station" assures by its very form that Wilbur is no antiquarian; a swoop of cantilevered concrete does as well as a "ragged, loose / Collapse of water."

If all that Wilbur offered in "For the New Railway Station in Rome" were something new to offset the decline of civilization, he would tacitly concede the doomsayers' point. (And, as the reviewer suggested, Wilbur would merely be good-natured.) Instead, the poem interrogates the means by which hurt pillars are taken as signs of decline—or concrete swoops as signs of progress. Wilbur's doomsayers "would not take the sun standing at noon / For a good sign." This line cuts two ways, for it suggests both that the doomsayers are insensitive to the daily particularity of their world and that they are incapable of taking anything for a good sign. Neither the Roman forum nor the railway station stands for our future, just as the song of the cicada doesn't naturally stand for anything: the human imagination invests these objects with meaning, producing signs whose arbitrariness the doom-sayers have forgotten. Here, as in so many of his poems, Wilbur champions a deductive looking at particular shapes of things rather than an inductive attribution of qualities. But—again typically—he doesn't believe that things can speak to us outside the parameters of human thought or formal ingenuity. The speaking shards at the end of the poem are the product of a self-consciously flagrant act of human imagination, and their final words ("What does it say over the door of Heaven / But *homo fecit?*") could stand over all of Wilbur's paeans to particular things, beginning with "Italy: Maine."

"It is easy to prophesy against us," said Wilbur in "Poetry and Happiness";[34] the title poem of *Advice to a Prophet* builds on "For the New Railway Station," suggesting that prophecy will be believable only if it catalogues the simple, apparently insignificant things we could lose: "The dolphin's arc, the dove's return, / These things in which we have seen ourselves and spoken." But *Advice to a Prophet* as a whole seems a little disappointing after *Things of This World*, in which one glorious poem seems to topple over the next. The disappointment is perhaps inevitable, given the midcareer achievement of *Things*, but Wilbur himself has said that there are poems in *Advice to a Prophet* that he wishes he had never published. Any great writer's career has its lulls, but I think this moment in Wilbur's career is especially revealing of his strengths. A comment Wilbur once made about Day Lewis's later work may also describe the predicament of his own career: "He is left with his earnestness, his good-will, a poetic manner appropriate to a matter [the political turmoil of the 1930s] which has deserted him."[35] The poems of *The Beautiful Changes* and *Ceremony* grew quite directly from Wilbur's engagement with wartime struggles, physical and ideological. In the poems of *Things of This World* those struggles are more distant, but they lurk beneath the surfaces of the poems (to continue with Eliot's metaphor) in identifiable ways. By the time Wilbur wrote *Advice to a Prophet* that historical ballast was lost: a few poems retain a sense of urgency, but too many others finally seem like the extenuation of a *manner* after the *matter* that provoked it has dropped away.

Together with *Walking to Sleep*, published in 1969, *Advice to a Prophet* nevertheless confirms my sense that Wilbur's best writing comes in response to the events of his time: while the connection is too often missing in *Advice to a Prophet*, it is prominent throughout the poems of *Walking to Sleep*. Wilbur seems to have been reinvigorated by the 1960s in general and by his opposition to the Vietnam War in particular. His manner faced a newly urgent matter, and the result was, with "In the Field" (the first section of *Walking to Sleep*), the finest group of poems that Wilbur has written.

Several pages away from this group stands "A Miltonic Sonnet for Mr. Johnson on His Refusal of Peter Hurd's Official Portrait." The octet's long subordinate clause compares Johnson's escalation of the Vietnam War with Jefferson's legacy of Enlightenment ideals; the sestet addresses Johnson directly:

> Rightly you say the picture is too large
> Which Peter Hurd by your appointment drew,
> And justly call this Capitol too bright
> Which signifies our people in your charge.

These lines are Miltonic in several ways, not least in the stern intrusion of a trochee ("Rightly") at the sonnet's volta. But they are Wilburian too. After turning Johnson's criticism of the official portrait against him, Wilbur doesn't leave himself, one of the people, untainted by criticism. This turn was important to Wilbur for reasons he explained in an interview conducted a few months after the sonnet was written: "I recall that Allen Ginsberg recently asked an audience whether they would consent to the proposition that the United States government, in its foreign policy, is psychotic. Something like a third of the audience voted for that idea. They and Mr. Ginsberg are setting themselves up as supersane. . . . Though I can share all their objections to our Viet Nam policy,

I'm all for institutions."[35] That last comment—as Wilbur well knew—
could make him no friends in 1968. (And there might be a touch of
grandstanding here too: in middle age as in his youth Wilbur sometimes
enjoys the notoriety of standing apart.) But Wilbur's sonnet embodies
the sentiment with greater power—both thematically, in its meditation
on the office of the president, and formally, in its rejuvenation of Milton's trumpet for political poetry.

"A Miltonic Sonnet" is the only conventionally political poem in the
volume, but even if Wilbur had not included it, *Walking to Sleep* would
still seem like a book provoked by wartime visions of carnage and wartime lapses of conscience. The book (and the group of poems called "In
the Field") opens with "The Lilacs," which offers a simple story of the
lilac's growth, cast in the Anglo-Saxon alliterative line. Recalling "When
Lilacs Last in the Dooryard Bloom'd," Wilbur's metaphors tell a somewhat more complicated story: the stalks begin "Like walking wounded
from the dead of winter"; their "bullet-shaped buds" grow out of "present pain and from past terror"; the blooms are "Healed in that hush,
that hospital quiet." But the lilacs themselves ultimately reveal nothing
of "their mortal message"—unless we can measure the depth of hell by
"the pure power / of this perfume." This concluding line of the parable
offers Wilbur's characteristic moral about the hidden potency of earthly
things. And the poem following "The Lilacs" gives historical weight to
the parable's metaphors, forcing us to return to these lines with a more
vivid sense of what the "present pain" may be: "some dirty war" pre-
occupies Wilbur in "On the Marginal Way," transforming even casual
fancies into images of violence.

Several of the poems of "In the Field" are themselves about this
dialectic between metaphor and historical reality (or what Wilbur several times calls "fact"). But throughout "In a Churchyard" and "In the
Field" itself (the poem that gives this section of *Walking to Sleep* its title),
even the slightest reference to the "dirty war" drops away, leaving only
the struggle of the dialectic. These poems seem to me even stronger
than "A Miltonic Sonnet" or "On the Marginal Way": Wilbur works
best when he feels the challenge of history but records the more sur-
reptitious ways in which the challenge enters our lives and poems.

"In the Field" begins with a recollection of a nighttime walk. Wilbur
and his wife gaze at a sky that seems almost domestic in its familiarity:
the field-grass through which they wade is like "the cloudy dregs" of
a teacup, and Andromeda, transformed into a constellation, is self-
sufficient, requiring neither Perseus to protect her nor Euripides to tell
her tale. "But none of that was true": Wilbur is caught short, reminded
that he's speaking of metaphors, of stories spun on filaments of light,

and the sky suddenly seems emptied of human relevance. Initially he doesn't let this emptiness include him:

> The heavens jumped away,
> Bursting the cincture of the zodiac,
> Shot flares with nothing left to say
> To us, not coming back
>
> Unless they should at last
> Like hard-flung dice that ramble out the throw,
> Be gathered for another cast.
> Whether that might be so
>
> We could not say, but trued
> Our talk awhile to words of the real sky,
> Chatting of class or magnitude,
> Star-clusters, nebulae.

Wilbur is an experienced fiction-maker, knowing that to have abandoned one metaphor is only to have tried on another; dice replace the shapes that Greece or Babylon discerned. But he slips—perhaps knowingly, at first—when he imagines that he "trues" his thought with words of the real sky. This is the movement toward "fact" that "In the Field" shares with "On the Marginal Way" and "In a Churchyard," and throughout these poems the facts are anything but stable. In "On the Marginal Way" Wilbur fights off a vision of the Holocaust with geological facts; but the violence of volcanic eruption and glacial movement offers no haven from imaginative vision. It is not simply the imagination's waywardness that leads him to find new horror in "the facts"; it is "the time's fright," his knowledge of "some dirty war." Wilbur is less specific about the "nip of fear" that approaches him in "In the Field," but its effect is the same: metaphor takes the upper hand, and Wilbur is left with nothing—"All worlds dashed out without a trace, / The very light unmade."

This dialectic between imagination and fact is a messy one, for "fact" is conceived of unusually as something comforting rather than something to escape; later, as imagination works on fact, the distinction between the two collapses, and there is nowhere to seek refuge but in the dialectic itself—the process of time and the mind's ability to conceive of it. Similarly, when fact interrupts the reverie of "In a Churchyard" (a pendant to Gray's "Elegy") in the form of a ringing bell, the real sound is "far more strange" than the imagined, the "things that are" more mysterious than any vision. This is because the world of "things that are" includes mortality—"the darker dead"—the undeniable fact as well as the ultimate mystery.

The project of "In the Field" is to remain aware of this final reality but not be overwhelmed by it. In the second half of the poem Wilbur returns to the field during the day, his metaphor-making skills rejuvenated. Stars, invisible in daylight, are now "holes in heaven [that] have been sealed / Like rain-drills in a pond." The only starry sky now visible is on earth: "galaxies / Of flowers, dense and manifold." At night, Wilbur only felt these flowers (he had mistaken them for field-grass the night before) brushing against his legs. As in so many poems, he is saved by a close look at the physical world: daisies, heal-all, and hawkweed, all of them committing "to air / The seeds of their return."

Behind that heal-all lurks the flower of Robert Frost's "Design," and Wilbur follows Frost in suggesting that no "design of darkness," independent of the mind's ability to imagine it, may "govern in a thing so small."

> We could no doubt mistake
> These flowers for some answer to that fright
>     We felt for all creation's sake
>         In our dark talk last night,
>
>     Taking to heart what came
> Of the heart's wish for life, which, staking here
>     In the least field an endless claim,
>         Beats on from sphere to sphere
>
>     And pounds beyond the sun,
> Where nothing less peremptory can go,
>     And is ourselves, and is the one
>         Unbounded thing we know.

Just as Frost knows that birches aren't broken by boys, Wilbur knows that the field, imagined as an earthly heaven, is not really an answer to his fright. More importantly, just as Frost knows that a spider is not brought to a heal-all by some force of evil, Wilbur now knows better that no design of darkness determines his place—or some dirty war's place—in the universe. Wilbur achieves no higher eloquence than the final lines of "In the Field": the poem is worthy to stand with "Directive," "The Idea of Order at Key West," or "At the Fishhouses."

This is company Wilbur wanted to keep from the beginning of his career. Discussing his first book, I concentrated on Moore's presence in the poems, but traces of Frost, Stevens, Eliot, and Williams are also apparent, sometimes overwhelmingly so. And while it is a commonplace to notice Wilbur's early ventriloquism (he was sometimes chastised for it), I mention it again to suggest that the magnanimity of "In the Field" is the ultimate fruit of Wilbur's openness to his immediate predecessors. Reviewing Robert Graves in 1955, Wilbur quoted this statement about modernism: "the mainly negative work begun by the 'modernists' of the Twenties in exploring the limits of technical experiment is finished and done with." With Laura Riding, Graves had first voiced this opinion as early as 1928, in *A Survey of Modernist Poetry*. But Wilbur added a sentence to Graves's: "and indeed there are styles of the Thirties and Forties, *not* technically extreme, which would seem to have had their time of prevalence."[37] Unlike Graves, Wilbur is not battling modernism by suggesting that it has passed; casting his historical net a little wider, Wilbur sees that the first wave of postmodern reaction has also passed.

For reasons I've explored, Wilbur is often understood as a reactionary poet, but he worked past that position early in his career, learning from a wide variety of poets even as his own poetry became utterly distinctive. Or perhaps I should say that the poetry became so utterly itself precisely because of Wilbur's undogmatic openness. As Wilbur has explained in "On My Own Work," there is only one aspect of modern poetry that has not appealed to him.

> The revolution [in American poetry during the second decade of the century] was not a concerted one and there was little agreement on objectives; nor is there now any universal agreement as to what, in that revolution, was most constructive. But certainly it has been of lasting importance that Robinson and Frost chose to enliven traditional meters with the rhythms of colloquial speech; that Sandburg and others insisted on slang and on the brute facts of the urban and industrial scene; and that Pound and Eliot sophisticated American verse by introducing techniques from other literatures, and by reviving and revising our sense of literary tradition.

Visible here is the same Wilbur who, as a young man, fostered an open political debate, even as his own convictions were clear. Visible too is Wilbur's lifelong caginess: he chooses his forebears carefully, knowing that few poets will champion Carl Sandburg and Ezra Pound in the same breath. Wilbur's one disagreement with these modern poets is that he won't "exclude anything in the name of purity."[38] But I suspect that Wilbur knows, for example, that Pound's taste was rarely dogmatic; Pound promoted Sandburg, reviewed Frost glowingly when others rejected him, and even had a kind word for A. E. Robinson. This is why Wilbur is so careful to point out that the modernist movement was neither concerted nor single-minded—really not a movement at all. He knows that, at their best, the moderns were not manifesto writers but poets who worked to extend the possibilities of poetry. One of the joys of reading Wilbur is our knowledge that, with a long and productive career behind him, he is still continuing to extend those possibilities today.

# JOHN ASHBERY'S
# INDIVIDUAL TALENT

After the accidental death of Frank O'Hara in 1966, John Ashbery wrote several commemorative essays about his friend. Ashbery was at the time the author of three relatively unknown books of poetry; he had recently returned to New York after a decade of living in Paris—a city Ashbery praised (in contrast to any American city) for providing a "neutral climate in which one can work pretty much as one chooses."[1] Although his poetry had been included in Donald Allen's partisan anthology, *The New American Poetry*, Ashbery's allegiances in the wartorn world of American poetry were not clear. O'Hara's early death occurred at a precarious moment in Ashbery's own life, and the loss inevitably became an occasion as much for self-examination as for commemoration.

In "Frank O'Hara's Question," Ashbery championed O'Hara's independence from both the mainstream and the avant-garde at a time in America when "the loyalty-oath mentality has pervaded outer Bohemia." The very distinction between a mainstream and an avant-garde—between the academics and the beats, the New Critical and the confessional—seemed meaningless to Ashbery in the mid-sixties: "Like most truly original artists today, when tradition menaces the individual talent in ways undreamed by T. S. Eliot, O'Hara and his achievement are caught between opposing power blocs." The reason for O'Hara's singular position, Ashbery explained, was his blithe disregard for the exigencies of American politics.

> Frank O'Hara's poetry has no program and therefore cannot be joined. It does not advocate sex and dope as a panacea for the ills of modern society; it does not speak out against the war in Viet Nam or in favor of civil rights; it does not paint gothic vignettes of the post-Atomic Age; in a word, it does not attack the establishment. It merely ignores its right to exist, and is thus a source of annoyance for partisans of every stripe.

Ashbery did not mean, in a debased New Critical sense, that poetry had no relationship to social concerns; his appropriation of the language of the House Committee on Un-American Activities ("the loyalty-oath mentality") suggests otherwise. But Ashbery was suspicious of claims that were being made for poetry's political power, on both the right and the left. To Ashbery, O'Hara's flagrantly uncommitted poems seemed to carry more clout than poems pledging their allegiance to social protest: "unlike the 'message' of committed poetry it incites one to all the programs of commitment as well as to every other form of self-realization—interpersonal, Dionysian, occult, or abstract."[2]

Coming in the midst of the Vietnam War, this was a dangerously subtle argument; Ashbery must have known that (like the O'Hara he celebrated) his comments were likely to please nobody. Louis Simpson grabbed the bait. Writing for a symposium on poetry in the *Nation*, Simpson argued that poets like Robert Bly, Robert Creeley, Allen Ginsberg, W. S. Merwin, Gary Synder, and presumably Simpson himself belonged to no school but were linked by their common opposition to the war. More importantly, these poets were also linked by their stylistic choices; the sternly antiwar Wilbur had no place in this brotherhood because (unlike Simpson) he continued to work in traditional meters and forms. Ashbery's style might have given him a place, but (again, unlike Simpson) Ashbery did not put any stock in the "breakthrough" narrative's association of stylistic rebellion and political protest. "John Ashbery," Simpson concluded, " . . . complimented [O'Hara] on not having written poetry about the war. This struck me as a new concept of merit—praising a man for things he has not written. But it was not amusing to see a poet sneering at the conscience of other poets."[3]

These words forced Ashbery to make an uncharacteristically explicit gesture of self-defense. In two letters to the *Nation* he quoted his original remarks about O'Hara and then responded to Simpson's charges: "All poetry is against war and in favor of life, or else it isn't poetry, and it stops being poetry when it is forced into the mold of a particular program. Poetry is poetry. Protest is protest. I believe in both forms of action."[4] Especially since Ashbery's disjunctive poetry has often been justified in political terms (the poems disrupt the reified terms of cultural discourse), it is startling to see Ashbery making such an explicit disavowal of the politics of poetic form. But because Ashbery's poetry is as often condemned as apolitical as it is justified in political terms, it's crucial to see that he does not deny that poems may have a political valence; he believes that poetry cannot perform the substantive work of social protest. Traditional poetic decorum does not carry any particular moral weight for Ashbery (just as it doesn't for Richard Wilbur), and he doesn't believe that his disruption of decorum is necessarily a mark of his political commitment. The terms of "international politics," Ashbery concluded, are too important to be clouded by the terms of "poetry politics." However inextricably related these terms may be, one will not account adequately for the other.

Obsessed as he is with minute variations in the flux of experience, Ashbery is necessarily the least oppositional of poets: as he says in "Houseboat Days," "To praise this, blame that, / Leads one subtly away from the beginning, where / We must stay, in motion." However distinctive his own poems, Ashbery has stayed resolutely in motion, refusing to choose sides in the debates that have preoccupied so many American poets after modernism. In a 1967 review he noted that an opposition between "open" and "closed" form "underlies much of the art of our time." But for Ashbery himself, open form was no rallying cry, aesthetic or political: each formal possibility, he concluded, reveals "a different aspect of the same aggressive, enigmatic planet."[5] This unwillingness to choose seems appropriate to a poet who writes both sestinas and aleatory free verse; in Ashbery's hands, strict formal patterns hardly seem to offer a rational organization of experience.

But in the nearly thirty years that have passed since his exchange with Simpson, Ashbery has been conscripted in support of a variety of oppositional postmodernisms. Comparing his poems with *The Waste Land*, Marjorie Perloff grants that Eliot's modernism may prefigure aspects of Ashbery's postmodernism but concludes that in *The Waste Land* "there is, after all, a coherent core of relational images." Similarly, comparing Ashbery with Stevens, she cautions that "obscure as Stevens's poems so often are, they do convey particular meanings."[6] One could as easily say that Ashbery's poems, however dysfunctional, contain a core of relational images (think of "The Skaters") or convey particular meanings (think of "Self-Portrait in a Convex Mirror"): champions of the Language poets have in fact said so. For Jerome McGann, Ashbery, the poet who once seemed to represent "a swerve from the poetries of the fifties and sixties," has failed to exploit "his own work's 'opposi-tional' features and potentialities," turning instead to "suburban and personal interests."[7]

One of the revelations of John Shoptaw's *On the Outside Looking Out,* the most complete treatment of Ashbery's career to date, is that Ash-bery's poetry can hardly be discussed without almost constant reference to an extraordinarily wide range of precursors (among whom Eliot looms prominently): any effort to limit strategically our sense of Ash-bery's openness to his modernist past is bound to do the poetry an injustice. And even if the poems seem (to those who accept postmod-ernism's progressive narratives) more "advanced" than Eliot's—more open to demotic language, more accommodating to popular culture, more suspicious of the lyric's unified voice—the poems are nonetheless unthinkable without Eliot's example.

Ashbery's invocation of the terms of "Tradition and the Individual Talent" in "Frank O'Hara's Question" ("when tradition menaces the individual talent") was only one of many such invocations throughout the essays Ashbery wrote in the late sixties. Even without its title, "Tradition and Talent" would seem indebted to Eliot's dialectical sense of literary history. Ashbery praises Stanley Moss for his ability to be different from and yet indebted to his predecessors: Moss's work eludes "classifications of traditional and avant-garde."[8] In "The Invisi-ble Avant-Garde," a lecture delivered at the Yale Art School in 1968, Ashbery gave a more carefully nuanced version of this position.

> In both art and life today we are in danger of substituting one conformity for another. . . . We feel in America that we have to join something, that our lives are directionless unless we are part of a group, a clan—an idea very different from the European one. . . . Is there nothing then between the extremes of Levittown and Haight-Ashbury, between an avant-garde which has become a tra-dition and a tradition which is no longer one? In other words, has tradition finally managed to absorb the individual talent?[9]

This is Ashbery's characterization of O'Hara recast as a general ar-gument. As in "Tradition and Talent," Ashbery wants to encourage an art that renders the opposition between the avant-garde and the tradi-tion obsolete. He will champion neither a rejection of nor a devotion to the tradition. And just as Eliot wanted to see a dynamic interchange between tradition and the individual talent ("the present only, keeps the past alive," said Eliot[10]), Ashbery is interested in the past only in-asmuch as it is continuously modified by innovation. Art emerges from this argument not as a singular achievement but as an ongoing process of discovery: to move forward, it will accept whatever it can use.

The argument of "The Invisible Avant-Garde" no longer seems to describe the state of the arts accurately; the essay should be read as an analysis of the world as Ashbery found it in 1968. Even more accurately, the essay (like "Frank O'Hara's Question") should be read as a meditation on the direction of Ashbery's own career in the sixties. Ashbery concluded "The Invisible Avant-Garde" by holding up Ferruccio Busoni as an ideal artist, one who avoided the "extremes" in modern music (Arnold Schoenberg's innovation and Max Reger's reaction) by "taking what was valid in each and forging a totality." Hovering between the nineteenth and twentieth centuries, Busoni is crucial to any history of Western music but remains oddly unplaceable: Ashbery aspired to this position. In "Clouds," a poem written soon after "The Invisible Avant-Garde," he considered his isolated place in an artistic climate in which "there was no joining, / Only separate blocks of achievement and opinion."

> The old ideals had been cast aside and people were restless for
>     the new,
> In a wholly different mass, so there was no joining,
> Only separate blocks of achievement and opinion
> With no relation to the conducive ether
> Which surrounded everything like the clear idea of a ruler.
>
> And it was that these finally flattened out or banded together
> Through forgetting, into one contemporaneous sea
> With no explanations to give. And the small enclave
> Of worried continuing began again, putting forth antennae into
>     the night.

While the "separate blocks" eventually became indistinguishable, unified by their rejection of the "old ideals," there remained a "small enclave" dedicated to "worried continuing"—the harder work of moving forward without denigrating the past.

Ashbery was a part of this small enclave. *The Tennis Court Oath*, published in 1962, remains his most controversial achievement even today, either dismissed as a self-indulgent dead-end or praised as an indication of the more daringly oppositional course that Ashbery should have followed. Ashbery himself remains uncomfortable with the book, maintaining that while he wrote the poems to shake up his own early achievement, he didn't expect them to be published. But having done so, having exerted his individual talent so flagrantly, Ashbery needed to renegotiate his relationship to the tradition. *The Double Dream of Spring* (in which "Clouds" was published) represents not a rejection of Ashbery's previous experiments but, like Busoni's music, a reconciliation of tradition and innovation that is not a compromise—an expression of "worried continuing." Writing in the wake of *The Tennis Court Oath*, Ashbery himself learned how to write poems that do not confuse "poetry politics" with "international politics"—poems that do not presuppose any particular relationship between formal and ideological freedom.

In the same issue of the *Nation* in which Simpson turned on Ashbery, Stephen Koch wrote about the members of the so-called New York School: "Ashbery is concerned," he said, "with the imaginative problem of embodying poetic time."[11] Like Yeats, who began his career worrying about old age, Ashbery is a poet who discovered his characteristic preoccupation early on. As early as 1957 he praised Gertrude Stein and Henry James for embodying a constant sense of temporal flux in their prose—"life is being constantly altered by each breath one draws, just as each second of life seems to alter the whole of what has gone before"—and twenty years later he praised Elizabeth Bishop for what his own poems portray with varying fortitude: "our coming to know ourselves as the necessarily inaccurate transcribers of the life that is always on the point of coming into being."[12] This triple sense of contingency (life, transcription, and a self-conscious awareness of the act of transcribing) is embodied most grandly—which is also to say, without admonition, most tediously—in *Flow Chart*, the long poem published in 1991. But the poems of *Some Trees*, Ashbery's first book, are often equally as effective in describing these processes: "Perhaps this valley too leads into the head of long-ago days," begins "Grand Abacus." Ashbery literalizes this metaphor, so that a journey into the past ("the head of long-ago days") becomes an encounter with a monumental head.

> "I'd like to see it," someone said about the head, which has stopped
>     pretending to be a town.
> Look! A ghastly change has come over it. The ears fall off—they are
>     laughing people.
> The skin is perhaps children, they say, "We children," and are
>     vague near the sea. The eyes—
> Wait! What large raindrops! The eyes—
> Wait, can't you see them pattering, in the meadow, like a dog?
> The eyes are all glorious! And now the river comes to sweep away
>     the last of us.
> Who knew it, at the beginning of the day?

These lines almost seem like an answer to the challenge with which Elizabeth Bishop ends "The Monument": "Watch it closely," she demands, implying that the decaying monument will continue to change.

Ashbery's "head of long-ago days" changes unpredictably: the past is not a stable object of inquiry. And as if illustrating the parable Bishop once told, apropos of Hopkins, about a hunter and his target (both of which are in motion), Ashbery concludes "Grand Abacus" by suggesting that the position of inquiry is equally unstable.

> It is best to travel like a comet, with the others, though one does not
>     see them.
> How far that bridle flashed! "Hurry up, children!" The birds fly
>     back, they say, "We were lying,
> We do not want to fly away." But it is already too late. The
>     children have vanished.

"Grand Abacus" is, like many of Ashbery's early poems, divided against itself: the children, who may be part of the monumental head itself ("The skin is perhaps children"), resist being swept up into an unknown future, but they nevertheless disappear as the poem abruptly ends. The well-known final section of "The Picture of Little J.A. in a Prospect of Flowers" is similarly ambivalent: Ashbery describes an imaginary photograph of himself as a child, sensing that this transient version of his former self paradoxically feared change.

> Yet I cannot escape the picture
> Of my small self in that bank of flowers:
> My head among the blazing phlox
> Seemed a pale and gigantic fungus.
> I had a hard stare, accepting
>
> Everything, taking nothing,
> As though the rolled-up future might stink
> As loud as stood the sick moment
> The shutter clicked. Though I was wrong,
> Still, as the loveliest feelings
>
> Must soon find words, and these, yes,
> Displace them, so I am not wrong
> In calling this comic version of myself
> The true one. For as change is horror,
> Virtue is really stubbornness
>
> And only in the light of lost words
> Can we imagine our rewards.

Randall Jarrell's favorite word—*yet*—is the most important word in this poem: the past is lost yet we remember it; the past seems permanent in memory yet it changes with time. "Truth" is not undermined by these realizations; it is reconceived by the adult Ashbery as a contingent qual-ity even as his former self, frozen in the photograph, continues to think of it as permanent and unchanging. Yet the final lines disrupt this sym-metry, seeming to merge the child's illusion ("For as change is horror, / Virtue is really stubbornness") with the wisdom of the grown man ("And only in the light of lost words / Can we imagine our re-wards") as if one followed logically from the other.

"It becomes plain," says Ashbery near the end of his capacious *Three Poems*, "that we cannot interpret everything, we must be selective." In my brief reading of *Some Trees*, I've had to ignore many details of Ashbery's poems in order to present a coherent narrative. And while this is true in our reading of any text, Ashbery makes us deeply aware of what we must ignore in order to make sense of his poems; "underneath the talk," he says in "Soonest Mended," "lies / The moving and not wanting to be moved, the loose / Meaning, untidy and simple like a threshing floor." One way to make sense of Ashbery's apparently dramatic leap from *Some Trees* to *The Tennis Court Oath* is to see that he includes much more "loose meaning" in his increasingly untidy poems. " 'How Much Longer Will I Be Able to Inhabit the Divine Sepulcher . . . ' " or "Our Youth" are (in comparison to "Little J.A.") merely baggier descriptions of the same dy-namic sense of time. In the manner of Marianne Moore, the first line of "Our Youth" follows on the title: "Of bricks . . . Who built it?" But this period of our youth, which seems as steady as bricks, is also like "some crazy balloon": it seems both permanent and impermanent, both some-thing that made us and something that we made. We see that "Our youth is dead" at "the minute we discover it"; yet (the poem omits this crucial word but at every turn implies it) what we desire in the present is the in-carnation of a past that will not die: "You will never have that young boy, / That boy with the monocle / Could have been your father." The poem ends by reiterating the inescapability of this Oedipal romance; the old people persist, and dreams offer no refuge.

> It's true we have not avoided our destiny
> By weeding out the old people.
> Our faces have filled with smoke. We escape
> Down the cloud ladder, but the problem has not been solved.

"Our Youth" is one of the more approachable poems of *The Tennis Court Oath*; but strategically selective reading will make almost no sense of other poems in the volume. The opening lines of "Leaving the Atocha Station" sound like nothing but loose meaning.

> The arctic honey blabbed over the report causing darkness
> And pulling us out of there experiencing it

he meanwhile . . . And the fried bats they sell there
dropping from sticks, so that the menace of your prayer folds . . .
Other people . . .         flash
the garden are you boning
and defunct covering . . . Blind dog expressed royalties . . .


Ashbery has in fact admitted that he self-consciously produced two different kinds of poems in *The Tennis Court Oath*. Before he wrote the collage poems like "Leaving the Atocha Station" or "Europe," he achieved in poems like "Our Youth" what he has called an "intermediate" or "compromise" style between the poems of *Some Trees* and the poem "Europe": "I don't know quite why I stopped writing that way, but I feel that those are valid poems in a new way that I might well have gone on pursuing, but didn't." In the poems of the "intermediate" style, Ashbery continued to *describe* his moments as they passed, however waywardly; in "Leaving the Atocha Station" he attempted to *embody* the process: he has explained that the "dislocated, incoherent fragments of images which make up the movement of the poem are probably like the experience you get from a train pulling out of a station of no particular significance." Over and over again Ashbery justified the disjunctive quality of these poems in mimetic terms. In the dust-jacket statement to *The Tennis Court Oath* (which Ashbery did not intend to publish) he said his goal was to reach "a greater, more complete kind of realism." And he subsequently maintained that the "polyphony" of his poetry is "a means toward greater naturalism"—that the poet's work "is like that of Penelope ripping up her web into a varicolored heap that tells the story more accurately than the picture did."[13]

In statements like these, Ashbery comes closest to replicating the logic of the "breakthrough" narrative, essentializing the relationship of formal strategy and historical power. Several problems arise from this logic. In Elizabeth Bishop's "In the Waiting Room" a child realizes for the first time that selfhood is an arbitrary social construction, that experience as it comes to her has no coherent order or meaning. Bishop does not embody this realization in a poem that is "consequently" incoherent or arbitrary: she remains perfectly comfortable with a simple narrative, aware that its shape is, like all systems of meaning, arbitrary but nevertheless useful. In contrast, Ashbery paradoxically asserts in his justifications of "Europe" that its incoherence is *not* arbitrary or contingent; it is essential to the poem's embodiment of the inherently disorganized nature of experience: this is the potential danger with an exaggerated aesthetic of embodiment. Ashbery could not go on writing in the more disjunctive style of *The Tennis Court Oath* because its logic offered no room for development. Seeming to break down a supposedly truthful version of reality, the book established a harsher, more restrictive scale of truth in its place.

The experiments that Ashbery conducted with Kenneth Koch in the early sixties are more easily justified because they flaunt their arbitrariness; Koch's note to the uncollected "Crone Rhapsody" explains that the poem was written "according to the following requirements: that every line contain the name of a flower, a tree, a fruit, a game, and a famous old lady, as well as the word *bathtub*; furthermore, the poem is a sestina and all the end-words are pieces of office furniture."[14] There's no way to justify "Crone Rhapsody" as a representation of the way experience comes to us, outside of the arbitrary constructions of narrative: its form is flagrantly arbitrary, like the unrhymed trimeter of "In the Waiting Room." Nor is it possible to justify "Crone Rhapsody" as an embodiment of a postmodern condition, and, to Ashbery's credit, he has never succumbed to this weak historicism. (In "Lithuanian Dance Band," from *Self-Portrait in a Convex Mirror*, he mocks it: "Today is suddenly broad and a whole era of uncertainties is ending / Like World War I or the twenties.") Yet the specter of this way of reading *The Tennis Court Oath* is difficult to dispel; the poems demand a weighty justification for their obscurity. Frank O'Hara made the inevitable comparison, calling "Europe" the "most striking thing" since *The Waste Land*.[15] Today, *The Tennis Court Oath* is most commonly understood as a vanguard turn away from Eliot's tradition; but it once seemed like a return to Eliot's individual talent.

How then should a poem like "Leaving the Atocha Station" profitably be read? John Shoptaw offers a more compelling reading by historicizing the poem precisely: Ashbery visited Madrid with O'Hara in 1960, and though "it is doubtful that either of them ate (or shunned) 'arctic honey' or 'fried bats' " these surreal particulars "represent the experience of the overwhelming impenetrability of a foreign culture."[16] But even the best interpretation of "Leaving the Atocha Station" will inevitably seem a little like special pleading. The power of the poem stems from the fact that, like a Jackson Pollock painting, it is basically unacceptable; no interpretation will justify its extravagance. But the poem can also seem, from a different perspective, all too acceptable. For all of its aura of the prodigious feat, "Leaving the Atocha Station" might be the warped but inevitable conclusion of a secondhand New Critical aesthetic: the poem that does not mean, but is.

In retrospect, the place of *The Tennis Court Oath* in Ashbery's career appears similar to that of *As We Know* and *Shadow Train*: these more labored, idea-driven books (Ashbery has expressed his dissatisfaction with both of them) cleared the way for the synthetic poems of *A Wave*.

*The Tennis Court Oath* similarly made *Rivers and Mountains* possible, if only by revealing the potential hazards of a poetics of embodiment. For "The Skaters," the very long poem in *Rivers and Mountains*, returns to the descriptive idiom of "Grand Abacus" and "The Instruction Manual" in *Some Trees*, employing spatial metaphors to describe a temporal process: "Here I am then, continuing but ever beginning / My perennial voyage, into new memories, new hope and flowers / The way the coasts glide past you." But *Rivers and Mountains* represents two crucial stages in Ashbery's development. "Clepsydra," the last poem Ashbery wrote in Paris is (as Ashbery himself has emphasized) a watershed in his career: "Wouldn't it be nice, I said to myself, to do a long poem that would be a long extended argument, but would have the beauty of a single word? 'Clepsydra' is really a meditation on how time feels as it is passing."[17] What differentiates "Clepsydra" from "The Skaters" is that Ashbery attempts, once again, to embody that feeling rather than describe it.

But he does so with a difference, avoiding his earlier idealization of poetic form. One of Ashbery's goals throughout the period of *The Tennis Court Oath* (as he put it in his 1962 essay on Reverdy) was to "give their true names back to things, to shake off the eternal dead weight of symbolism and allegory."[18] Useful though it might be for a poet to think about cleansing words of their accretions of meaning, it isn't possible to do it. After completing *The Tennis Court Oath*, Ashbery seems to have realized that a writer can't stand outside discourse, thereby limiting its power; as he has recently admitted in *Flow Chart*, "the words have, as they / always do, come full circle, dragging the meaning that was on the reverse side / all along, and one even / expects this, something to chew on." So if "Leaving the Atocha Station" is an attempt to embody a temporal process by moving beyond the usual connotations of words (by standing outside of the ordering principles of language), "Clepsydra" is an attempt to embody that process within discourse—to "chew on" the meaning of words rather than escape them. There is no delusion of getting outside or beyond, and the result is a far more satisfyingly mysterious poem.

As any reader of Ashbery knows, "Clepsydra" is nominally about the way in which one moment supersedes another, slipping from the future to the past without any sense of a teleology; more important, Ashbery makes his reader experience this sense of flux in a poem whose grammar and rhetoric conspire to disperse any clear sense of cumulative meaning. While Walter Pater cajoled us in *Studies in the History of the Renaissance* to savor our moments as they pass, Ashbery isn't sure if it's worth the effort to isolate any particular moment—even if it were possible to do so: "Each moment / Of utterance is the true one; likewise none are true." But if this utterance itself seems true, consider how the rest of the sentence forces us to reconsider.

> Each moment
> Of utterance is the true one; likewise none are true,
> Only is the bounding from air to air, a serpentine
> Gesture which hides the truth behind a congruent
> Message, the way air hides the sky, is, in fact,
> Tearing it limb from limb this very moment: but
> The sky has pleaded already and this is about
> As graceful a kind of non-absence as either
> Has a right to expect: whether it's the form of
> Some creator who has momentarily turned away,
> Marrying detachment with respect, so that the pieces
> Are seen as parts of a spectrum, independent
> Yet symbolic of their spaced-out times of arrival;
> Whether on the other hand all of it is to be
> Seen as no luck.

Writing about de Chirico's *Hebdomeros* (a chapter of which he translated in 1965), Ashbery said that "the novel has no story, though it reads as if it did."[19] In stark contrast to the collage poems of *The Tennis Court Oath*, "Clepsydra" reads *as if* it had a story: if we ignore the semantic content of this sentence, one clause follows logically from the other, linked by a vocabulary of cause and effect: *likewise, which, in fact, about as, either, whether, so that,* and *yet*. The result is that while the meaning of the first two lines is gradually dispersed, we feel as though there ought to be an accumulation of meaning. The first six lines of the sentence might be paraphrased this way: *If each moment is true, then it is equally valid to say that none of them is true. But in fact, only the movement from one moment to the other (which is like a bounding from air to air) is true. This bounding is in turn like a serpentine gesture which paradoxically hides the truth behind a message that looks like the truth. In the same way, air hides the sky, and, in fact, the sky is tearing the air limb from limb at this very moment.* But such a paraphrase doesn't get us very far, especially if we extend it to encompass the entire sentence: why should moments be like air and sky which are tearing each other limb from limb? The movement, alternately sinuous and tortuous, from one metaphor to another (the temporal experience of the poem itself) is more important than any totality to which the metaphors point.

Ashbery's way of wedding logical syntax with illogical content in "Clepsydra" is not in itself remarkable; it would become his primary mode of writing in most of the poems that have followed. What is crucial here is that Ashbery has given up the idea of breaking through the normal discursive function of language. He can now reveal how much room for slippage there is within those boundaries, gaining not just a more absorbing embodiment of temporal flux but (more important) a greater discursive freedom. In "Decoy," from *The Double Dream of Spring*, Ashbery no longer wants to cleanse words of their usual meanings but to exploit those meanings.

> We hold these truths to be self-evident:
> That ostracism, both political and moral, has
> Its place in the twentieth-century scheme of things;
> That urban chaos is the problem we have been seeing into and
>     seeing into,
> For the factory, deadpanned by its very existence into a
> Descending code of values, has moved right across the road from
>     total financial upheaval
> And caught regression head-on. The descending scale does not
>     imply
> A corresponding deterioration of moral values, punctuated
> By acts of corporate vandalism every five years,
> Like a bunch of violets pinned to a dress, that knows and ignores
>     its own standing.

In "Clepsydra" Ashbery could use a cliché like "tearing it limb from limb" not with irony but as one among the many expressive possibilities the language has to offer. Here in "Decoy" Ashbery writes even more resolutely from within American public discourse. The syntax is not nearly as congested as in "Clepsydra," but the poem unfolds with a similarly deceptive logic, beginning with the declarative opening of *The Declaration of Independence* and mimicking the turns of Jefferson's periodic sentence. Within this normative structure—not in spite of it—a series of disruptions thwarts our effort to make common sense out of language that we think we already know: though we can easily integrate "ostracism" rather than "all men are created equal" with the opening line, we then expect ostracism to have "no place" rather than "its place" in the twentieth-century scheme of things. By the time we reach the last line of this passage ("Like a bunch of violets pinned to a dress"), the line feels startlingly disruptive—even though it offers the one remotely lyrical phrase in the opening movement of the poem.

"Decoy" was first published in September 1967, four months after Ashbery responded to Louis Simpson's attack in the *Nation*: with its brash use of the language of the establishment, the poem seems driven by Ashbery's sense that no poet could write with the cleanly oppositional conscience that Simpson recommended. As the poem moves on, Ashbery says that there is "every reason to rejoice with those self-styled prophets of commercial disaster, those harbingers of gloom": as he suggested in his essay on O'Hara, a repetition of the accepted terms of revolt, however pessimistic, only serves to make us more complacent.

> To sum up: We are fond of plotting itineraries
> And our pyramiding memories, alert as dandelion fuzz, dart from
>     one pretext to the next
> Seeking in occasions new sources of memories, for memory is profit
> Until the day it spreads out all its accumulation, delta-like on the
>     plain
> For that day no good can come of remembering, and the anomalies
>     cancel each other out.
> But until then foreshortened memories will keep us going, alive,
>     one to the other.

> There was never an excuse for this and perhaps there need be none,
> For kicking out into the morning, on the wide bed,
> Waking far apart on the bed, the two of them:
> Husband and wife
> Man and wife

Recalling Jorge Luis Borges's "Funes, the Memorious," in which the remarkable Funes can remember everything and consequently make sense of nothing, Ashbery suggests that any itinerary will eventually be overwhelmed by the events it seeks to order. Only a "foreshortened" memory, one that ignores uncommon events, will continue to be profitable. Ashbery recognizes the inevitability as well as the inadequacy of such discrimination; he forces his readers to confront both of these feelings ("to sum up") in response to the poem itself. What bothers him is the way in which the prophets of doom pretend that their itineraries are uncompromised. The end of "Decoy" is consequently divided. Perhaps there need be no excuse for plotting itineraries, yet the final image of routine seems inexcusable. Having begun the poem with *The Declaration of Independence*, he ends it with *The Book of Common Prayer*: the modernized phrase "husband and wife," with its suggestion of gendered itineraries, degenerates into "man and wife," its more purely sexist form.

In reconceiving a poetics of embodiment in "Clepsydra," Ashbery left description almost completely behind. A successful reading of the poem depends almost exclusively on attention to the poem's movement; the subject matter, minimal as it is, remains pretty much beside the point. In "Decoy" Ashbery both embodies and describes his moments as they pass, and it consequently seems to me representative of his strongest mode: "Syringa" and "Self-Portrait in a Convex Mirror" are its closest relations.

Yet Ashbery himself is oddly resistant to any preference for his more explicable poems—as if the wisdom of "The Invisible Avant-Garde" were too reasonable for its author to face. "Syringa" (from *Houseboat Days*) is hung on the Orpheus myth as clearly as "Self-Portrait" is spun around Parmigianino's painting, but the poem's purpose is to undermine its own reliance on subject matter. Like so many of Ashbery's poems, "Syringa" warns that "one cannot guard, treasure / That stalled moment"—that "it is the nature of things to be seen only once." The second death of Eurydice is consequently not worthy of undue notice: even if Orpheus had not turned around, she would have disappeared anyway, since everything we love disappears. Eurydice, the subject of both Ashbery's and Orpheus's song, drops away, and even poetry itself cannot forestall change: "it isn't enough / To just go on singing." Once the moment disappears, it is no longer material for a poem, since poetry is itself in motion:

> Its subject
> Matters too much, and not enough, standing there helplessly
> While the poem streaked by, its tail afire, a bad
> Comet screaming hate and disaster, but so turned inward
> That the meaning, good or other, can never
> Become known.

The subject matter—the occasion behind the poem's cry—is not only inconsequential but unknowable. Yet Ashbery makes this point in a poem that is notable for its explicable presentation of a story: even as description, the act of recounting the past, is dismissed, it continues to control our experience of the poem.

"Self-Portrait in a Convex Mirror" is less conflicted about the availability of its own meaning, but Ashbery has maintained, somewhat defensively, that the poem is really as chaotic as any of his more notoriously disjunctive work. In a sense, he is right, just as he is right to say that Eliot's *Four Quartets* "may be just as purposefully chaotic [as *The Waste Land*] beneath its skin of deliberateness."[20] And at other times, Ashbery has more logically declined to wear chaos as a badge of authenticity. Elizabeth Bishop pleased him by calling his poetry "sort of semi-abstract," poised between sense and nonsense: "I thought that was a good thing to be," said Ashbery, "because that's what everything is."[21] But if, given the slippery nature of language itself, radical disjunction may be found in the most normative text, why set out merely to exaggerate—or be self-conscious about—what all texts do?

Given the lingering power of the "breakthrough" narrative in American poetry—our continuing trust in a poetics of authenticity—we should welcome a poetry that (in Charles Altieri's words) "earns and explores a self-conscious rhetoric in reaction against rhetorics that claim naturalness." But a healthy distrust of what seems natural (a coherent sense of selfhood, a clear sense of closure) does not necessitate rejecting a poetics of normative sense (or of selfhood and closure). Since all po-etries are arbitrarily conceived, historically constituted, we need not conclude that "the poet's awareness of the duplicity of discourse" par-adoxically becomes "a mark of authenticity"; if anything, an increased self-consciousness about the rhetoric of authenticity should free us to explore a wider variety of rhetorical stances.[22]

To think of Ashbery's stylistic extravagance as a mark of authenticity is to reinforce the mimetic logic of the "breakthrough" narrative: the self-consciously employed rhetoric is not in itself arbitrary but in fact provides a clearer picture of the arbitrary way in which language stages our world. The logic may seem more sophisticated because what is at stake here is a semiotic process rather than a poet's suffering, but the logic is nevertheless the same. For many years, an uncritical acceptance of the terms of the "breakthrough" narrative helped to limit our sense of what is possible in poetry after modernism: an authentic poem, nec-essarily written in free verse, uncovers the poet's subjectivity, revealing it as the true mirror of his or her time. Today, an uncritical acceptance of the terms of Ashbery's career (as it's commonly understood) threat-ens to enforce similar limitations: an authentic poem, necessarily high-lighting its own rhetoricity, dismantles the illusion of a poet's subjectivity, revealing the process of unraveling as the true mirror of his or her time. But Ashbery's poems almost never succumb to this idealization of language (his statements about the poems succumb slightly more often). John Koethe, one of the few younger poets to have harnessed Ashbery's powerful influence, ponders the right question in "The Narrow Way."

> I was wondering the other day
> How poetry still manages to move people
> (Since any illusions about its ability to do so
> Should by now have been definitively dispelled).[23]

Koethe goes on to offer his own answer to this question, but it's more important that the question continue to be asked, reminding us that we remain at the mercy of language (thankfully so), no matter how stra-tegically we employ it.

Ultimately, as Koethe implies, the only unimpeachable justification for writing the way Ashbery does is the same justification for writing any other way: pleasure. Discussing the obscurity of John Wheel-wright's poems, Ashbery has suggested that when a clear subject matter is lacking, "we are forced back on the tributary beauties of the language, which are however frequently so substantial as to carry the poem alone." This is frequently true of Ashbery's poems as well; and it is equally true, as he also says of Wheelwright, that the poems necessarily risk "occasional lapses into tedium."[24] Ashbery's poems, in all their extravagance, are finally justified (or not) by the pleasure aroused by their language—their seductive movement, reproduced in the mouth or mind of the reader, of nonsense and sense. Which is not to say that the poems do not make us consider various linguistic and social issues: but if the poems are to stand as poems, then pleasure must be a criterion as well. The poet who so bravely resisted any political justification for O'Hara's poems—and did so at a time when a culturally sanctioned justification could easily have been appropriated—would have agreed. And so would the poet writing three decades later. In these lines from "Like a Sentence" (collected in *Can You Hear, Bird*, his most recent book), Ashbery suggests that in our lives as in our sentences, only unexpected pleasure, the payoff of waywardness, can sustain us.

> Time only has an agenda
> in the wallet at his back, while we
> who think we know where we are going unfazed
> end up in brilliant woods, nourished more than we can know
> by the unexpectedness of ice and stars
> and crackling tears.

# AMY CLAMPITT'S
# UNITED STATES

*W*estward: the word appears in many of Amy Clampitt's early poems (most prominently in "Procession at Candlemas"), and in 1990 it became the title of her fifth full-length collection. Clampitt was a poet finely tuned to a word's accretion of usage, so while "westward" has a natural place in her vocabulary, it inevitably came to her enriched by Henry James. Marianne Moore quoted one of James's descriptions of the American sensibility in her essay "Henry James as a Characteristic American."

> Some complain of his transferred citizenship as a loss; but when we consider the trend of his fiction and his uncomplacent denouements, we have no scruple about insisting that he was American; not if the American is, as he thought, "intrinsically and actively ample,... reaching westward, southward, anywhere, everywhere," with a mind "incapable of the shut door in any direction."[1]

For Clampitt, born like Moore in the American Midwest, westward is the most difficult direction to face. When she speculates in her own essay on James that America offered him "no sense of inwardness," her thoughts carry the weight of experience: "It was as though the seemingly unlimited spaces of the New World had proved so daunting as not to lend themselves to any true enclosure—or indeed to a sense of the sacred, except as a halfhearted borrowing from the Old World."[2] Clampitt doesn't mean to say that James indulged in such borrowing; she wants to suggest how difficult it is for any writer to discover a true sense of inwardness in what T. S. Eliot called (apropos of James) "a large flat country which no one wants to visit."[3]

Clampitt herself was sometimes accused of such borrowing, as James and Eliot were accused. She often remarked about the "formlessness" of her native Iowa landscape, and, like other Midwesterners (Clampitt invokes Crane and Pound as well as Eliot and Moore), she sought what Pound called a "foreign fastness" by looking east. Her travels first to New York and then to Europe, especially England and Greece, were crucial to her art. Mental traveling was equally important: Clampitt attempted to be influenced by a wide variety of predecessors ("There is less originality than we think"), and she wore the marks of their work proudly.[4] The result is a body of work that listens boldly to the courtly muses, as Emerson said the American artist should not.

This debate is an old one, older than Emerson, but Clampitt's work has provided a new locus for contention. "Especially on the East Coast," wrote one reviewer, "Amy Clampitt has been widely hailed as the latest wonder woman of contemporary poetry." The implication is that the West Coast (not the Middle West) thinks differently: "The phenomenon represented by this suddenly made and meteorically ascending reputation is an interesting one, suggesting that some readers are almost desperately nostalgic for the good old pre-'Beat,' pre-'Deep Image,' pre-'Confessional' days when poems were well-wrought urns, [and] poets' personalities were (as T. S. Eliot had recommended) decorously 'extinguished.' " This response to Clampitt's highly rhetorical poetry is predictable. Less so is the East Coast's discomfort with the same qualities. "Many readers view Clampitt as a formalist poet," wrote an editor of the *New Criterion*, justifying her absence from an anthology of New Formalist poetry: "In truth, Clampitt seldom writes metrically. Just as problematic, however, is the conflation in many of her poems of 'high' poetic language and a kind of surrealism that was popular in the sixties and seventies. The result . . . is an unlikely and finally unsatisfying juxtaposition of the poetic spirits of Marianne Moore and John Ashbery."

It's true that Clampitt rarely employs regular meter and rhyme; but her poems don't take up the rhetorical stance associated, in the wake of modernism, with the rejection of these tools. To some readers, consequently, her poems seem decorous and traditional—the kind of poem Richard Wilbur is supposed to have written in the fifties; to others, they seem garrulous and unmannerly—the kind of poem John Ashbery is supposed to be writing today. Clampitt's poetry *is* a hybrid, but it is not an unlikely one; as she herself recognized, Ashbery has learned a great deal from Moore (he once called "The Octopus" the great poem of the century). But while Clampitt has been championed noisily by such readers as Richard Howard and Helen Vendler, her poems are not easily accommodated by the terms with which the history of American poetry is usually written. "East was East and West was West," said Louis Simpson, recalling the standoff between *The New American Poetry* and *New Poets of England and America* in the early sixties.[5] The lay of the land hasn't changed much. For if Ashbery must be considered antithetical to Moore—if confessional, deep-image, or formalist poetry still seems like an affront to Eliot—then Clampitt has no home on either coast.

Clampitt thought of herself as a kind of nomad, shuttling between East and West, so I suspect that she was happy to ignore the divisions of the American poetic continent. No other poet of her generation (she was born in 1920) could say this about T. S. Eliot: "I've tended to forget all about him when it came to the naming of influences."[6] Clampitt rightly complained about the attention given to the late start of her career (her first book was not published until 1973); like the attention given to Stevens's career in insurance, it implies that only a lifetime of poetry goes into the making of poems. Still, it's worth remembering Clampitt's birthdate if only to understand why she has seemed so blissfully unconcerned with the debates that have preoccupied American poets since the Second World War: Clampitt was somewhere else. Her work is often likened to Wilbur's, since both poets delight in baroque rhetoric and European landscapes. A more telling difference is that, unlike Wilbur, Clampitt did not have to be aware of the academy's highstrung relationship with Eliotic modernism: in this regard, only much younger poets are her contemporaries. Clampitt's poems are occasionally marked by the wide-eyed enthusiasm of the autodidact (I sense this more often in the notes to her poems), but by schooling herself she never had to choose sides. The poems reach for any influence, any landscape, that will nurture. And if Wilbur and Moore are instructive, so are Ashbery and Olson, whose *Call Me Ishmael* Clampitt invokes in the notes to *The Kingfisher* as "a book no American poet should fail to read."

Moore thought that James's openness, his inability to shut the door in any direction, made him a characteristic American, and the same may be said of Clampitt. Like James she looks "westward, southward, anywhere, everywhere": her use of the word *westward* must be understood in this context. Clampitt's preoccupation with European places and literatures does not replace her troubled fascination with the Midwest; on the contrary, it makes that fascination possible. All of Clampitt's finest poems find their subject, however circuitously, in her native Iowa—its landscape, its people, its sordidness. Even her most ambitious poems about European culture (such as "Voyages," her sequence about Keats) are propelled by her effort to understand the stranger place from which she came: these poems become interesting in direct proportion to their concern with the American Midwest. Conversely, Clampitt's most ambitious poem about the Midwest, "The Prairie," doesn't stop looking eastward; its power grows from Clampitt's yoking of her native Iowa with the Russian steppe. Auden said of James that it may be necessary for writers to leave their homes, "not to get away from them, but to recreate them."[7] In Clampitt's case, one would have to add Elizabeth Bishop's terse qualification to the word *home*: "wherever that may be."

The example of Bishop's life and work was important for Clampitt, probably more so than those of Moore and James. But the impetus behind Clampitt's work is not exclusively literary, no matter how strenuously she courted influences. A more compelling, even more haunting impetus is suggested by *Some Incidents in My Life: A Saga of the "Unknown" Citizen*, published by Frank T. Clampitt when his granddaughter was sixteen years old.

> Father and mother were of pioneer stock and had themselves done pioneering in the Middle West when the land was crude and new. They had endured many privations courageously. . . . Some day these staunch foundation-builders of their own fortunes and of civilization on a new front should be accorded the large place in the history of this inland empire which they deserve.[8]

Frank Clampitt, whose life is one of the subjects of "The Prairie," was born in 1860. When he turned eighteen, his father offered him a choice: a college education or a tract of land. Clampitt took the land, hoping he could somehow attend college too: planting corn, he studied Latin while the horses rested. He also read Emerson late at night; he wrote sonnets; he wrote a metrical account, modeled on *Hiawatha*, of his experience in the Dakotas. He suffered from migraines; he developed a twitch. His son Roy graduated from Grinnell College, attending every other year so he could work on the farm. His granddaughter Amy graduated from Grinnell and headed east, thinking she would never look back.

Clampitt lived in New York City, more or less, from 1941 until her death in 1994; her first trip to Europe came in 1949. She worked as an editor and librarian, wrote novels that were never published, and finally turned to poems in the late sixties. The grand reception accorded *The Kingfisher* in 1983 tended to obscure the virtues of Clampitt's first book,

*Multitudes, Multitudes*, published ten years earlier. Many of Clampitt's most treasured motifs are present there: Andersen's "The Little Mermaid" and the statue of Ornithe that would become the presiding deity in *Archaic Figure*. So are many other abiding concerns: the Holocaust, the Vietnam War, the lives of women, and the landscapes of Iowa and Greece. The poems themselves have the discursive breadth of Clampitt's later work, and they often display her characteristically ornate rhetoric, yoking the highest diction with the grubbiest slang. What they most often lack is the particular syntax, ingrown yet sprawling, of Clampitt's later work. The absence is most apparent in the poems about Iowa: Clampitt asks the right questions ("O my own America, what are you?"), but she hasn't yet discovered their real difficulty—she's not sufficiently estranged from the place she called home. So while in her later books the poems about the Midwest are consistently the best, the poems about Greece are the finest in *Multitudes, Multitudes*.

> In solitude, among marsh-orchises and calendulas
> a last unstable column lurches and staggers.
> No one comes to stroll here now.
> The sea's rush is diminished to a whisper,
> a closed susurrus like the bloodstream
> in the dusk of a shuttered room. Voiceless
> at its back, and savage with waiting,
> hangs the blue headland. There Asia begins.

In these opening lines of "Hera of Samos," Clampitt's mature style is fully present. So is her characteristic interest in landscapes long deprived of meaning—only here the landscape is Grecian rather than Middle Western. Throughout *Multitudes, Multitudes* it is not a large flat country but the washed-out corners of ancient civilization that nobody wants to visit. In "Delos" Clampitt offers an even bleaker history of deprivation: "an island so high on civilization / that after a few shifts of hegemony / it had no populace at all except looters."

> It's still true.
> Humped like sleeping seals, the other islands
> rim a horizon of impossible blue.
> Nine sightless lions beside a dried-up lake,
> these led herds, all this
> pedantic litter of pillage and cupidity,
> debris of so much intellect—
> dust, and very little else.
> Why is it one feels happy here?

Clampitt faces the present condition of Greece directly, unwilling to indulge in any easy nostalgia for a past culture's glories. But in the poem's final lines she admits that Delos can nevertheless satisfy her as her native landscape, equally vacant, cannot: a long history, even of deprivation and violence, seems better than none.

In a famous passage in his book on Hawthorne, Henry James offered a list of everything American culture lacked: "no literature, no novels, no museums, no pictures, no political society, no sporting class—no Epsom nor Ascot!"[9] The effusiveness of this list (I quote only a part of it) is meant to be self-mocking; the New World had a different, not a "thinner," culture than the Old. But that difference has been notoriously difficult to appreciate. Clampitt once recalled that while growing up in Iowa, she had no consciousness of history: "It wasn't really until I got to Oxford and went into Christ Church Hall, and *smelled* it, that I believed in the presence of the past."[10] Like James, Clampitt would eventually be able to express some irony about these feelings (that self-awareness will mark the difference between *Multitudes, Multitudes* and her later work), but in her earliest poems she takes her history straight. In "The Christmas Cactus" (the best of the very few poems in *Multitudes, Multitudes* that attempt any connection between Greece and Iowa) Clampitt remembers her grandmother's cactus as something "gorgeous and wicked" in a place that otherwise said "NO NO NO the blizzard leaning / woodpile and shrubbery drifted full of NO."

> It remembers
> the equator's dark Brazilian underside
> where day and night cohabit
> dividing the globe between them
> like a ripe pomegranate.

This allusion to Persephone allows Clampitt to register her grandmother's momentary and possibly unintentional leap from the dull rounds of prairie life. Greek myth offers an escape from the Midwest, not the terms for rethinking the Midwest as a landscape with its own long history of violence and deprivation.

The landscape of coastal Maine does not appear in the poems of *Multitudes, Multitudes*, but it dominates much of *The Kingfisher* and all of *The Isthmus* (a chapbook published in 1981). After focusing on Greece, Maine probably seemed to Clampitt an easier subject than Iowa, an inroad to a more formidably American locality. In *The Isthmus* Marianne Moore's influence can also be felt for the first time. The rigor of more meticulous description, focused on Maine, helped to curb the heavily prophetic sensibility that occasionally dominates *Multitudes, Multitudes*. But in some ways Maine may have been too easy a subject. In "Vignetting" Clampitt attempts to dignify the American landscape by imbuing it with European history ("Cloudlets in a ceiling hued by

Tiepolo"), but the comparisons don't carry much weight. She would offer a variation of this poem in "Remembering Greece," published in *The Kingfisher*, in which the Maine cove is so blue that

> it halfway dislocates itself to the Aegean
> and becomes, if only in the way events can weigh
> upon events, the bloodied bath of Agamemnon.

Though the weight of myth is added to the landscape here, the comparisons still seem tired, especially if we think of Eliot's invocation of the bloodied bath in "Sweeney Among the Nightingales."

In *What the Light Was Like* Clampitt offers a third variation: the title "A Baroque Sunburst" is the subject of the poem's single sentence.

> struck through such a dome
> as might await a groaning Michelangelo,
> finding only alders and barnacles
> and herring gulls at their usual squabbles,
> sheds on the cove's voluted
> silver the aloof skin tones
> of a Crivelli angel: a region,
> a weather and a point of view
> as yet unsettled, save for the lighthouse
> like a Venetian campanile, from whose nightlong
> reflected angelus you might suppose
> the coast of Maine had Europe
> on the brain or in its bones, as though
> it were a kind of sickness.

The last three lines make "A Baroque Sunburst" a very different poem from "Vignetting" or "Remembering Greece." Maine's relationship to Europe is no longer the subject; instead, the act of conceiving of that relationship becomes the reason for the poem. Clampitt is no longer trying to lift an American landscape to the level of Italy or Greece: the urge to make the comparison has been diagnosed, and it looks like a disease. Clampitt had earlier seen the depravity of Greece; she had no illusions there. Now she sees the shallowness even of looking to Greece for something she lacks.

A much richer poetry hinges on this realization. In "Beethoven, Opus 111," for instance, Clampitt suggests that the "sole ironic function" of the American home's Steinway may be "to demonstrate that one, though he may / grunt and sweat at work, is not a clod." This skepticism does not undermine the poem's carefully argued link between Beethoven's music and her father's farming; it makes the self-consciously tenuous comparison meaningful. As in "The Christmas Cactus," Clampitt sees only one small aspect of a relative's life (her father's grappling with the givens of nature) that could be identified with a European's (Beethoven's grappling with the givens of art); but the link is no longer presented as a momentary reprieve in an otherwise dreary life. By confronting the potential self-deception of her own need for European culture, Clampitt finds the terms for articulating the higher purpose of an entire life, however mundane.

As part of her interrogation of her own motives, Clampitt remarks that there's "no dwelling on the sweet past here, / there being no past to speak of / other than the setbacks." She's trying to provide a legitimately nurturing history for the prairie—but she's aware of the pretentiousness of doing so. In the poems that follow "Beethoven, Opus 111" in *The Kingfisher* (in the section of the book called "Heartland"), Clampitt continues this balancing act, but she's not so much providing a history as discovering it: the history of her native Iowa turns out to be as long and as sordid as Delos's. Watching the wind blow over fields of grain, Clampitt always imagined the prairie as a vast, shapeless sea. Geology confirmed the intuition: "Geologically, the Midwest—the Missouri-Mississippi basin—has been underwater more often that it has been above. . . . It's real bottom. It's never been up. It's always been down. And there's something depressing about being from there. The Midwest seems to have no form."[11] The trilogy of poems that opens "Heartland" ("The Quarry," "The Woodlot," and "Imago") ultimately suggests that formlessness, of a certain kind, could be a virtue.

In "The Quarry" Clampitt conflates geological time with the westward expansion, imagining "prairie schooners" sailing across the Eocene sea. Whether literally or figuratively under water, the landscape has no landmarks, no locality; it is "a flux / that waterlogs the mind." Clampitt juxtaposes two ways of giving this landscape a shape, one that ignores its long history of flux, and one that attempts (more tenuously but more potently) to accommodate it. Before there were any roads through the territory, Clampitt recalls, a man named Lyman Dillon drove a plow southwestward for a hundred miles, "the longest furrow / ever, straight into the belly of the future." In this narrative, the "future" is the old capitol building in Des Moines, built from imported marble: the "broken loam" would be given a shape, be "mounted, as on a howdah," by

> a marble capitol, the glister
> of whose dome still overtops
> the frittered sprawl of who we are,
> of where we came from,
> with its stilted El Dorado.

As in "Beethoven, Opus 111," but more stringently, Clampitt is suspicious of this imposition of European form; her metaphors invoke several varieties of pillage or domination, suggesting Clampitt's possible discomfort with her own style—"glister" laid over the "frittered sprawl." And though "The Quarry" ends with this passage, emphasizing the lasting power of European domination, the poem includes another story about the Midwest's origins and ends. Since it involves De Soto's search for American gold, this story is not completely distinct from the one ending in the capitol's glistering dome. But what interests Clampitt here is De Soto's *failure* to find the "least corruptible" metal, his dead body sinking, literally and metaphorically, into the corrupt, shapeless ooze of the Mississippi delta.

> Will
> some shard of skull or jawbone, undecomposed,
> outlast his name, as the unquarried starfish
> outlast the seas that inundated them?

Clampitt cannot answer this question, but in it lies her desire for an American history of the vanquished, one that includes the reality of European domination but is not determined by it—a history that honors formlessness rather than purity.

"The Woodlot" offers one idea of what this history might be. Clampitt again presents the prairie as a watery mire, except that she emphasizes the violence of its blizzards and tornados, imagining the latter as a devouring mother ("frightful udder") that sucks up any shape imposed on the landscape: "luck and a cellarhole were all / a prairie dweller had to count on." Clampitt can think of two things that survive this violence: the barbed wire invented by an anonymous Iowa farmer and the few outcroppings of trees that "gave the prairie grid / what little personality it had." Could that farmer, Clampitt asks, ever have imagined that his invention, stringing together "orchard, barnyard, bullpen, feedlot," would have led to a child's discovery of

> an enclosure
> whose ceiling's silver-maple tops
> stir overhead, uneasy, in the interminably
> murmuring air? Deep in it, under
> appletrees like figures in a ritual, violets
> are thick, a blue cellarhole
> of pure astonishment.
> It is
> the earliest memory. Before it,
> I/you, whatever that conundrum may yet
> prove to be, amounts to nothing.

In this poem, which recounts Clampitt's own earliest memory, barbed wire leads to the first glimpse of what she would call, apropos of James, a true sense of inwardness or enclosure. Clampitt can refer to this image as *the* earliest memory because, for her, all sense of selfhood depends on discovering that sense of enclosure in a place defiantly vast. The farmer's grubby work merges with the growth of an aesthetic sensibility—not the "fine manners" of Europe, but something more primal. And that sensibility, though protected from the formless landscape, is not completely separate from it: the apple trees are "like figures in a ritual," but the patch of violets beneath them becomes "a blue cellarhole / of pure astonishment." The cellarhole, all the prairie-dweller can count on after the storm has passed, now seems like an image of possibility rather than necessity. As J. D. McClatchy has pointed out, the words *tornado* and *astonishment* come from the same root: *extonare*, which once meant something like "leave one thunderstruck."[12] That no such root connects *violets* with *violence* doesn't prevent us from hearing one.

Clampitt enacts this accommodation of formlessness within the movement of the poems themselves; their forms seem (to borrow the metaphors of "The Sacred Hearth Fire") less like an "object" or even a "process" than an "unshaped / accretion." "Imago," the last poem in this informal trilogy, moves the way Elizabeth Bishop's "Santarém" does, accumulating details unpredictably, almost randomly, but at the same time developing a sturdy coherence. Metamorphosis is the vehicle for this movement: arrowheads in a furrow become seashells from the Eocene; the little mermaid becomes a human being, walking "on a parterre of tomahawks"; and—most potently—the European past, known only through cheap imitations of antiquity, becomes something far more threatening when its dark secrets are discovered close to home.

"Imago" is also about metamorphosis: a young girl's maturation, sexual and intellectual, connects all these transformations. She is the "shirker," reading Hans Christian Andersen in the farmhouse parlor; she becomes the "scribbler" whose writing, like the place where she lives, has no form. She travels to Europe, which in comparison seems "hard and handsome," but is also a "hodgepodge of ancestral / calamities." Anything exotic is scorned on the prairie ("the whispered 'Cathlick' "), so while European antiquity seems like an "adjunct of schoolhouse make-believe," it is also "a slough to be pulled out of"— "a knothole / you plugged with straw." Clampitt is once again separating a debased importation of history from something more astonishing. The plugged knothole becomes the black eyeholes in a theatre mask: "the tragic howl, the comic rictus, / eyeholes that stare out of the crypt / of what no grownup is ever heard to speak of." This "crypt" is, like the Eocene, older than antiquity. It is discovered by the girl, at the moment of sexual maturity, when she sees both herself and the mask's black eyes in the wings of the luna moth: *imago* means both an idealized image of the self and a sexually mature insect. While the grown-ups attend a prayer meeting, being "born again," the girl experiences a more profound transformation.

> On prayer-meeting night, outside
> the vestibule among multiple
> bell-pulls of Virginia creeper,
> the terrible clepsydra of becoming
> distils its drop: a luna moth, the emblem
> of the born-again, furred like an orchid
> behind the ferned antennae, a totem-
> garden of lascivious pheromones,
> hangs, its glimmering streamers
> pierced by the dripstone burin of the eons
> with the predatory stare out of the burrow,
> those same eyeholes. Imago
> of unfathomable evolvings, living
> only to copulate and drop its litter,
> does it know what it is, what it has been,
> what it may or must become?

In these densely packed lines, the girl discovers the aspect of sexuality grown-ups don't speak of: an overpoweringly biological urge that transcends not only love but desire. That urge lurks within the eyeholes of European antiquity, but it also lurks within the girl's own body: she doesn't need to leave home to find it, and she can't leave home to escape it. The moth, as exotic as the Europe she craves, as lascivious as the body she inhabits, becomes an image of what she both wants and fears most deeply. In the final question of "Imago," Clampitt invokes Yeats's "Sailing to Byzantium," a poem that faces squarely eastward, but she allows "what is past, or passing, or to come" to become the story of one Midwestern woman, not simply all of human history.

In an interview conducted several years after *The Kingfisher* was published, Clampitt said that she'd only begun to "puzzle out" what her experience of Europe "means in relation to the place I came from."[13] Given how powerfully "The Quarry," "The Woodlot," and "Imago" do just that, this remark may seem disingenuous, but I don't think it is. *What the Light Was Like* contains several powerful poems about Clampitt's Iowa childhood ("Black Buttercups" is a kind of sequel to "Imago"), but in other poems the subject has grown a little stale. In her note to "The Reedbeds of Hackensack," Clampitt explains that her allusions to Williams, Dante, Milton, Keats, and Shakespeare "may be regarded as a last-ditch effort to associate the landscape familiarly known as the Jersey Meadows with the tradition of elegiac poetry." The poem is less schematic than this note suggests, but its effort to dignify an American landscape is predictable after "Imago" or "Black Butter-cups." Instead of resting on the achievement of these poems, Clampitt needed to rethink them more radically: like the poems of *Multitudes, Multitudes*, those of *What the Light Was Like* and *Archaic Figure* turn to England and to Greece—but only to put more pressure on Clampitt's relationship with the American Midwest. Some readers find these volumes less satisfying than *The Kingfisher*, a response that may be inevitable, given the praise lavished on *The Kingfisher*. But Clampitt's need to shake up her most polished conclusions has something to do with the response too.

"Voyages: A Homage to John Keats," the centerpiece of *What the Light Was Like*, is a retelling of the story of Keats's life; it is also an oblique reconsideration of the story of "Imago." Clampitt's fascination with Keats intensified when she discovered that he too had watched the wind transform a field of grain into an "alien corn's inland sea- / surfaces"; she associated this image so deeply with the American Midwest that Keats began to seem connected to that landscape. The link is not completely fortuitous. After Keats's brother George emigrated to Kentucky, Keats wrote a little poem on hearing that George's wife was pregnant; he said he would be happy if the child "should become the first American poet."

> Bard art thou completely
> Little Child
> O' the western wild.

Keats's idealization of the land "where furrows are new to the plough" (as he called it in another poem to his brother) was sullied when George lost all his money to the financier John James Audubon, later to become famous (ironically) for his efforts to conserve the American frontier. In "Lines to Fanny," one of Keats's last poems, America becomes "that most hateful land, / Dungeoner of my friends, that wicked strand / Where they were wreck'd and lived a wreckèd life."[14]

Throughout "Voyages" Clampitt uses Keats's complex attitude toward America to mirror her own. In "The Elgin Marbles," third in the sequence, she imagines Keats spending his last evening with George and Georgiana before they sail for America: "imagination failed," says Clampitt of Keats's inability to comprehend the western landscape, but the failure is hers too: "—and still fails: what can John Keats / have had to do with a hacked clearing / in the Kentucky underbrush?" However, Clampitt also remembers that in Keats's "Fall of Hyperion," the dreamer looks north and south, finding only mist; then eastward, "where black gates / Were shut against the sunrise evermore." The only vista left is westward. When Moneta appears there, she tells him that Hyperion is "sloping to the threshold of the west.—/ Thither we tend." In "Wincester: The Autumn Equinox," the seventh poem of "Voyages," Clampitt merges Keats's turn westward with her own:

> The opening of the West: what Miltonic
> rocketry of epithet, what paradigm
> of splendor in decline, could travel,
> and survive, the monstrous region (as he'd
> later depict it) of dull rivers poured
> from sordid urns, rank tracts unowned
> by any weed-haired god he'd ever heard of,
> that had fleeced his brother George?

This is Keats's question—how to make an epic poem of a diminished thing?—and it is also Clampitt's. Having first looked eastward (to the sunrise, to spring, to Italy and Greece) Keats must ultimately turn westward: to the sunset, to autumn, to death, and at least symbolically to America. For Clampitt's Keats, the unplowed prairie stands for the unimaginable, monstrous region with which he must come to terms; for Clampitt herself, the prairie simply is that place.

Considered as a comment on Keats's life and work, "Voyages" is interesting, but the poem becomes much richer when considered as a kind of displaced autobiography. This is what distinguishes the European poems of *What the Light Was Like* or *Archaic Figure* from those of *Multitudes, Multitudes*: Clampitt tries not to escape the prairie but to discover a more difficult and lasting rapprochement with it. More difficult because, especially in the poems of *Archaic Figure*, Clampitt confronts the sordid underside of the westward expansion. In "Venice Revisited" she tells a familiar story about the cohabitation of an appreciation of beauty and a lust for power; as in "Voyages," the poem become interesting when the settling of the Venice mud flats merges with the settling of the prairie. America also becomes a "faltering empire," its promise indistinguishable from its plunder, and the sequence ends with twin images of American expansion.

> while crusaders of our own
> rampaged in Asia, one set foot also
> on the maskless, indubitable
> wasteland of the moon.

More pessimistic is "The Mirror of the Gorgon," a group of poems tracing the creation and subsequent dissemination of the Medusa in

Western culture; once again the sequence comes alive (in "The Nereids of Seriphos") when the foreign landscape merges with the Iowa prairie. Here, it doesn't matter if one turns east or west: both are places of filth and sexual terror.      .

> Exposure. Rape. Abortion. The mute
> gropings of the wedding night
> locked up in fright. Fright
> locked in for life. Mere allegation.
> Headed west, they say. Or was it
> east? Nobody knows the story.

Robert von Hallberg has written suggestively about the vogue for American poems about Europe in the 1950s: given the dominant position of the United States in Europe after the Second World War, American poets' concentration on "poems that display taste, sophistication, intelligence, and inventiveness" was not only natural but "responsible."[15] As much as this logic accounts for the early poems of Anthony Hecht or Adrienne Rich, it cannot account for Clampitt, who wrote no poems in the fifties. Clampitt spent most of the following decade protesting the Vietnam War, and when she began to write poetry, her attitude to American dominance was necessarily more uneasy: like the later Hecht or Rich, she could not return to the aesthetic positions of the fifties even if she wanted to. As in *The Kingfisher* (following *Multitudes, Multitudes*), Clampitt returns in *Westward* (following *Archaic Figure*) to a more direct engagement with American culture: the poems are now driven by a more capacious sense of what constitutes that culture, for better and for worse. The girl of "Imago" remains a protagonist of these poems, but her personal relationship to the prairie becomes one aspect of the larger historical narrative of what Clampitt's grandfather ominously called the "inland empire."

If American culture once seemed thin to Clampitt, it finally seemed overwhelmingly thick, as it ultimately did to James too. In "Nothing Stays Put" a greengrocer's shop packed with out-of-season fruit and exotic flowers becomes a metaphor for the culture at large: "The strange and wonderful are too much with us." Even the American landscape now seems incomprehensibly rich to her. In the opening poem of the volume, "John Donne in California," Clampitt plays off the fact (as she did in "Voyages") that the American West figured in Old World mythology long before it was actually seen by Europeans. Donne wondered in "Hymne to God my God, in My Sicknesse" whether his home was in Jerusalem or the Pacific, but he was confident, facing death, that east and west met in his body, as they do on any map. Clampitt is not so sure. She's daunted by the "utter strangeness" of the sun setting in the Pacific: it is "beyond imagining" for her, as it was for Keats.

> Is the Pacific Sea my home? Or is
> Jerusalem? pondered John Donne,
> who never stood among these strenuous,
> huge, wind-curried hills, their green
> gobleted just now with native poppies'
> opulent red-gold, where New World lizards run
> among strange bells, thistles wear the guise
> of lizards, and one shining oak is poison.

Even more than Donne's "Hymne," Elizabeth Bishop's "Brazil, January 1, 1502" stands behind these lines: like Bishop's, Clampitt's New World appears ominously perilous, already infected with Old World myths of innocence and seduction. It is a landscape created and subsequently nurtured by imperialism. In "Nothing Stays Put," the greengrocer's exotic commodities are the spoils of empire, and throughout *Westward* Clampitt is constantly aware of her own place in (as she puts it in "The Prairie") "empire's westward course." Like Faulkner in *Go Down, Moses*, she sees the impossibility of "relinquishing" the history of oppression bound up in the American landscape even today. "The Prairie," Clampitt's longest and finest performance, is also her most stringent account of that history.

"The Prairie" is a sprawling, associational poem of 477 lines divided into eight sections, but it accumulates a moral force that feels sternly at odds with its meandering narrative: connections, both thematic and aural, provide this growing sense of purpose. (Clampitt writes in "My Cousin Muriel," one of *Westward*'s quiet, discursive elegies, that her "function" is to "try for connections.") The poem's movement is determined by such "chance facts" as that Chekhov and Clampitt's grandfather were born in the same year. These fragile associations reinforce one another, leading to the conclusion that "everything connects." At the same time, certain phrases recur throughout the poem ("hot baths," "forced marches," "the wind a suicidal howling"), garnering new significance with each repetition.

Before these refrains accumulate, the narrative's connections necessarily seem more arbitrary. "The Prairie" begins in New York City with a scene of homeless people in the street: by keeping "every pittance under lock and key," Clampitt is herself "a party to the general malfeasance." This look in the mirror makes her think of Chekhov's "The Steppe," in which a Jew burns his inherited rubles in a stove. "The Steppe" leads in turn to Chekhov himself, who lived with the nomads of the Russian steppe. And the nomads, "who smelled, up close, / as

all unbathed and houseless wanderers do," recall New York's homeless.
This string of connections culminates in Clampitt's conviction that
"however much has changed, still nothing changes." A catalogue of
oppressions follows: here, as throughout *Westward*, some of Clampitt's
trademark stylistic "glister" is abandoned in the effort to confront the
"frittered sprawl" of American history.

> Demagoguery. Boundaries. Forced marches.

> Monoculture on the heels of slash and burn.
> Land reform. Drought. Insects. Drainage.
> Long-term notes. Collectives. Tractor lugs.

> Names: brunizem and chernozem; culm,
> rhizome and stolon. A fibrous, root-fattened
> hinterland of grass. The steppe. The prairie.

With this final link between steppe and prairie, we reach the heart of
the poem. Chekhov and Emerson, along with the landscapes of New
York and the steppe, will reappear; Clampitt couldn't tell the complicated history of the westward empire in anything but a circuitous fashion—especially given her sense of her own vexed, complicitous
relationship to that history. But as the most crucial and most tenuous
"chance fact" (the concurrence of Chekhov's and Frank Clampitt's birth-
days) "leaps into place," "The Prairie" becomes a chronicle, however
wayward, of the hard fate of the Louisiana Purchase.

By the time the Purchase was negotiated in 1803, the land had already accumulated a long history of subjugation: "lush midriff / of an
empire Napoleon, having retaken it / from Spain (who didn't exactly
own it) was now / hard pressed to trade for cash." Before the Europeans found it, the land was "so rich" that "the nomad / aborigines
for centuries had shunned it." With New York's homeless and the
steppe's nomads in mind, Clampitt turns to the fate of the prairie's
Native Americans.

> Treaties
> and forced marches brought them to it—treaties

> made by chiefs who knew no better. Boundaries
> were drawn; section by quarter section
> platted, parceled, sold, speculated on,

> built on it; torn open, for the first time ever,
> by plowshares.

Clampitt often wrote (not only in "The Prairie" but in "The Woodlot" and "Westward") of the unmanageable vastness or namelessness of the Midwest. Here the invention of barbed wire doesn't seem so romantic: a true sense of psychological enclosure seems indistinguishable from the basest forms of land ownership. In 1860, the year in which Clampitt's grandfather was born, the prairie is "yet unturned"; a mere decade later, the people he thought of as Indians are "long gone." In *Some Incidents in My Life* Frank Clampitt writes fervently of his opposition to slavery (he was a devout believer in social justice with strong leftward leanings, but, as late as the Depression, the Democrats remained for him the party of secession). And in "The Prairie" Clampitt is ruthlessly impatient with her grandfather's blindness to racial injustice much closer to home: "No slaves on the prairie . . . merely treaties and forced marches."

Clampitt is herself filled with Emersonian fervor throughout "The Prairie," but she manages to avoid self-righteousness. Her grandfather was initially a reluctant farmer, but he found he enjoyed landownership when he became a surveyor—someone who divides the prairie into a "neat and fearful grid of settlement." For Clampitt, this geographical grid becomes a metaphor for the prairie culture's intolerance of difference (as will her grandmother's carefully constructed quilts and gardens). Not only Native Americans, external to the grid, were "dismissed" because they "didn't match." The American West seemed to promise freedom from Old World values, but a system of internal oppression, replicating the Old World's, grew easily within the grid or garden; it dismissed, among many others, "the drifter from nowhere; the sinner / found out out of wedlock." Frank Clampitt, as he was observed by his granddaughter, seemed to pay for his responsibility for the grid: always prone to severe headaches, he developed a twitch—"a lurking / hint of something wrong." Sitting in church on Sunday mornings, Clampitt noticed "how many [others] were likewise afflicted." Generously, she describes the twitch as both an "assent" to and a "denial" of the grid. But to save herself from being likewise afflicted, Clampitt must find a way to avoid both these responses to her culture: she must extricate herself from its history of oppression without "relinquishing" (to use Faulkner's word) her inherited responsibility for it.

Clampitt built "The Prairie" on *Some Incidents in My Life* in much the same way that she made use of Walter Jackson Bate's biography of Keats in "Voyages." And like "Voyages," "The Prairie" is an autobiographical poem, whatever its manifest subject. In its eighth and final section, Clampitt admits that as a younger woman she thought she could "escape" the grid by moving to New York and on to Europe. She then offers a long catalogue of everything the grid excludes, ending with these lines:

> excess, androgyny, the left wing: anonymity-
> celebrity: escape achieved that's no escape,
> the waiting misstep, the glassy fjord-leap.

> Living anxious. The wind a suicidal howling
> in the elevator shaft. The manholes' stinking,
> steaming entrails. Dreams, now and again,

> lopsided fantasies of going back, weak-kneed,
> through the underbrush, and getting even.

This passage recalls the opening line of "The Prairie" ("The wind whines in the elevator shaft") and merges the prairie's grid with the grid of New York City's streets. In "Sed de Correr" (from *A Silence Opens*, Clampitt's final book), she meditates further on her early move to New York, remembering that she wanted to discover "things / beyond systems." But like so many refugees before her, Clampitt discovers that nothing exists beyond the grid or system—that her move to another landscape was an "escape that is no escape." The very structure of "The Prairie," linking the Midwest with so many other tainted landscapes, shows that escape isn't possible. The dream of "getting even" nevertheless remains to be exploded. At the beginning of "The Prairie," Clampitt is overwhelmed by the world's "general malfeasance": "nothing changes," she says. But by going back to where she came from to "get even," she discovers that everything changes. Her forebears are dead, the land gone "strange": there is nothing left to avenge but herself.

Change becomes Clampitt's consolation at the end of "The Prairie." If the life that Frank Clampitt bequeathed to her still seems inadequate, there is another life, one he almost lived. Before he settled into landowning and surveying, Clampitt's grandfather was a restless nomad, moving uneasily between Iowa, the Dakotas, and California, where he lived for two years before he thought to stand before the Pacific Ocean. By identifying with this aspect of her heritage, Clampitt can also identify with the drifters, nomads, and aborigines who populate the various landscapes of her poem: it is a heritage of healthy discomfort with the land, not of dominance easily achieved. In the last lines of "The Prairie," Clampitt returns to California (the same landscape with which she began in "John Donne in California") to find, as she did in Iowa, that "No one / I know or ever heard of lives there now." But the poem ends with Clampitt gazing resolutely westward, out at the Pacific, as her grandfather, who turned back to settle down, could not: standing beside her is not only Donne but Keats (who placed "stout Cortez" at the Pacific) and Henry James, who ended his journey across the American continent at Coronado. Clampitt faces this "brim of an illumination / that can't be entered" (as she calls it in "Westward") with less fortitude than Donne, but she is determined to keep moving with a world that, like Bishop's Santarém, ultimately sloughs off the surveyor's grid.

In an interview published in 1987, Clampitt wondered if there was a place in the landscape of American poetry that she could think of as home: "T. S. Eliot was born in St. Louis and settled in London. Marianne Moore was born in St. Louis and settled in Brooklyn. Elizabeth Bishop began life in Nova Scotia . . . and can hardly be said to have settled anywhere. I feel a certain kinship with her nomadism, if that is what it is: though I've been based in New York for many years, I feel less and less as though I've really *lived* anywhere." Throughout "The Prairie" Clampitt refers to various nomads as "houseless" rather than "homeless" because she wants *home* to be a movable rather than stationary condition: "Is that kind of uprooting possibly an American tradition?" Just as Clampitt came to terms with the landscape of the Midwest by reconceiving its formlessness as a virtue, she came to terms with the landscape of American poetry by refiguring its grid. In her reading, such predecessors as Eliot, Moore, and Bishop neither "deny" nor "assent" to their places of origin; they exist in a perpetual state of uprootedness that disregards the terms (east and west, formal and free) with which the map is drawn.[16]

There are times when Clampitt falls away from this ideal condition, not least when she rails against the "vulgarity" of American culture, measuring it by standards derived from an impossibly idealized past. Ezra Pound once remarked that the "star turn of the ancientists" is to play "the cream of antiquity" against "the unselected product of a particular decade or century."[17] Ironically, Pound himself occasionally offered such comparisons, and among Clampitt's poems, "The Godfather Returns to Color TV" (from *What the Light Was Like*) is a particularly schematic example of the strategy. The poem is a relatively isolated example, for it seems to me that in *Westward* Clampitt's more complicated notion of American culture no longer allows such neatly ironic comparisons to be made: for Clampitt as for Ashbery, motion is the key. "Nothing Stays Put," which is strategically placed just before "The Prairie," begins (as I've mentioned) with a diatribe against the extravagance embodied by a greengrocer's well-stocked shelves: "The strange and wonderful are too much with us." The grocers themselves are from

South Korea, their orchids from Hawaii; the hybrid gladioli are "estranged from their piercing ancestral crimson," the bachelor's buttons only slightly less "altered from the original blue cornflower / of the roadsides and railway embankments of Europe." But as the poem moves on, Clampitt sees that the wayward processes that brought orchids to New York, that derived the bachelor's button from the cornflower, are themselves valuable. As Clampitt turns from diatribe to celebration, the poem itself begins to move quickly, arcing from one association to another: American bachelor's buttons lead away from European cornflowers and back to the prairie.

> But it isn't the railway embankments
> their featherweight wheels of cobalt remind me of, it's

> a row of them among prim colonnades of cosmos,
> snapdragon, nasturtium, bloodsilk red poppies,
> in my grandmother's garden: a prairie childhood,
> the grassland shorn, overlaid with a grid,
> unsealed, furrowed, harrowed and sown with immigrant grasses,
> their massive corduroy, their wavering feltings embroidered
> here and there by the scarlet shoulder patch of cannas
> on a courthouse lawn, by a love knot, a cross stitch
> of living matter, sown and tended by women,
> nurturers everywhere of the strange and wonderful,
> beneath whose hands what had been alien begins,
> as it alters, to grow as though it were indigenous.

In these lines Clampitt rethinks the significance of many of her most cherished images for the stultifying society of the prairie: most potently, she reaches back to "The Christmas Cactus" and forward to "The Prairie" to reconceive her grandmother's garden as not only a structure of exclusion—an imposed grid—but as the kind of structure (necessary, for better and worse, to any society) through which difference is enabled—a massive field "embroidered" by the "strange and wonderful." Choosing "Nothing Stays Put" as the penultimate poem of *Westward*, Clampitt implies that even the confident affirmation of these final lines is fleeting, only to be recaptured by the harder work of "The Prairie."

> Nothing stays put. The world is a wheel.
> All that we know, that we're
> made of, is motion.

# EIGHT

# RICHARD HOWARD'S
# MODERN WORLD

In 1969 a book called *Alone With America* examined the careers of forty-one members of the third wave of twentieth-century American poetry—poets who like Ashbery, Merrill, and Rich were born with both T. S. Eliot's and Elizabeth Bishop's generation behind them. Its author, a poet who belongs to this third wave, does not appear. Not only does he not write about his own work: unlike most poet-critics, Richard Howard rarely seems to be addressing his own aesthetic principles when he discusses other poets. Reading Stevens's or Lowell's criticism, one always has the sense that it is made from the chips and sawdust on the workshop floor. But throughout the almost six hundred pages of the first edition of *Alone With America* (it was expanded in 1980), there are almost no sentences that could be used to characterize the work of Richard Howard. He attempts neither to own nor to disown his contemporaries, but receives them.

Howard is equally at home admiring poets as different as Snyder and Hollander, and he revels in this diversity, making little effort to characterize generally the third wave of twentieth-century American poetry. Six months after *Alone With America* was published, however, Howard quietly tipped his cards in "Reflections on a Strange Solitude."

And now I should like to hover, to loiter a little over the an-
nounced perception of a generalized impulse in all this poetry of
ours; something in the burden, to use an old word for subject or
content when it takes a special form, the burden, then, of our
forty-one poets as I have seen them to hang or fall or even lie
together—a mistrust, a questioning, indeed an indictment of all
the overt ceremonies which constitute—which always *have* constituted—the means of poetry. . . .

Conventions are . . . conveniences, and without them the poet,
alone with America, must indeed fall back on his unpropped nature, the terms, merely—merely! yet how much they determine!—
of a temperament, an identity.[1]

This is Howard's version of the "breakthrough" narrative: a conversion
from a traditional poetry of meter and rhyme to a more supple instru-
ment, freed from the constraints of tradition, that allows—forces—the
poet to sing more intimately of the self.

Howard would never have told the story this bluntly. His hesitation
over the word *terms* suggests that there finally is no unpropped or un-
mediated identity to fall back on, no matter how dramatically a poet
spurns the traditional ceremonies of poetry: the drama of the "fall" is
itself ceremonious. And while there is evidence enough to support the
story (even the most elegant poets of the third wave, Hecht or Merrill,
have moved closer to what might appear to be an unpropped temperament), the poet whom the story suits least is Howard himself. In 1969,
the year he brought out *Alone With America*, Howard also published
*Untitled Subjects*, his Pulitzer Prize-winning series of apostrophes and
dramatic monologues. Considered thematically or stylistically, nothing
could be further from "a poetry of forgetting."

Unlike most of the poets in *Alone With America*, Howard has not
moved toward an ostensibly more personal poetry. Instead, his career
seems to follow the opposite pattern, beginning with two books that do
contain autobiographical poems and then, with *Untitled Subjects*, in-
augurating a long series of dramatic poems. But Howard's career does
not simply invert the terms of the "breakthrough." James Wright, another poet of the third wave, always insisted that his turn to free verse
in *The Branch Will Not Break* was in no sense a breakthrough: "I was
simply trying to expand my understanding of what the form of poetry
can be. I do not think that there is any opposition between traditional
iambic verse and free verse."[2] At a time when most poets had to choose
sides, Howard similarly exploded this opposition in his essays by treat-
ing poets as different as Snyder and Hollander with equal respect. In
1971, after he had served with his old friend Allen Ginsberg on the
selection committee for the National Book Award, Howard seemed

wounded by Ginsberg's public dismissal of the winner, Mona Van Duyn. While Ginsberg condemned her as merely "excellent," formal and safe, Howard responded not by scorning the "ecstatic," open and daring, but by lamenting "the separation, the line you would draw between art and genius, between excellence and ecstasy—as if the one had to, or could, preclude the other."[3]

While Howard's criticism makes this point, his poems embody it, following Marianne Moore in their conjunction of highly artificial syllabic patterns with the various rhythms and dictions available to speech. The poems are immediately recognizable as no one's but Richard Howard's; their distinctiveness is in no way compromised by ecumenical taste. On the contrary, the poems are enabled by open-mindedness. "There is a dialectical impulse we all endure," wrote Howard in *Alone With America*, ". . . a vexed energy forever urging the meaning of our loves by means of our hates, the justification of gardens, say, by the weeds we guard them from, the hope of selfhood to be found by expelling the foreign self rather than frequenting it."[4] Much has happened in American poetry since Howard first published *Alone With America*, including the whole of Amy Clampitt's career. But the reception accorded her work suggests that Howard's sensibility remains threatening to many readers, especially those who justify their gardens by their weeds. In his own poems, Howard never indulges in the idealism of an "unpropped" identity, and he frequents the "foreign self" with a vengeance, reaching out to other voices, other lives, other literatures: by relying on a more sophisticated sense of what has happened in American poetry since Whitman, he provides a more capacious vision of what the future of American poetry might be.

Howard was born and raised (like Hart Crane) in Ohio, and went on to study (like John Berryman) at Columbia with Mark Van Doren. Before he was thirty, he had translated novels by Robbe-Grillet and Simon, and he had become a regular reviewer for *Poetry*, *The Nation*, *Partisan Review*, and *The New Leader*. Some of those early reviews were well-armed ("I shall give one further quote from Mr. Bridgewater to discredit him forever"), but a particular conversation with W. H. Auden brought Howard's sensibility into sharper focus. Howard has described this encounter several times, most delightfully in the poem "Audiences," published in *Fellow Feelings*.

> No use being a writer unless you offer praise. Lacing-in
> may be good for style (though I don't think it's good
> for yours, my dear), but so bad for character. For example,
> Stravinsky: you can't take revenge in words, the one revenge

to take is writing music. No more of either now:
he's gone, poor dear. At last. That's what my call was about.

Why write unless you praise the sacred places, encounters
when something is given over, something taken as well?

It's probably too simple to say that Howard's entire career was shaped
by this moment, but it's tempting to do so anyway. Howard became a
critic who was capable, without compromising his own temperament,
to honor an astonishing variety of writers. Simultaneously, he became
a poet whose goal was to praise the sacred places and encounters. Both
of these achievements (along with his work as translator and editor)
have depended on his ability to receive other people with a scrupulous
but impassioned disinterestedness: to say that Howard does not appear
in *Alone With America* is to emphasize that he is everywhere. "If you
have received well," said Howard in *Quantities*, his first book of poems,
"you are what you have received."

Like the first books of many poets of the third wave, *Quantities* (published in 1962), is very much infused by Auden's sensibility. Its poems
are often distinguished by a formal virtuosity and a knack for aphorism,
but those very qualities sometimes make the poems seem too clever,
confined within their own brilliance of insight and sound. The book's
first poem, "Advice from the Cocoon," has become a touchstone in discussions of Howard's work since its final lines seem—too perfectly—to
prefigure the entire shape of his later career.

> Would you, like him, survive at any cost?
> Then seal yourself in layers of yourself,
> Warm as a worm, until there is enough
> To eat your heart away and still have left
> Enough for the hungriest winter and beyond.

With these lines, so the story goes, Howard expressed his preference
for the dramatic guise, even though *Quantities* and *The Damages* are not
by any means dominated by monologues. *The Damages* was quickly
overshadowed by the tour-de-force of *Untitled Subjects*; that book's complete devotion to drama made *The Damages* seem like a stepping stone
rather than an achievement in its own right. But along with *Two-Part
Inventions* and *No Traveler*, *The Damages* is one of Howard's most revealing productions, and I want to examine it in some detail.

The book's crucial place in Howard's career is easier to see if more
attention is paid to the opening lines of "Advice from the Cocoon."

> This leaf, delivered to your empty hand,
> Is crumpled like a letter from the fall:

> Unfold it gently, it is legible
> If you are patient with mortality.
> Perhaps it bears a message for your loss
>
> Among its broken veins.

Mortality and loss: these are Howard's great subjects, and he has always been an elegiac poet (a talent that he has sadly been able to put to use in poems about friends who have died of AIDS). The poems of *Quantities* often rely on seasonal metaphors to establish this "climate / Of loss"—

> Decay is in the poplar,
> Darkness gathers
> On even the simplest
> Leaf, and withers

—but in *The Damages* the losses (the damages) seem richer and more intimate, less obscured by the universality of seasonal metaphors. In "A Far Cry After a Close Call," the volume's opening poem, the poet lies in a hospital bed beside a priest who is brought "pralines, not prayers for the next world" by a group of nuns. The poem is all for pralines—for the acceptance of the body's pleasures with (and not in spite of) a knowledge of their diminished, fragile condition. Pleasures, the final lines suggest, are to be had no other way.

> For as Saint Paul sought deliverance from
> The body of this death, I seek to stay—
> Man is mad as the body
> Is sick, by nature.

To achieve this realization, Howard lies in bed, "remembering the future now, / Foreseeing a past I shall never know." In the second poem of *The Damages* Howard conjures up the moment in the past when a child first confronts his mortality: once again, it is a bodily experience—but also a linguistic one.

The first half of this poem, "Seferiades: A Poem in Two Parts," describes a poetry reading by George Seferis. Listening to the Greek, Howard can make out only a few words—*man, life, river, god.* Then the translator, a friend of his, reads the poem in English:

> What is a god?
> What is not a god? What is the life
> in between god and not-god?

This movement from confusion to understanding mirrors the process through which the past is conjured into presence: in the second half of the poem, Howard recreates a scene from childhood, pieced together from the words *man*, *life*, *river*, and *god*—a moment "discovered, created, lost." At summer camp, six boys swim across the mile-wide lake, meeting on the other side a Circe-like woman who offers them jasmine tea and toadstools: " 'The cup,' she said, 'drink this, it will / make you immortal—take it.' " Back across the lake, the boys line up on the dock ("the wood / was slimy, rotting, cold") before their counsellor, eager for him to search "for places where / immortality would show / first." This Nestor figure does so, but not in a way the naked boys might expect.

> his hands, withered by water
> more than by the years, sounded out
> our bodies, easy over
> the clammy limbs, expert, depraved,
> relentless, palpating where
> the portal skin lay slack, prying
> at the reluctant muscles,
> smoothing flesh where it would pucker
> and the hair, already rough
> in hollows where it soon would curl.

This initiation into the adult world of sexuality seems at first an introduction to mortality as well, but Howard's point is the one Stevens made in "Peter Quince at the Clavier": while beauty is "momentary in the mind," in "the flesh it is immortal." It is only in a slimy, rotting world that anything we might call immortality could show itself—just as in "A Far Cry After a Close Call" the will to live turns only on the realization that "the body / Is sick, by nature." When the counselor speaks at the end of the poem, his pronouncement rings true, even though he may have taken advantage of the boys' confusion.

> "not one boy among you could I
> dare to single out and say,
> 'You, my friend, you are not a god.' "
> Across the water, the beach
> winced now and wrinkled in the glare:
> she was going away and
> we could see her going: once gone,
> the sun's white circle widened.

Ultimately, anything lost in this poem is something saved. As the Stevensian final lines in the next poem in *The Damages* put it, "It was enough to stay, / To inhabit earth, where we do not stay / But unlike God in heaven, come and go."

Howard would eventually reconsider "Seferiades" as an adult experience in "Oracles," published in *No Traveller*, but throughout *The
Damages* childhood remains as potent a world for Howard as it was for
Jarrell: the book's most ambitious poem is an elegy for a childhood
playmate who killed herself after discovering a darkly sexual adult-
hood. Astonishingly moving, "Private Drive" mingles the discovery of
sexuality with the discovery of death, but the poem's most potent drama
lies in Howard's conjuring of the dead Lois. Peter Sacks says of elegies
in general that they "create a believable fiction that returns the dead to
us"; in the process (more important than the product), "the living come
to recognize their role within that overarching career [of life and death],
involving as it does a close alliance with the dead."[5] That close alliance
is the key to Howard's poem. Recalling a childhood visit to a garden
where Lois ran away and reappeared, Howard compares her to Pros-
perine (an elegiac topos), and then invokes the other garden (a ceme-
tery) in which Lois now resides. Who will bring her back from this
underworld? The flowers are "replaced / With Everlasting Care"—

> but you
> Not—you never, you
> Nowhere, now, save in that past I don't suffer
> But create, in a ritual
> Precious to me for
> Its banality. Nobody will be there
> To see you in your bush of hair
> Dance burning away,
> But to me you will come, I will make you come,
> Your face saturated in sleep
> And nothing else left
> In the landscape garden these late days of ours
> But darkness, Lois, and disgrace.

This self-consciousness about his own role in the process of elegiac recovery—itself always intimate—is what will lead Howard so effortlessly
from his private to his public past: in the rhetoric of his poetry, there is
no difference between the two.

In the poem preceding "Private Drive," the aptly titled "Intimations
of Mortality," Howard makes this point clear by invoking his childhood
self as an other—*he*: "This little boy I was / Collected other lives," the
poem begins, recounting a childish fascination with bees and mice. One
mouse refused to drown when thrust into a milk bottle, leaving the boy
with an uncanny sense of everlasting life. In the second part of the
poem, Howard speaks of a failed love affair, considering his adult role
as a collector of other lives.

How else do we know what we are,
Save by tokens of what we have ruined?
How else read right the signs
Of our surrender to ourselves, save
In terms of what we are scared to save?

Howard recognizes that the effort to "save" is essential both to the process of a life and the rhetoric of the poem (*"save /* In terms of what we are scared to *save"*); but he also recognizes that the effort is futile: "Today there is no more such saving up, / Lives inevitably / Having come to mean deaths." Paradoxically, a life saved (in the sense of cherished) comes to mean the opposite of a life saved (in the sense of rescued). Yet the act of saving, understood as both doomed and necessary, appears in Howard's poems over and over again:

Will you
do as I say, save it all—
the rest of the things are mere images,
not medieval—only middle aged:
lifelike but lifeless, wonderful but dead.
These are mine. Save them.
I have nothing save them.

These are the concluding lines of "1915, A Pre-Raphaelite Ending," the final dramatic monologue of *Untitled Subjects*: they could serve as the conclusion of "Intimations of Mortality" as well. As she speaks these lines, Jane Morris sifts through letters and photographs from William Morris, Dodgson, Rossetti, and Ruskin (all of them players in the previous poems of *Untitled Subjects*), and her meditation on the difficulties of "saving" extends Howard's thoughts in "Intimations of Mortality." Both poems are marked by a strong sense of an unrecoverable past. And the future in both poems is clouded by a foreboding sense of violence—presented in "Intimations of Mortality" with an image from Howard's private past ("A murdered mouse sliding down the glass") and in "1915" with an image from the historical past ("Once the Zeppelins are gone /—and I shall be gone too").

Similar as the sentiments of these poems might feel, however, it is important to recognize that throughout his monologues Howard is more keenly interested in the otherness of other people than in expressing a hidden self through others. He has always written as an openly gay poet, and his adoption of personae does not feel strategic or defensive in the way that Jarrell's sometimes does. While Jarrell both disguises and composes himself through female personae, Howard more clearly recognizes a difference between himself and his speakers: what he calls the "foreign self" is given greater integrity. This difference does not constitute a distance between Howard and his speakers, however. In "1915" Jane Morris seems like a relic of her own past in a way that Howard himself never does ("I am not certain . . . what Zeppelins *are*"), yet Howard's poem about her is as moving and revealing as any of the more private poems in *The Damages*. Howard has suggested that he may find it even more so: with the poems of *Untitled Subjects*, he discovered "a way [of writing] which could be intimate without being private; which could be personal without being direct; a way I could speak through other people, or rather they could speak through me."[6]

Howard chooses his terms carefully here: *intimate* but not *private*. Accounting for the shape of Howard's career, it is tempting to emphasize "Bonnard: A Novel" (a dramatic monologue in *The Damages*) as the turning point that leads to the far more ambitious adoption of personae in *Untitled Subjects*. But "Bonnard: A Novel" does not seem to me *intimate* in the way that both "1915" and "Private Drive" do. The constant note in Howard's poetry, lyric or dramatic, is the elegiac—the intimate process through which the past is recreated. To map Howard's career on his use of the monologue as such is consequently to draw too sharp a line between an apparently personal poem, dealing with the author's life, and an apparently impersonal poem, dealing with an historical life. As I've already pointed out, many of Howard's poems are designed to blur these distinctions, and the distinction is worth blurring, since it depends on one of the most overdetermined shibboleths of modern poetry—a shibboleth that Howard's poetry reveals to be subtly but powerfully inflected by sexist and homophobic assumptions.

As his letter to Ginsberg suggests, Howard has always been well aware of the war between personal and impersonal poetries, and, in a literary climate that has favored the former, Howard has sometimes seemed peculiar to readers who think that a poet's purpose is to display the inner workings of the devouring self: "There is too much of the dandified manner and not enough of the presence of a man," says one reviewer; Howard keeps "himself and his life—even when he does write about these things—at such a distance from the poems that they emerge as snowflakes under glass rather than the prowling animals they have every right to be." These incongruous metaphors for poetry beg a question that Howard has often dismantled. In a 1965 review of Valéry's prose, he wrote (inevitably invoking Eliot) that "the surrender of personality is an important means of achieving and retaining identity." Valéry is best, he went on, "when he is merely himself, and indeed he is more 'himself' in this volume on aesthetics than any professional intimist could be in any number of lengthy autobiographical avowals."[7] The reviewer I've mentioned might respond by saying that Howard is still mired in an Eliotic (so-called modernist or New Critical) poetics of impersonality—a poetics that seems, in a time when decorums exist only to be transgressed, insufficiently masculine. From this point of view, Howard is a poet of high style rather than deep substance; but Howard himself wants to argue that for a "professional intimist," the uncovering of deep substance is equally dependent on a pose, a manner, a style.

Howard is first and foremost a stylist. I've suggested that his trademark rhetoric of *saving* distinguishes both the lyric "Intimations of Mortality" and the dramatic "1915," but the two poems are even more clearly marked as Howard's by their linguistic texture—the virtuoso way in which Howard's wayward gregariousness unfolds within his elaborately charted syllabic stanzas. The last line of "1915" ("I have nothing save them") is both an exception to the rule and a quintessential instance of Howard's art: the accumulating energy of speech is allowed to override the the severe and arbitrary limitations of the stanza's final five-syllable line. Howard's characteristic penchant for aphorism is indulged in lines like these, but the line now feels in motion, at once an integral unit of wisdom and a part of an ongoing verbal performance. This tension distinguishes any poem by Richard Howard, makes it intimately his own, no matter what he happens to be writing about. "It was the most personal poetry ever written," Howard has said of Marianne Moore, "yet it had become so by a refusal to be autobiographical."[8] Throughout Howard's own work, the poet is similarly present in the idiosyncratic movement of the poems—the surface is the self, the manner is the man. Because Howard understands so well that this is true of all poets—even of those who pretend to have sacrificed manner for substance, excellence for ecstasy—he is free to let style alone be his signature, the mark of his deepest commitment.

For this reason, I'm not sure that David Bergman's argument about Howard's "weak sense of selfhood" accounts for the utter distinctiveness of the poems, even if it does account for larger questions of homosexual identity.[9] Because the "breakthrough" narrative is so dependent on notions of an inner self (the "presence of a man" rather than the "dandified manner"), it is tempting to counter the narrative with a Wildean fable in which selflessness, surface, and dispersion take the place of selfhood, depth, and integrity. But the power of Howard's work is that it does not allow us to accept either of these stories unconditionally: "gay is to straight *not* as copy is to original," argues Judith Butler in a passage especially appropriate to Howard, "but, rather, as copy is to copy."[10] Just as he refuses to invert the terms of the "breakthrough" narrative, Howard refuses simply to invert the codes of heterosexuality in writing. He not only allows us to see the authenticity of the "professional intimist" as a pose; by revealing all expressions of identity as performance, he also prevents us from granting an equally limiting authenticity to the more egregiously posing poet.

Howard also denies us the complacency of rejecting the professional intimist. Writing in 1965, at the height of Robert Lowell's popularity, Howard did not praise Lowell for having dramatized the inner self but neither did he blame him; all that mattered was that Lowell had enlarged the discursive arena of poetry: "we welcomed Lowell's recovery for poetry of material which by cultural drift or the complacencies or talent had defected to the novel."[11] If this critical remark sounds for once like Howard's own goal, then we should remember that in 1965 Howard was known only as the author of *Quantities*, not the master of dramatic utterance: he was learning from Lowell, professional intimist, how to become himself. Howard could do this because he has always maintained an unpolemical vision of literary history in which Whitman, Wilde, Eliot, Stevens, and Moore are participants in the same unfolding drama. Not having narrowed his vision of the past, he can learn from a wide variety of his contemporaries, intuiting the common ground of ostensibly antagonistic writers.

Howard is consequently attracted to periods of transition, moments when he can measure what has been lost against what is saved. The moment of what he calls "ante-modernism" (when a *fin-de-siècle* sensibility hung on into the early years of the twentieth century) is of particular interest: Howard sees in this moment the fruitful conjunctions and the pointless antagonisms that continue to shape his culture—and his own life—even today. In "1907," from *Untitled Subjects*, he imagines a letter Richard Strauss sends Arnold Schoenberg after hearing Debussy's *Pelléas et Mélisande*. Strauss is about to reveal *Elektra*, one of the most harmonically advanced scores of the time, but in Debussy's equally revolutionary score Strauss hears "nothing"—"no development, / no melody, / no consecutive phrases." The young Schoenberg seems to him just the man to do justice to Maeterlinck, but Strauss seems unaware that Schoenberg had already done so in 1903. Schoenberg's *Pelléas* is a late romantic tone-poem, and by 1907 Schoenberg was well into the freely atonal world of *Das Buch der hängenden Gärten*, while Strauss would soon retreat (never to return) into the reactionary harmonic vocabulary of *Der Rosenkavalier*.

Like Jane Morris, Strauss is caught between the past and the future, not fully aware of how fully the future has arrived. But his objection in aesthetic terms to Debussy's music masks nationalistic and sexual biases. Strauss attends the opera with the (to him) distastefully feminine Ravel ("he was rouged and powdered, and I *know* / he was perfumed"). The words *French* and *feminized* are synonymous words for Strauss, and the music seems to him as lacking in phallic energy as Ravel himself.

> there is no . . . no *Schwung* in it
> (I defy you,
> Herr Privatdozent, to find a French word
>      proper for *Schwung*).

What is at stake for Strauss is the hegemony of German music as well as the strength of what, as he remarks at the opening of the poem, a column "always suggests."

What is at stake for Howard is clarified by his response to an act of vandalism that took place in Cleveland, where he grew up: in 1970 someone dynamited the city's cast of the statue known as *The Thinker*. "I realized as surely as if I had heard the nymphs crying 'the great god Pan is dead' when Christ was born, that an era was over," wrote Howard in "Fragments of a 'Rodin.'" The era he had in mind was both the moment of attenuated "ante-modernism" and the moment of Howard's own childhood, both of which are epitomized for him by the library in the house he grew up in.

> Under a framed lithograph of Brahms playing the piano and puffing on a cheroot—a Brahms bearded like Whitman, like Ibsen, like God and like Rodin himself (whose hand, I knew, already partook of divinity)—there was a shelf of books in our house, and the biggest book . . . was to be found in the houses of all my parents' friends, if not under Brahms then on top of the piano, among the folds of an art-scarf which might have been snatched from Isadora's chubby shoulders. This was the book republished now by Horizon Press, and on its spine were but two words, though they appeared in very large letters: ART, and beneath that, a trifle larger, RODIN.

For Howard's parents, these two large words were synonymous, just as the word *literature* was synonymous with Maeterlinck or Anatole France, and *music* with Massenet or Strauss.

> Certainly, after the Great War there was a Great Snobbery about the other side of the Atlantic, a great craving for spoils. But more than any other creative figure—even more than Richard Strauss (music, after all, even music orchestrated by Strauss, could not be *owned* in the way marble and bronze and mere clay could be owned, as chthonic trophies)—Rodin satisfied that craving, fulfilled the needs of the class and circumstance in which I grew up—the class defined, abruptly, by the circumstance of having "been"—by which was meant having been to Europe. A class which is, today, a has-been, for it has been had—by its own possessions, despoiled by its own spoils, among which few were so proudly carted home as the statues of Auguste Rodin.[12]

Howard retains some affection, certainly some fascination, for this moment just preceding modernism proper, but he feels impatient with it too—impatient with the way a taste for Strauss and Rodin defined an American bourgeoisie and consequently stood in the way of a taste for, say, Stravinsky and Picasso. To Howard, then, the dynamited *Thinker* looked "like a 'modern' statement"; it "had a new pertinence, a deeper significance." What had been blown from its pedestal was not simply the statue but a whole set of social and aesthetic values—a *fin-de-siècle* world that lasted long after it should have passed away, a world in which the precocious Howard could still be raised in the thirties. "You had been done in, long since," says Howard in "Anatole France," when "Mother was grateful / for glimpses vouchsafed into the Grand Salon."

Howard doesn't want to dismiss Strauss or Rodin (or blow up statues), but he does want to wrench them from this world—make them "modern"—by uncovering neglected or obscured aspects of them. He wants to remember that Rodin's fetishized *Thinker* should preside over the Gates of Hell; he wants (as he says in *Lining Up* of his effort to "continue" Rossetti) to ravel "a sow's purse out of that silk ear." Thinking of the dynamited *Thinker*, Howard suggests that an "emblem of an abject ideology" has been replaced by "the ecstatics of a released identity," and that release is precisely what Howard accomplishes in his poem about Strauss (and later, with *Two-Part Inventions*, in his poems about Rodin, Ibsen, and Wharton). The identity released in the process belongs not only to these artists but to Howard himself: the poems re-read the cultural matrix that shaped him as a child—redecorate the house he grew up in—discovering there a genealogy for the person he is today. In the poems of *Fellow Feelings* Howard has written more openly about being Jewish, homosexual, and adopted; more precisely intimate are his poems about modern culture, for they represent his effort to find the place where he did and (as in the poem uncovering Strauss's nationalism and homophobia) did not come from.

I want to show how Howard found the former place, the place where he belongs, in two long poems: "Wildflowers" from *Two-Part Inventions* and "Even in Paris" from *No Traveller*. Together, these two poems offer an account of modernism's unantagonistic relationship with the literatures that preceded and succeeded it. "Wildflowers" dramatizes the legendary meeting of the aging Walt Whitman and the budding Oscar Wilde. In the process, the poem belies the association of any particular notion of style with sexual orientation: the meeting of these two men is also the meeting of past and future, reaction and rebellion, surface and depth, a man and a mask—though it's often difficult to decide which qualities should be assigned to which protagonist. "Give me enemies / rather than these *disciples* of mine," says Whitman before Wilde arrives.

But Wilde, who like Arthur Symons and Lionel Johnson kept a candle
burning beside two sacred books (*Leaves of Grass* and *Les Fleurs du mal*),
is intent on playing the latter role: *"You are with the prophets, Walt,"* he
proclaims, to which Whitman responds, "spare me / the responsibility."
Still, as Wilde takes the old man's chilled fingers in his own, Whitman
warms to him, and consents to hear a recitation of Baudelaire's
"Spleen." For Wilde this is a great moment—the meeting of two heroes,
two great "moralists." But the moment is destined from the start to
misfire ("Do moralists sing?" asks Walt, "I thought they expurgated
poems"). This is Whitman's response to Baudelaire.

> if the world is unjust to you,
> you must take care not to be unjust to the world.
> I don't get much beyond that
> with "Spleen": what I hear
> is a sickly sensuality in it
> ...........................................
>
> Is it not verse written of malice prepense,
> all laid out, rhymed, designed on
> mathematical
> principles—is it not a machine,
> a kind of enslavement?

The irony here is that Wilde is not mistaken about the strong continuity
between Whitman and Baudelaire; but Whitman's kindred spirit is not
the smoky decadent Symons and Wilde adored (translating "Spleen,"
Howard's Wilde produces phrases like *"incredulous of doom"* and *"dark
corruption"* for lines which Howard himself translates as "is not
amused" and "impure substance"). The conversation consequently
turns to what is in this context the most superficial difference between
the two poets, and the positions Wilde and Whitman take up prefigure
the terms of the debate for the following century. Wilde: *"I want only
Form. / Is it not Form, Walt, that keeps things together?"* Whitman: "Breaking loose is the only thing, / opening new ways." Wilde and Whitman,
Howard and Ginsberg: the opposition continues through modernism
and beyond, but in "Wildflowers" Howard shows how the terms of the
debate are germinated only by misunderstanding. "Do not suppose that
the *Leaves* / is a mask. It is the man," says Whitman in response to
Wilde's claim that *"Not until / you permit a poet a mask does he dare / tell
the truth."* By exposing the partial truth of both these statements, Howard educates his own readership, alerting us to the more intricate ways
in which the man, however surreptitiously or flagrantly dramatized, is
the mask.

"Wildflowers" is, like all Howard's poems, historically accurate.

Though Wilde's two visits to Whitman were cordial and affectionate, Whitman would later say this in *November Boughs*: "No one will get at my verses who insists upon viewing them as a literary performance . . . or as aiming mainly towards art and aestheticism." Wilde saw himself in this remark, and when he reviewed *November Boughs*, he said that the value of Whitman's work lay "in its prophecy not in its performance. . . . If Poetry has passed him by, Philosophy will take note of him."[13] In "Wildflowers" Wilde does learn something, however: asking to receive Whitman's blessing he discovers instead that he must "give himself away." This gesture of renunciation (which is simultaneously an act of self-exposure), passed from Whitman to Wilde, becomes the lesson Wallace Stevens passes on to Richard Howard in "Even in Paris."

Since all of Howard's poems are accurate, I am tempted to entertain the possibility that the story told in "Even in Paris" might be true: in 1952, while studying at the Sorbonne, Howard met the legendary stay-at-home Wallace Stevens in Sainte Chapelle. Throughout the poem, Howard impersonates his earlier self in much the same way that he impersonates historical figures: "Even in Paris" consists of a sequence of letters to Roderick from the frivolous Ivo, who is skeptical of the poet's identity, and from the charmingly overbearing "bald Richard," who leads "my great poet" around Paris. Ivo first describes the recognition scene.

> All at once, sitting there, bald Richard began
>            staring (across me) at this
>      fat man under the windows, red or blue
> as the famished light devoured the famous glass . . .
>            He might have had anybody's
>      face—absolutely unremarkable,
> as though he had been obliged to put up with
>            something ready-made until
>      more suitable features could be made
> to order—and since the proper article
>            had never been delivered,
>      he had gone about in this blank disguise
> the greater part of his life! Richard went on
>            peering at . . . what? What appeared
>      matter-of-factness at the expense of
> matter *and* of fact. Splendor crept over
>            our row until it covered
>      even Monsieur X with medieval grace—
> Rod, you'll never guess! He fell on his knees,
>            arms out, as if receiving
>      stigmata from stained glass! And then got up

> as if nothing had occurred, dusting his pants
> and muttering (Richard heard),
> "A little kneeling is a dangerous thing."

This is the best description of Stevens's elusive, contradictory sensibility that I know (the atheist's deathbed conversion to Catholicism is here perfectly explained): Stevens's studied ordinariness is enabled by an equally strong extravagance; his extravagance is reined in—but never trounced—by delicate irony. In "Wildflowers" Whitman is glad that he never "ventured abroad," and Stevens, however much he lamented his stationary life, usually seemed glad too: Paris was an idea that he could entertain but it remained an extravagance that—equally satisfying—he could deny himself. In suggesting that Stevens did travel, Howard makes the poet's intricate system of checks and balances even clearer. Ivo remarks that in Paris during January one must endure "the punishing presence of the commonplace." Nothing could have pleased Stevens more. When Richard takes him to see Monet's *Nymphéas*, he asks if Stevens is happy. "Happy here?" responds Stevens, speaking here as throughout the poem in Wildean aphorism, "—how hideous the happiness one wants, / how beautiful the misery one has!"

Compelling as this portrait of Stevens is, Howard keeps his long poem in the air by both building up and tearing down the plausibility of Stevens's secret trip to Paris. Ivo takes care of the latter task, going so far as to ask if Roderick can find out if Stevens is still in Hartford. Meanwhile, Richard shows his great poet around Paris.

> Roderick dear, today was to be the last
> my poet would spend in Paris—although *spending*
> is hardly the verb for what I've hauled him through.
>
> He's always praying life not to give him more
> than what it can take back.

*Spending* is close to the right verb, for the pecuniary metaphor helps to account for Stevens's almost compulsive need to give away what he desires most. At the climax of "Even in Paris" Stevens acts out the lesson Wilde received from Whitman. Passing the bookstalls along the Seine, Stevens finds an 1897 volume of the *Mercure de France* that includes Léon Bazalgette's translation of *Leaves of Grass* (which Gide criticized for "heterosexualizing" Whitman). Wilde mismatched the worlds of Baudelaire and Whitman, but their real conjunction produces the modernism of Wallace Stevens. The twenty-fifth section of "Song of Myself" had already come to Stevens's mind in response to Monet ("'We also ascend dazzling,' is all he said, / or all I could make out—

is it a quote?"), but Stevens is less interested in remembering than in letting the mind's contents go.

> "The future of the past is never sure.
> This must be the one place in the world
> where a man can realize what he writes
>
> is a river too. It is continuous,
> no burden on the memory, but a way
> —made up of all ways—of reaching the sea."

Following this meditation, Stevens literalizes its metaphors: he purchases the *Mercure* and stands at the top of the river stairs, "extending the book / and a fistful of hundred-franc notes as well! / to every passer-by, muttering his phrase, / *'lancer ce livre comme un bateau.'* " Finally, a boy snatches the money and launches the book out over the water, and the poet's response to this ritual of giving up what he has received is both predictable and astonishing: "a ceremony bought is a ceremony still." Though Richard could not know it in 1952, he has witnessed the making of a great poem: Stevens's meditation on "Song of Myself," combined with his ceremony on the Seine, will produce "The River of Rivers in Connecticut," one of the late poems about the necessity of relinquishing everything: "The river that flows nowhere, like a sea." Looking back to the world of 1952, Howard makes his earlier self the unknowing catalyst for a poem that would in turn shape his own career.

"Even in Paris" is Howard's most delightful and instructive creation of a legacy: the poem is both a highly entertaining wish fulfillment and a serious engagement with literary history. Today, in the wake of Harold Bloom's powerful reading of Stevens's debt to Whitman, we might forget that in 1952, when modernist meant metaphysical, most readers would have been puzzled to hear Stevens quoting "Song of Myself." Throughout "Even in Paris," Howard creates a world in which it was inevitable for the "excellent" Stevens to learn from the "ecstatic" Whitman, just as Howard himself has learned from both of them. But Howard's reading of the debt is different from Bloom's in one crucial way. Unlike Bloom, for whom literary history is relentlessly antagonistic, Howard is most interested in moments of literary fellowship—the feeling Eliot described in "Reflections on Contemporary Poetry" (the essay Hart Crane admired) as one "of profound kinship, or rather of a peculiar personal intimacy, with another, probably a dead author." Howard sustains these moments because he has never been willing to accept strategically distorted readings of his precursors—Rodin, Strauss, Whitman, Wilde, Stevens—in order merely to distinguish himself. "It has been a week, Rod," writes Richard in "Even in Paris": "Who would have thought / there was so much to learn about the moderns?" Even by the early 1940s the great moderns seemed like ancient history to readers like Jarrell ("Who could have believed that modernism would collapse so fast?" he asked), but today, half a century later, Richard Howard sees that we have a lot to learn.

Howard's Stevens is, not surprisingly, the great elegist, the poet of renunciation who spoke most eloquently in late poems like "The River of Rivers" or "As You Leave the Room." Near the end of "Even in Paris," Ivo remarks that if we do not meet our heroes in Sainte Chapelle, "we invent them." Howard has invented his Stevens—not because the story of "Even in Paris" is true or false but because, as the poem's final line suggests, we have no choice but to "make something out of ourselves." Reading "Private Drive," I mentioned Peter Sacks's Stevensian observation that elegies "create a believable fiction that returns the dead to us." "Even in Paris" is not an elegy as such, but it is built (like most of Howard's poems) around this elegiac process. And like any elegiac poem, "Even in Paris" is ultimately about its author—where he came from, where he may go from here. At the same time, it is a genealogy of American modernism—a poem that describes where we have come from and where we may go from here.

Set in 1952, "Even in Paris" is also a nostalgic account of the interactions of gay men before AIDS. Even before *No Traveller* was published, Howard had the occasion to write many formal elegies for friends who died of AIDS—poems that have seemed to mark a new direction in his career. Reviewing *No Traveller*, Robert Richman noted that a poem published since that volume appeared "seems to signal an end to [Howard's] own disinclination to speak about himself in the first person. It will be interesting to see if this new poem is a prologue to writing the kind of poetry his critics have always wanted."[14] The poem to which Richman refers is "For Robert Phelps, Dead at 66" (an elegy for a friend who died of Parkinson's disease), which is now among the many elegies collected in *Like Most Revelations*, Howard's most recent book. Richman wants to see in these poems, however late it is in coming, a Lowell-style "breakthrough." In contrast, I think it is crucial that these poems not seem like the kind of "personal" poetry that Howard's critics have always wanted. Near the end of " 'Man Who Beat Up Homosexuals Reported to Have AIDS Virus,' " the long poem that concludes *Like Most Revelations*, Howard offers a meditation on the historical imagination that asks to be read as a comment on his own career. "Remembering is not even the word," writes a victim both of AIDS and of the nameless attacker, *"making* comes closer."

> Whatever's left of my life, I am *making*,
> the way I made it happen all along
>     —I replay the scenes
> from the movie The Past, starring not
> Mr. X playing opposite myself
>         but Endymion,
> Narcissus, Patroclus, all the fellows
> I have welcomed to the tiny duchy
>         of my bed . . .

These lines suggest that any account of the past, whether private or historical, is an act of personal *making*. For years Howard has been speaking to and for the dead in his poems, and throughout *Like Most Revelations* the dead are more often friends than historical figures: in either case his investment does not waver.

The poems in *Like Most Revelations* differ from those of *No Traveller* (just as "Homage to Nadar" differs from *Untitled Subjects*), but they were written because of the earlier work, not in spite of it. It is precisely because Howard has for many years developed a poetry of inclusion—poetry that reclaims vast discursive territories—that he can turn naturally to subjects not easily contained by the vocabulary of an apparently "private" poet. All of Howard's poems "make something" of his self, collapsing easy notions of interiority; the work's engagement with contemporary issues has always been clear. Only when the dust has settled on the literary debates of the twentieth century, when the party of ecstasy lies down with the party of excellence, will we read Howard more clearly. Paradoxically, Richard Howard himself has been clearing away the dust for years.

# NINE

# ROBERT PINSKY'S
# SOCIAL NATURE

A poet's mark may be measured by his or her ability to expand the language available to poetry. The effort is usually subtle (we don't need to think of Shakespeare as a formally innovative writer), and it always depends on an openness to a variety of poetries, past and present. For a legitimately postmodern poet, argues Robert Pinsky, "formal freedom feels assumed, and matters of technique [are] no longer fighting issues in the old modernist sense."[1] Pinsky himself not only admires both the formal terseness of J. V. Cunningham and the capacious waywardness of Frank O'Hara; his poems also partake of both these qualities. Unlike other writers who seem, mostly because of their formal choices, more programmatically postmodern, Pinsky has consequently become the more truly innovative poet—the poet who increases the possibilities available to poetry. When his first book of poems appeared in 1975, two years before the death of Robert Lowell, Richard Howard could immediately see that its "unfashionable" virtues constituted "the antidote and the recourse in a period of over-valued madness, oneiric inflation and suicide-worship."[2] But even if the publication of *Sadness and Happiness* helped to signal the end of the Age of Lowell, Pinsky could still write admiringly of Lowell and Berryman in *The Situation of Poetry*, the critical book that appeared two years later. If Pinsky is a postmodern poet, it is not because he belittles the moderns in the way that some of the moderns rejected their romantic forebears; the label sticks because he has no need to balance his enthusiasms with antagonisms.

I think it's especially important to make this point about Pinsky, because his influential criticism has been used to widen the poetic canon's artificial oppositions. This is in part understandable, since Pinsky is a writer with clear opinions; but he is not a writer who would say that he is "denying the hegemony of such dominant twentieth-century conventions as the subjective modernist lyric." Pinsky is too sophisticated a critic to put together the words subjective, modernist, and lyric, secure that the phrase means something coherent enough to deny. It's true that Pinsky has criticized what we might think of as a strain of attenuated modernism—much smaller than the practice of any modernist poet—that privileges the "image" to the exclusion of other kinds of poetic discourse. But to capitalize polemically on this aspect of Pinsky's work is to diminish the scope of what he's doing. Pinsky did not set out to replace one orthodoxy with another; his goal is to resist any vocabulary for poetry that becomes exclusionary and taken-for-granted. The point of *The Situation of Poetry* is that all poetic language is more or less arbitrary, none of it closer to the heart than any other. Though he has his preferences, Pinsky's argument is not with the "image" as such but with the unquestioned acceptance of its values.

Throughout *The Situation of Poetry* Pinsky discusses this issue in what seem like purely formal terms. But as the title of his most recent critical work (*Poetry and the World*) suggests, Pinsky understands that any formal issue in poetry is simultaneously a social issue: "The poet's first social responsibility, to continue the art, can be filled only through the second, opposed responsibility to change the terms of the art as given— and it is given socially, which is to say politically."[3] Except that it's not afraid of the word *art*, this statement is similar to many "New Historicist" ideas about literature. (In fact, the essay it's taken from, "Responsibilities of the Poet," was first published in a special issue of *Critical Inquiry* on politics and poetic value: unlike most poet-critics, Pinsky seems in touch with academic literary criticism in profitable ways.) But the wisdom of this statement also resonates beyond critical fashion. Over the course of his career, Pinsky has made his finest poems not by harnessing beautiful language but by forcing the language of his time (the language that didn't yet seem beautiful) into poetry. This skill, discovered in the poems of *Sadness and Happiness* and perfected in *The Want Bone*, is the product of Pinsky's strong sense of poetry's historicity. Like the poets of his past, Wordsworth or Bishop, Pinsky resists not subjectivity itself but the dramatization of subjectivity uncomplicated by an awareness of the subject's social nature: this is Pinsky's inheritance, romantic and modern.

Pinsky was born and raised in Long Branch, New Jersey, a town that by 1940 was already a dilapidated resort. Graduating from Rutgers University in 1962, he wrote his senior thesis on T. S. Eliot. Then he enrolled as a graduate student at Stanford, and, quite by accident, became aware of Yvor Winters, the poet-critic who would become a kind of mentor to him—the same poet-critic who had served as a kind of mentor to Hart Crane. During his first semester, after reading Lowell's review of Winters's *Selected Poems*, Pinsky was impressed enough to show Winters his poems. On more than one occasion Pinsky has described this meeting with self-deprecating irony.

> He asked me to sit down, and he thumbed through the manuscript while I was there. It took him perhaps four minutes, stopping once or twice at certain ones. Then he looked up at me, and said, "You simply don't know how to write."
>
> He added that there was some gift there, but because I was ignorant of what to do with it, he could not estimate how much of a gift it was. If it was blind luck or happy fate or smiling Fortune that must be thanked for leading me to Stanford, let me congratulate myself for having the sense not to leave the room when he said that.[4]

Pinsky stayed in the room for several years, taking directed reading courses with Winters and writing poems. He has subsequently expressed his debt to Winters many times, most wonderfully in the penultimate section of his "Essay on Psychiatrists," the long poem that concludes *Sadness and Happiness*: "*My friend Hart Crane died mad. My friend / Ezra Pound is mad. But you will not go mad; you will grow up / To become happy, sentimental old college professors.*" But unlike many writers who have identified with Winters, Pinsky has never seemed like a Wintersian, repeating the old man's idiosyncratic take on literary history. He did inherit Winters's preference for a Jonsonian clarity of statement in poetry; and he did share Winters's skepticism towards poetic madness, a trait that (as Richard Howard recognized) made Pinsky's poems stand apart from confessional poetry: "it is all bosh, the false / Link between genius and sickness," said Pinsky in "Essay on Psychiatrists." Ultimately, however, I think Winters was important to Pinsky as a poet-critic who stressed the necessity of coming to terms with the entire history of poetry: it was Winters's generosity rather than his crankiness that made an impression on the young Pinsky. In addition, I think Winters stressed in usable terms what Pinsky probably knew intuitively: that the reading and writing of poetry was a moral act.

Three years after he showed Winters his work, Pinsky published his first poems in the October 1965 issue of the *Southern Review*, then a journal where many of Winters's students and friends appeared. These poems sound almost nothing like the work Pinsky would produce three or four years later, but they are distinguished by a formal clarity and ease. Of the four poems, Pinsky preserved only "Old Woman" in his first collection, *Sadness and Happiness*.

> Not even in darkest August,
> When the mysterious insects
> Marry loudly in the black weeds
> And the woodbine, limp after rain,
> In the cooled night is more fragrant,
> Do you gather in any slight
> Harvest to yourself. Deep whispers
> Of slight thunder, horizons off,
> May break your thin sleep, but awake,
> You cannot hear them. Harsh gleaner
> Of children, grandchildren—remnants
> Of nights now forever future—
> Your dry, invisible shudder
> Dies on this porch where, uninflamed,
> You dread the oncoming seasons,
> Repose in electric light.

Like one of the poems that accompanied it in the *Southern Review* (the others were set in rhymed couplets or in terza rima), "Old Woman" is organized syllabically, the eight syllables of each line variously accented. The subtlety of their rhythm does stand apart from the lines of the other poems ("The marriage bed awakes to hear / A voice reciting, without fear"), but "Old Woman" showed only half of what Pinsky would become: the expert craftsman.

Pinsky published no more poems until 1969-70, when he appeared again in the *Southern Review* and also in *Poetry*: most of these poems remain uncollected, as do four additional poems that appeared in a 1971 issue of *Poetry*. Pinsky included one of these four, "The Destruction of Long Branch," in *Sadness and Happiness* but subsequently deleted it from *The Figured Wheel: New and Collected Poems*. "The Destruction of Long Branch" might not compare with Pinsky's later work, but in retrospect the poem seems like a watershed.

> When they came out with artificial turf
> I went back home with a thousand miles.
>
> I dug a trench by moonlight from the ocean
> And let it wash in quietly

And make a brackish quicksand which the tide
Sluiced upward from the streets and ditches.

The downtown that the shopping centers killed,
The garden apartments, the garages,

The station, the Little Africa on (so help me)
Liberty Street, the nicer sections,

All settled gently in a drench of sand
And sunk with a minimum of noise.

It's tempting to say that the new power of these lines comes from Pinsky's focus on the peculiarity of his hometown. In some sense, the poem does represent the finding of a "subject matter," and Pinsky has subsequently written in sophisticated ways about the importance of subject matter and of poems that are organized by the earnest presentation of their meaning. But this advance happened when it did because Pinsky broke through an earlier idea about poetic language. He has recently said that "Old Woman" represents a kind of poetry that no longer interests him because of its "overt lyricism." In contrast, the force of the language of "The Destruction of Long Branch" depends not on an extravagance of image or wit or metaphor—not even on the sonorous quality of lines like "Deep whispers / Of slight thunder, horizons off, / May break your thin sleep"—but on the unfolding of an argument that includes words like *shopping center*. Pinsky has joked that he tends to be suspicious of a poet who hasn't gotten a shopping center into his poems: his point is to stress not only the place of the everyday world but the place of everyday language— language not yet poetic—in poetry. The phrase *shopping center* could never appear in "Old Woman," just as Yeats could never have gotten the words *greasy till* into "To the Rose upon the Rood of Time"—even if he'd wanted to.

"The Destruction of Long Branch" sounds even more like the mature Pinsky because the introduction of phrases like *shopping center, artificial turf,* and *so help me* does not disrupt the formal clarity evident even in his earliest work. In "American Poetry and American Life" (collected in *Poetry and the World*) Pinsky has described the social qualities of Anne Winters's poetry.

I don't intend anything as quixotic or odious as prescribing a subject matter, or proscribing one. Rather, the point is that a certain kind of fluidity, a formal and moral quality, seems to have been demanded of American poets by their circumstance. . . . Winters's laundromat with its *"I mean to live"* seems simultaneously to challenge and embarrass poetic language, and to incorporate it: to defy poetic form, and to demand it.[5]

These sentences describe perfectly later poems like "At Pleasure Bay," "The Hearts," or "Impossible to Tell" (the long, fluid poems that "The Destruction of Long Branch" looks forward to). They also describe the values that give those poems their idiosyncratic movement (Williams's diction plugged into Stevens's pentameters). Pinsky has no interest in the "freedom" so often associated with the breaking of poetic forms, since he understands that forms are, as part of the historicity of his writing, unbreakable; but like Bishop he is interested in bending them, testing them against the warp and woof of his experience.

Perhaps it isn't coincidental that "The Destruction of Long Branch" embodies thematically this double attitude toward history and culture—defying it and demanding it. The poem isn't about the slow decay of Long Branch; rather, it's about Pinsky's desire to flood the place and pave it over—an act which he accomplishes, like any romantic poet, "by moonlight." But the loving specificity of the poem's catalogue of everything that disappears belies his desire to destroy, and the poem ends not with destruction but with Pinsky's "cautiously elegiac" recreation of his hometown. In the process, the words that threatened to make him what he is (*artificial turf, shopping mall*) become the words with which he names the world and makes it his own.

Comparing Elizabeth Bishop to Wordsworth, Pinsky has said that "her great subject is the contest—or truce, or trade-agreement—between the single human soul on one side, and on the other side, the contingent world of artifacts and other people." This is Pinsky's great subject too, and it accounts for Pinsky's emphasis of the historicity of his language: it is only through the social structure of language that the self is constituted, and it is only through language that the self asserts its power over the social structure. "Naming and placing things," says Pinsky apropos of Bishop (though he could have been talking about "The Destruction of Long Branch"), "is an approach to genuine liberty. This is true even though the very means of naming things . . . are also part of the terrain."[6]

This concern unites the poems of *Sadness and Happiness*. If Bishop's "In the Waiting Room" dramatizes the difficulty of realizing that the self is a social construction (the individual merely "one of them"), then the first poem in *Sadness and Happiness* is about the opposite difficulty of seeing the individual as anything but a product of the categories that constitute it—"an I." The opening stanzas of "Poem About People" offer a comfortable account of other people seen less as individuals than as exemplars of a kind of Johnsonsian "general nature." The difficulties begin here:

> But how love falters and flags
> When anyone's difficult eyes come
>
> Into focus, terrible gaze of a unique
> Soul, its need unlovable.

Pinsky offers several examples of this problem, the last of which explores the sentimentality of his earlier remark that it is "possible / To feel briefly like Jesus," crossing the "dark spaces" between individuals.

> In the movies, when the sensitive
> Young Jewish soldier nearly drowns
>
> Trying to rescue the thrashing
> Anti-semitic bully, swimming across
> The river raked by nazi fire,
> The awful part is the part truth:
>
> *Hate my whole kind*, but me,
> Love me for myself.

The truth is partial because single selves have meaning only as the parts of whole kinds; the difference is frightening, and difficult to calibrate. But it is not impossible, as the poem's final lines suggest, restating the opening stanzas' hope in darker, more tentative terms: "we / All dream it, the dark wind crossing / The wide spaces between us."

Two years after *Sadness and Happiness* appeared, Pinsky published *The Situation of Poetry*. But as his fugitive essays and reviews from the early seventies reveal, the book's argument had been in his mind for some time. Its thesis appeared in concentrated form in the June 1973 issue of *Poetry*.

> Some contemporary poems tend, pretty distinctly as such matters go, toward coolness: the aspect of modernism which effaces or holds back the warmth of authorial commitment to feeling or idea, in favor of a surface cool under the reader's touch.
>
> A previous generation sought coolness through concentration on objective images. But the techniques implied by the term "imagism" have come to look rhetorical and warmly committed. . . . When it fails, it resembles other forms of "poetic diction."[7]

This was the problem. In the January 1974 issue of *Poetry* Pinsky offered a solution.

Most people who read poetry have some loose idea of what the prose virtues are—a demanding, unglamourous group, including perhaps Clarity, Flexibility, Efficiency . . . ? This is a drab, a grotesquely puritanical bunch of shrews. They never appear in blurbs. And yet when they are courted by those who understand them—Williams, Bishop—the Prose Virtues, which sound like a supporting chorus, perform virtuoso marvels. They become not merely the poem's minimum requirement, but the poetic essence.[8]

The only word missing here is *discursive*: the word is Pinsky's, but it has become the word most often used to describe his poems, especially those from *Sadness and Happiness* like "Essay on Psychiatrists" and "Tennis." Throughout these poems, Pinsky tries to recapture the preromantic sensibility of Dryden or Virgil (the sensibility that was supposedly available, as Yvor Winters is made to say in "Essay on Psychiatrists," before "the middle / Of the Eighteenth Century" when "the logical / Foundations of Western thought decayed and fell apart"). If Virgil could write poems about the skills of farming, why not poems about the skills of tennis?

> Hit to the weakness. All things being equal
> Hit crosscourt rather than down the line, because
> If you hit crosscourt back to him, then he
>
> Can only hit back either towards you (crosscourt)
> Or parallel to you (down the line), but never
> Away from you, the way that you can hit
>
> Away from him if he hits down the line.

When these lines were first published, they seemed like an incredible breath of fresh air. After twenty years, however, the more egregiously discursive poems don't seem to me to be the finest achievement in *Sadness and Happiness*—necessary though they were for Pinsky's development. While the textures of "Essay on Psychiatrists" or "Tennis" do encourage the expansion of poetic language, they do so programmatically, making the inclusion in poetry of phases like *crosscourt* and *down the line* sound like a feat rather than an achievement that later poems will build on. Consequently, the poems seem more like attempts to write like Virgil (no more possible than it is to write like Keats) than efforts to adapt his preromantic sensibility to the poetry of today. In contrast, that is exactly what poems like "Poem About People," "Discretions of Alcibiades," or "The Beach Women" do.

In retrospect, then, how dangerous it was for Pinsky to embark on the long poem *Explanation of America*, published in 1979. This poem is as plainly discursive as "Tennis," but, unlike "Tennis" or even "Essay on Psychiatrists," *Explanation* is a poem in which Pinsky has something urgent to say. Halfway through, Pinsky offers this hope to his daughter, to whom the poem is addressed.

> The words—*"Vietnam"*—that I can't use in poems
> Without the one word threatening to gape
> And swallow and enclose the poem, for you
> May grow more finite; able to be touched.

This is what Pinsky had learned, writing his first book of poems. But the word that he chooses here, so much more charged than *shopping center*, reveals how much is at stake in his expansion of the language of poetry. Pinsky begins *Explanation* by stressing the vast multiplicity of images in American culture ("Colonial Diners, Disney, films / Of concentration camps, the napalmed child / Trotting through famous newsfilm"), and he wants his daughter to see all these images—just as he wants to build a poem ample enough to contain them. Such a poem might satisfy Pinsky's smaller hope:

> The Shopping Center itself will be as precious
> And quaint as is the threadmill now converted
> Into a quaint and high-class shopping center.

The larger hope—the larger word—is not dispatched with so easily:

> Someday, the War in Southeast Asia, somewhere—
> Perhaps for you and people younger than you—
> Will be the kind of history and pain
> Saguntum is for me; but never tamed
> Or "history" for me, I think.

J. D. McClatchy has called *An Explanation of America* Pinsky's "most capacious and aspiring work," but I agree with him when he says that *History of My Heart*, published in 1984, is an even more important achievement.[9] Pinsky's great subject (the dialectical relationship of the self and the social structure) was necessarily at the center of his meditation of what the word "America" might mean. But while the poems of *History of My Heart* and *The Want Bone* continue this meditation, they do so dramatically, enacting the dialectic as well as explaining it. These poems retain the discursive clarity of the long poem, but their narratives seem, even within their smaller compass, more comprehensive and complex, more a dramatization of a mind thinking than the product of thought (to borrow the distinction Elizabeth Bishop favored).

The opening poem in *History of my Heart*, "The Figured Wheel," de-

scribes the rotation of a great wheel throughout history. A catalogue of
culture, high and low, familiar and foreign, it begins with a *shopping
mall* rather than a *center* and ends with the creation of Robert Pinsky's
single self.

It is hung with devices
By dead masters who have survived by reducing themselves magically
To tiny organisms, to wisps of matter, crumbs of soil,
Bits of dry skin, microscopic flakes, which is why they are called
    "great,"
In their humility that goes on celebrating the turning
Of the wheel as it rolls unrelentingly over


A cow plodding through car-traffic on a street in Iasi,
And over the haunts of Robert Pinsky's mother and father
And wife and children and his sweet self
Which he hereby unwillingly and inexpertly gives up, because it is


There, figured and pre-figured in the nothing-transfiguring wheel.

These lines establish the terms in which the title *History of My Heart*
must be understood. Virtually all of Pinsky's poems are autobiographical, but they recognize that an autobiography, like the self it narrates,
is constituted by a wide array of cultural and historical forces. To get
to the "heart" of these poems is not to find some essential core but to
recognize that the heart is on the surface of everything the poet sees or
speaks. Any distinctions between private and public "history" become
difficult to sustain.

The second poem in *History of My Heart* adds a more plainly political
charge to this history. "The Unseen" begins with a group of tourists in
Kraków, touring the death camp. The scene is "unswallowable," both
unbearably familiar and unbearably horrific: "We felt bored / And at
the same time like screaming Biblical phrases." Stalled between these
extremes, Pinsky remembers a "sleep-time game"—an insomniac's
dream of heroic destruction: granted the power of invisibility, Pinsky
roams the camp, saves the victims from the gas chamber, and, as a
finale, flushes "everything with a vague flood / Of fire and blood." As
in "The Destruction of Long Branch," Pinsky dreams of having power
over his history, remaking what made him.

It's not possible to take that dream too seriously in "The Destruction
of Long Branch," of course: its act of destruction serves as a kind of
metaphor for the self's struggle with language and history. In "The
Unseen" the act is too literal, too historically charged, and Pinsky must
back away from it more distinctly.

> I don't feel changed, or even informed—in that,
> It's like any other historical monument; although
> It is true that I don't ever at night any more
>
> Prowl rows of red buildings unseen, doing
> Justice like an angry god to escape insomnia.

Though he feels unchanged, Pinsky describes an important transformation here. Having imagined himself as the "unseen," Pinsky now recognizes a more potent invisible presence.

> And so,
> O discredited Lord of Hosts, your servant gapes
> Obediently to swallow various doings of us, the most
> Capable of all your former creatures . . .

In Pinsky's lexicon, this force could be called "history" as easily as "Lord of Hosts." Having earlier found the scene "unswallowable," Pinsky realizes that he has no choice but to take in the past. And as "The Figured Wheel" suggests, the past—however sordid—is already inside him: in this sense, the force could also be called "my heart."

The historical wheel rolls through all of Pinsky's work, but these lines from *The Want Bone* point to a slight change in his attitude: "How can I turn this wheel / that turns my life?" Throughout *History of My Heart* Pinsky is amazed by the vast array of images that make up the self; throughout *The Want Bone* he is equally amazed by the images that the self can make. The desire—the want—to turn the wheel of history has certainly been present in Pinsky's work since "The Destruction of Long Branch"; but in *The Want Bone* Pinsky sometimes stands aghast at the potential hubris of the human imagination—or what in "What Why When How Who" he calls

> The old conspiracy of gain and pleasure
>
> Flowering in the mind greedily to build the world
> And break it.

Behind these lines stand Old Testament injunctions against idolatry— "they worship the work of their own hands, that which their own fingers have made"—but in an essay on the prophet Isaiah, Pinsky concludes that "all worship, even the most meticulous or elaborate, may be flawed by the spirit of idolatry."[10] Since idolatry is in some way essential to human action, good or bad, Pinsky's fascination is less with greed as such than with the point where pleasure begins to conspire unhappily with gain.

The first poem in *The Want Bone*, "From the Childhood of Jesus," is impatient with both Old and New Testament wisdom, both the laws of Judaism and Jesus' revision of them. Pinsky tells the apocryphal tale of a young Jesus who makes a little pond of mud and twigs and models twelve sparrows from clay. The scene seems innocent enough until "a certain Jew" (Pinsky incorporates the language of the anti-Semitic joke or story here) scolds the child for "making images." In response, Jesus makes the sparrows come to life, and, when the son of Annas accidentally ruins the little pond, Jesus makes the boy wither away. The petulant tone of Jesus' anger is familiar from the Gospels ("what did the water / Do to harm you?"), but his actions are merciless, filled with the childish self-importance that the tone suggests. (As Pinsky says in "Lament for the Makers," worship is "tautological, with its Blessed / Art thou O Lord who consecrates the Sabbath . . . And then the sudden curt command or truth: / God told him, Thou shalt cut thy foreskin off.") "From the Childhood of Jesus" ends like a parable gone wrong.

> Alone in his cot in Joseph's house, the Son
> Of man was crying himself to sleep. The moon
>
> Rose higher, the Jews put out their lights and slept,
> And all was calm and as it had been, except
>
> In the agitated household of the scribe Annas,
> And high in the dark, where unknown even to Jesus
>
> The twelve new sparrows flew aimlessly through the night,
> Not blinking or resting, as if never to alight.

Jesus is resolutely human in this story, granted the powers of a god but the emotions of a child, and, like any man, he cannot control the things he has made: the poem's final image is more frightening than the child's petulance. "From the Childhood of Jesus" is astonishing because, while it is ultimately about the consequences of the simple human desire for power, it tells that profane story in the vocabulary of the sacred. Consequently, this poem about hubris is itself startlingly hubristic—a paradox that embodies Pinsky's uneasy double attitude toward the human imagination.

"From the Childhood of Jesus" exemplifies one of the two kinds of poems that make up The Want Bone. The other kind, rather than adapting biblical rhetoric, combines a multiplicity of vocabularies and narratives into a shape that seems both wild and controlled, random and planned. Structually, these poems resemble Amy Clampitt's "The Prairie": they're organized something like a Baroque concerto with a ritornello or repeating motif that returns (though in a different key) after each episode of new material. In "The Uncreation" various ideas of singing hold the poem's disparate materials together. In "At Pleasure Bay" some version of the phrase "never the same" recurs. And in "Shirt" the repeated motif is neither a theme nor a phrase but simply a rhythm: "The back, the yoke, the yardage" or "The planter, the picker, the sorter." In "The Hearts" the *ritornello* is an unsentimental image of the heart, itself the sentimental image of desire, as "pulpy shore-life battened on a jetty."

> Slashed by the little deaths of sleep and pleasure,
> They swell in the nurturing spasms of the waves,
>
> Sucking to cling; and even in death itself—
> Baked, frozen—they shrink to grip the granite harder.

Between the recurrences of this image comes a catalogue of harsh desires. The victim of a suffocating lover is equated with a heroin addict who knows, the first time he shoots up, that he will suffer, go to prison, and probably die. But this knowledge doesn't stop the addict, whose consolation is that proposed by Enobarbus in *Antony and Cleopatra* when Antony laments "Would I had never seen her": "Then you would have / missed / A wonderful piece of work." This passage, in turn, invokes a sentence from Stephen Booth's commentary on Shakespeare's sonnets: "*Shakespeare was almost certainly homosexual, / Bisexual, or heterosexual, the sonnets / Provide no evidence on the matter.*" This link in the chain of associations provokes the poem's central question: why does human desire fuel, over and over again, the making of images—the singing of songs, the throwing of pots, the writing of poems?

All of these creative acts are invoked as the chain continues, one image leading almost arbitrarily to the next. The question of Shakespeare's sexuality invokes the rhetoric of courtly love (tears, crystals, hearts) which still infects the songs (Lee Andrews and the Hearts—"My tear drops are / Like crystals") we sing in the shower (falling like tears or crystals).

> To Buddha every distinct thing is illusion
> And becoming is destruction, but still we sing
> In the shower. I do. In the beginning God drenched
>
> The Emptiness with images: the potter
> Crosslegged at his wheel in Benares market
> Making mud cups, another cup each second
>
> Tapering up between his fingers, one more
> To sell the tea-seller at a penny a dozen,
> And tea a penny a cup. The customers smash

The empties, and waves of traffic grind the shards
To mud for new cups, in turn; and I keep one here
Next to me: holding it awhile from out of the cloud

Of dust that rises from the shattered pieces,
The risen dust alive with fire, then settled
And soaked and whirling again on the wheel that turns

And looks on the world as on another cloud,
On everything the heart can grasp and throw away
As a passing cloud. . . .

The image of the wheel returns here, but unlike "The Figured Wheel"
the potter's wheel is turned by a man: the result of all human *making*,
Pinsky suggests, is this absurd, this transient—not the potent images
with which the Old Testament God drenches the emptiness but the mere
images that the Buddha denounces as empty. And yet, as the poem
continues to unfold, the wheel continues to turn—perhaps productively.
The visions of the Old Testament are dismissed as "too barbarous for
heaven / And too preposterous for belief on earth" (Pinsky rehearses
the horrible vision in Isaiah 6, after which the prophet's unclean lips
are purified by a live coal), and "The Hearts" ends by returning to Lee
Andrews and the Hearts, their record spinning like the potter's wheel.
Pinsky's suggestion here is that the turning itself—the longing, the singing, the making—must constitute our human value.

As the record ends, a coda in retard:
The Hearts in a shifting velvety *ah*, and *ah*
Prolonged again, and again as Lee Andrews

Reaches *ah* high for *I have to gain Faith, Hope*
*And Charity, God only knows the girl*
*Who will love me—Oh! if we only could*

*Start over again!* Then The Hearts chant the chords
Again a final time, *ah* and the record turns
Through all the music, and on into silence again.

These lines of the poem answer the song: you can start again, though
you'll end up in pretty much the same place. Finally, Pinsky's suggestion is that the turning itself—the longing, the singing, the making—
must constitute our human value. If this seems like a paltry consolation,
the empty images condemned by the Buddha, we should remember in
contrast the uncontrollable, unsatisfying images conjured by the Son of
Man.

In "Impossible to Tell," one of the new poems in *The Figured Wheel:*

*New and Collected Poems*, Pinsky describes (among many other things) the way in which medieval Japanese poets worked together to write linked poems or *renga*: "The movement / Of linking *renga* coursing from moment to moment / Is meaning." This is a good description of what Pinsky tries to accomplish in poems like "The Hearts," creating the texture not only of one poet's mind but of a culture's accumulating stock of reality. In "Impossible to Tell" Pinsky cuts back and forth between the Japanese poet Basho, nurturing his disciples, and Pinsky's own friend, Elliot Gilbert, who was a consummate teller of ethnic jokes. The jokes Pinsky repeats in "Impossible to Tell" are sidesplitting, but the poem is also deeply moving. A kind of courtly community grows from the conventional yet idiosyncratic work of the joke-teller.

> But as the *renga* describes
> Religious meaning by moving in drifting petals
>
> And brittle leaves that touch and die and suffer
> The changing winds that riffle the gutter swirl,
> So the joke, just under the raucous music
>
> Of Fleming, Jew, Walloon, a courtly allegiance
> Moves to the dulcimer, gavotte and bow,
> Over the banana tree the moon in autumn—
>
> Allegiance to a state impossible to tell.

As these lines suggest, Pinsky often explores the racial and ethnic components of identity, and though all of the ingredients for an identity politics are contained within his poems, such a politics never emerges. Rather than asserting the importance of his lower-middle-class Jewish heritage alone, Pinsky emphasizes the mongrel, compromised heritage of everything: through poetry, through jokes, through any communal activity, our allegiance is to "a state impossible to tell." Pinsky's mature poems are rarely about Long Branch in the explicit way that the early "Destruction of Long Branch" is, but poems like "The Hearts" or "Impossible to Tell" feel like an effort to rebuild Pinsky's hometown's ambience in language: beautiful yet vulgar, poignant yet funny, preserved out of time yet, like the waves, relentlessly in motion. At first, the poems might seem to move haphazardly, jumping from the sacred to the vulgar to the commonplace; but as Pinsky suggests in "Impossible to Tell," the *movement* (or, as he puts it in "The Hearts," the *turning*) of the poem between these elements is what ultimately satisfies us.

Thinking about this quality of movement in "Poetry and Pleasure," Pinsky asks a question that has been implicit in his work since "The

Destruction of Long Branch": "if gorgeous, impressive language and profound, crucial ideas were all that poetry offered to engage us, would it seem—as it does to many of us—as necessary as food?" This strikes me as the most threatening question that can be asked of poetry at the end of the twentieth century, and Pinsky's answer is convincing because it neither dismisses nor exaggerates poetry's claim on our attention. What engages us in poetry is not the product (the achieved word or thought) but the process of moving through those thoughts and words: "This movement—physical in the sounds of a poem, moral in its relation to the society implied by language, and the person who utters the poem—is near the heart of poetry's mysterious appeal, for me."[11] In their sinuous investigation of desire, Pinsky's poems describe this appeal: at the same time, they make us feel it.

I've quoted "Poetry and Pleasure" to elucidate Pinsky's poems, but of course Pinsky is trying to say something about the pleasures of poetry at large; the phrase "Death is the mother of beauty" gets its power from its occurrence within the idiosyncratic movement of thought and sound in Stevens's "Sunday Morning." In "American Poetry and American Life" Pinsky returns to this quality of movement, emphasizing that it is visible in a wide range of American poetries.

> One could exemplify this fluidity of tone, including the insepa-rable blend of comic and ecstatic, formal and vulgar, in an enor-mous range of American poets, John Ashbery and Elizabeth Bishop, George Oppen and James Merrill, Allen Ginsberg and Marianne Moore. (I think that the stylistic trait I mean also char-acterizes poems that do not explicitly take up American cultural material such as bus rides or movies.)[12]

Pinsky is interested in developing categories for the discussion of American poetry that do not encourage the polemical oppositions of Oppen and Merrill, Ginsberg and Moore, or—even more culturally over-determined—the high and the low. His strategy not only clarifies the position of his own work but helps to insure the future health and diversity of American literature.

Even the most deeply entrenched battle positions of American poetry don't interest Pinsky. In an essay occasioned by the centennial of T. S. Eliot's birth, he has admitted that the subject of his undergraduate thesis first alerted him to the quality of movement he so values, the "clangor-ous, barely-harmonized bringing together of the sacred and profane."

> Eliot is above all the pre-eminent poet of this clash or yoking. . . .
> Because he identified and penetrated this dualism in the rhythms and noises and smells and surfaces of modern life, without sim-

plifying what he saw into false ideas of squalor or perfection, Eliot remains entirely essential for us. He is not merely whatever we mean by "great poet," but precisely what Pound means by "an inventor." For this, Eliot's readers forgive him his mean side, his religio-authoritarian claptrap, the plushy grandiosity of "Ash Wednesday," the tetrameter anti-Semitism, the genteel trivialities of the late plays.[13]

Today—more than thirty years after Eliot's death, sixty years after Bishop heard Eliot speak at Vassar, seventy years after Crane sent Eliot's "Reflections on Contemporary Poetry" to Tate—there still seems something daring about this expression of debt and affinity.

I began by proposing that it is through such acknowledgments of debt and affinity that Pinsky's originality is constituted. Tracing his artistic development, I think we can see that Pinsky's own work provides the terms in which my proposition must be understood. Since our selves are turned on the great wheel of history and language, we owe whatever combination of qualities that might distinguish us, formal and vulgar, comic and ecstatic, to mysterious forces we disregard at our own peril. Pinsky's is a poetry of acknowledgment, and its power grows from his deep awareness—sometimes wariness, sometimes worship—of the literary, linguistic, and historical precedents that continue to mold his life even as he writes today. Acknowledging Eliot, Pinsky calls him an "inventor," invoking Pound's sense of a writer who discovers "a particular process." Above inventors, said Pound, stands the small class of "masters," those "who, apart from their own inventions, are able to assimilate and co-ordinate a large number of preceding inventions."[14] This, near the end of the twentieth century, is what Robert Pinsky is doing.

# JORIE GRAHAM'S
# BIG HUNGER

Jorie Graham published her first book only sixteen years ago, but she has already produced a body of writing that feels like the accumulation of a lifetime. Like Yeats, who early in his career cautioned suspicious readers that "it is myself that I remake," Graham has been driven to turn against her own best discoveries, risking everything she has achieved. Each of her books is a new beginning; in *Materialism*, each poem feels like an interrogation of the one preceding it. Graham has been unwilling to settle for anything settled, and she sometimes discards achievements that other poets would be willing to nurture for a long time. A different kind of writer would winnow more scrupulously in private, sharing only the distilled residue of her dissatisfaction. But Graham's most self-conscious interrogations of poetry are driven by a kind of seriousness that impresses the most skeptical reader. The more she writes, the more necessary—the more truly elucidating—her public agon seems. Graham's achievement seems big because she is satisfied with so little.

Even individual poems seem poised between the contrary demands of the intimate and the cosmic. The linguistic texture of Graham's poems has always been distinguished by a tension between poetically precise and philosophically expansive kinds of diction; in *Materialism*, Graham transformed this tension into a structural principle. Her most recent poems tend to focus on an insignificant action—walking the dog, delivering her daughter's leotard, or picking up a dead butterfly. The poems themselves never seem little, however, for Graham creates (more than uncovers) the infinitely expanding web of psychic energies that makes each small moment possible. The result is a dramatization of what Husserl thought of as the "thickened" present: tracing the contours of a single action in the present, we feel the weighty convergence of the personal and cultural traces that cling to it. As Graham says in one of the five poems called "Notes on the Reality of the Self" in *Materialism*, she wants to "expand / each second, / bloating it up, cell-like, making it real." In the process, she forges a deeply sensuous poetry out of the slippage between language and sensation that so many American poets have worked to suppress—and she does so without capitulating to the opposite idealism, in which the claims of language supposedly override our desire to know the world intimately.

Graham's dramatization of consciousness can be so rapid and expansive that the insignificant action provoking the poem becomes difficult to find; but simple evidence for the action is always there. In "Recovered from the Storm" (collected in *The Errancy*, her most recent book), the action is simply and unexpectedly delineated in the poem's monosyllabic final line: "I pick up and drag one large limb from the path." The line is as unassuming as the action it describes, but because of the poem's breathless exfoliation of thought, the line is almost unbearably weighted with connotation.

> So this is the wingbeat of the underneathly, ticking—
> this iridescent brokenness, this wet stunted nothingness—
> busy with its hollows—browsing abstractly with its catastrophic
>     wingtips
> the tops of our world, ripping pleatings of molecule,
> unjoining the slantings, the slippery wrinklings we don't even
>     grasp the icily free *made-nature* of yet?
> Why are we here in this silly moonlight?
> What is the mind meant to tender among splinters?
> What was it, exactly, was meant to be *shored*?
> Whose dolled-up sorceries *against confusion* now?
> The children are upstairs, we will keep them tucked in—
> as long as we can, as long as you'll let us.
> I hear your pitch. How containment is coughing,
> under the leafbits, against the asphalt.
> How the new piles of kindling are mossily giggling
>     their kerosene cadenza

all long the block in the riddled updrafts.
I pick up and drag one large limb from the path.

The achievement of this poem is that its final line—in itself so plain—
is almost impossible to paraphrase. Negotiating the syntactical thicket
that precedes it, we are made to feel the existential terror that Graham
staves off by the necessary and yet poignantly inadequate act of dragging
one (just one) fallen limb from the path. On the one hand, that terror feels
threateningly domestic, the kind of fear that every parent of small children knows. On the other hand, the terror feels ominously metaphysical.
In this poem of tiny consequence, Graham is audacious enough to refer
openly to the two greatest modern poets of existential terror. She makes
already well-known lines from Eliot ("These fragments I have shored
against my ruins") and Frost ("a momentary stay against confusion")
ring in our ears again. There is nothing cagey about these gestures toward
the moderns. Graham wants us to feel the power of these lines, and she
needs to let us know that the lines—however familiar they might be—are
a necessary part of her poetic equipment. Her poems do not feel at all
similar to those of Pinsky, Howard, or Clampitt, but, like them, Graham
exemplifies what is best about contemporary American poetry: her distinctiveness is based on acts of inclusion, a hunger to align herself with a
wide array of contemporaries and precursors.

For Graham, the problem with Eliot, Frost, or Stevens is not that their
achievements are overpowering, but that their presence in contemporary poetry is not powerful enough. Having come of age at a time when
Eliot had as much or as little to do with contemporary writing as Cole-
ridge (Graham was born in 1951), she is young enough to feel that the
moderns are separated from her by several generations of equally formidable writers. But these poets tended, says Graham, to narrow the
scope of American poetry. However necessary and productive it was
for them to endorse a "strictly secular sense of reality (domestic, confessional)," we need to return to the ambitious questions of spiritual
and cultural redemption that preoccupied Eliot, Frost, and Stevens: "I
think many poets writing today realize we need to recover a high level
of ambition, a rage, if you will—the big hunger."[1]

I suspect that there is no postromantic poet who has not felt this
hunger (the elegantly circumscribed world of Richard Wilbur is hardly
unambitious), but Graham is right to suggest that a kind of expansive-
ness, a certain rhetoric of ambition, became difficult for poets after modernism. "We hear the *man* in *manifesto*," said James Merrill, thinking
about the vast productions of Eliot, Pound, Stevens, and Williams:
"these men began by writing small, controllable, we might say from our
present vantage 'unisex' poems. As time went on, though, through their

ambitious reading, their thinking, their critical pronouncements, a kind of vacuum charged with expectation, if not with dread, took shape around them, asking to be filled with grander stuff. As when the bronze is poured in the lost-wax process of casting, what had been human and impressionable in them was becoming its own monument." It was for this reason that Merrill was so deeply nourished by Elizabeth Bishop, a poet who (as Merrill put it in "Overdue Pilgrimage to Nova Scotia") refused "to tip the scale of being human / By adding unearned weight."[2] In contrast, Graham wants the "big hunger" to bring to American poetry a muscularity, not a flabbiness.

Merrill ultimately rejected the notion, implicit in his pun on *manifesto*, that "unearned weight" is accumulated only by men (though he was right to suggest that the conscious shirking of high ambition is often associated in American poetry with femininity). Similarly, Merrill's career makes us resist the notion that weight, earned or unearned, is necessarily accumulated more readily by the moderns than by their successors: *The Changing Light at Sandover* is one of the grandest poems produced by an American poet since Pound's *Cantos*. Merrill checked the portentousness of his poetic cosmology with a tone that varies from bemused to whimsical, and the moderns were similarly troubled by the specter of unearned weight, even when they indulged their appetites. Almost as soon as *The Waste Land* was published, Eliot began diminishing the poem as nothing but "rhythmical grumbling." Yeats was careful to publish "The Second Coming" beside "A Prayer for My Daughter," tempering his apocalyptic vision of "a rocking cradle" with a glimpse of his own child "half hid / Under this cradle-hood and coverlid." Lamenting the loss of the "big hunger," Graham does recognize that Merrill and Ashbery have kept modernist ambition alive: "the hugeness of their project seems so central," says Graham, "and the aesthetic differences that divide them ultimately so minor."[3] It consequently seems appropriate to say that a longing for the "big hunger" has coexisted with a fear of "unearned weight" in the poetry of both the moderns and their successors. As "Recovered from the Storm" suggests, Jorie Graham has embraced this tension and made from it a poetry all her own.

In her recent poems, Graham has perfected a style that is, in its own way, as grippingly idiosyncratic as Marianne Moore's. But her development has been swift; as I began by suggesting, Graham has not been shy about exposing her quest (a lesser word will not do) for new ways to dramatize the mind in motion. In retrospect, her career might be described in the way that Merrill characterized the careers of the moderns: her first two books, though different, contained small, controllable poems, while her third book, *The End of Beauty*, unveiled a far more challenging and ecstatic way of writing. This dramatic development was due mostly to a poet's passage from apprenticeship to an early mastery of her own language, a mastery that allows the poet to attempt more risky effects. But because Graham was precocious (the poems of her apprenticeship are highly crafted), it has been difficult not to read her passage from *Erosion* to *The End of Beauty* as an allegory for the play of larger forces. Bonnie Costello has ventured that *Erosion*, Graham's second book, "is essentially a modernist text, whereas Graham's later work may be characterized as postmodern."[4] Plausible as this statement is, our sense of what modernism was remains so fluid that Graham herself is able to read her own career in opposite terms. To her, the earlier work in *Erosion* is similar to the modest productions of poets who came of age in the wake of modernism, while *The End of Beauty* represents her first large-scale attempt to recover the "big hunger"—the formal audaciousness and cultural relevance she associates with modernism.

Graham has become, due in part to the heartfelt endorsements of Helen Vendler, the most prominent American poet born after the Second World War. It is consequently difficult to remember how controversial each of her books has seemed—how sharply she has turned against her own accomplishments and how unsympathetically those turnings have often been received. Costello, who admires *Erosion*, finds *The End of Beauty* and *Region of Unlikeness* problematic. Less thoughtful reviewers have said worse. But the controversy seems to me elucidating, because Graham so expertly resists the narratives we usually bring to postmodern poetry while, at the same time, she invites us to consider her poetry in relationship to those narratives. Like Ashbery, Graham does occasionally reinforce the logic of the "breakthrough," especially when she associates an idealized sense of aesthetic closure with an equally ahistorical notion of ideological oppression. But just as often she explodes this logic. If, as Costello has suggested, the recent work takes on the formal strategies currently associated with a garden-variety post-modernism ("darting images without explicit connections; a digressive, decentered approach to thought; the fragmentation of linear plots and arguments"), it is more important to remember, as Costello also points out, that Graham "has a fundamentally different orientation" from Ashbery and his cotillion: for them, poetry is not—as it is for Graham—"a matter of metaphysics, of sustaining the rigor of truth or opening words to ecstatic vision."[5] As "The Tree of Knowledge" suggests, Graham entertains "the old dream of an underneath," but she does so without complacency or idealism: she knows that "just appearance turning into further appearance" may as easily become an unexamined certainty as appearance giving way to the real thing.

Such contradictions—real or apparent—are the source of Graham's distinctive power. Especially since the publication of *Materialism*, it has become clear that Graham's poetry reaches in too many different directions to be accounted for by any linear narrative. Just as *Life Studies* looks like the crucial turning point only if we ignore the restless, searching quality of Lowell's entire career, *The End of Beauty* looks like a "breakthrough" only if we ignore the ways in which the book that followed it, *Region of Unlikeness*, now seems like a retreat to the presuppositions that underlie many of Graham's earlier poems. Until recently, this retreat was difficult to see: *Region of Unlikeness* appears to extend the stylistic extravagance of *The End of Beauty*, eschewing the controlled shapes of the earlier poems of *Erosion*. But style is not always linked unequivocally to vision, and one of the great strengths of Graham's poetry is that it weakens links that readers of postmodern poetry almost always take for granted. In other words, Jorie Graham is as frustrating and problematic a poet—I mean this as the highest compliment—as Eliot or Frost.

In "The Sense of an Ending," the long poem that concludes *Erosion* and foreshadows the concerns of her later work, Graham recalls her childhood acquaintance with "eyemachines" at a clinic: looking into the machine, each eye would see an "earthy thing, one to / each eye," and the mind would be "given the task: to bring them / together." These lines describe the way in which most of the poems from *Erosion* (and many from *Region of Unlikeness*) work: in contrast to recent poems like "Recovered from the Storm," these poems do not so much enact the processes of consciousness as create, through juxtaposition or implied analogy, a static puzzle that the reader is obliged to solve. In "At Luca Signorelli's Resurrection of the Body," for instance, Graham brings together Signorelli's fresco of "The Resurrection" in the cathedral of Orvieto with the story of Signorelli's dissection of his son's body. In the fresco, souls clamor to reenter human flesh that Signorelli has rendered perfectly; in the studio, Signorelli dissects cadavers in order to achieve that perfection. But the dissection of his own son suggests that something more than the demands of early modern empiricism was motivating the painter.

> It took him days,
>     that deep
> caress, cutting,
>     unfastening,
>
> until his mind
>     could climb into
> the open flesh and
>     mend itself.

Graham does not need to make any explicit gesture back to Signorelli's "Resurrection" for us to feel its relevance here. Looking at the fresco, she wonders if the souls are really "after" perfection as they hurry into human form; the people in the cathedral, muses Graham, could tell the souls that "there is no / entrance, / only entering." Similarly, the poem's hushed final lines suggest that the painter himself is "mended" not by seeking spiritual wholeness but by confronting the physical evidence of the most unbearable kind of human suffering.

"At Luca Signorelli's Resurrection of the Body" offers one of the most convincing examples of Graham's analogical method in *Erosion*; in other poems, this method produces poems that overdetermine their endings. "The Age of Reason" is divided into three discrete sections (as the Signorelli poem could have been): part one describes birds who settle on anthills, taking the insects—or sometimes cigarette butts or broken glass—into their bodies before they fly away; part two describes Werner Herzog's film of Georg Büchner's *Woyzeck*, in which the hero stabs his wife, throws the knife in the river, and "goes in" after it much as the knife "goes in" the body; part three attempts a synthesis, depending (as many of the *Erosion* poems do) on questions that instruct the reader: "How far is true / enough? / How far into the / earth / can vision go and / still be / love?" As in "At Luca Signorelli's Resurrection of the Body," Graham plays with different notions of "entering," groping for the place at which the mechanisms of violence and of love seem too similar to pull apart. If the poem is like the "eyemachine," however, it not only presents discrete narratives but conflates them, solving the poem's puzzle before we have a chance to feel its mystery. The poem may look more modest—more apprehensible, more controlled—than much of Graham's later work, but its shape is determined by a hunger for big solutions to big questions.

In offering this analysis, I am only repeating what Graham suggests about her own poems when, in "The Sense of an Ending," she describes a wolf pacing in a cage: "Too much clicks shut in that quick step / revolving on the one hind leg, bringing the other down just as / the swivel ends. . . . It's beautiful. You can hear / minutes stitching shut." Looking back to one of the most frequently invoked metaphors in *Erosion* (stitching), these lines also introduce the most prominent metaphor of *The End of Beauty* (clicking shut). Throughout both *The End of Beauty* and *Region of Unlikeness* (though in very different ways), Graham is appalled by the "click" of closure, having felt that she herself was seduced in *Erosion* by its beauty, its perfection. But in *Region of Unlikeness* she is once again seduced by closure even as she sustains her critique of it. The most ambitious poems from this volume ("Fission," "From the New World," "The Phase after History") do not read much like

*Erosion* poems; instead of juxtaposing different stories, Graham fragments and intertwines them, making the poems seem (at first glance) decentered and open-ended. Yet these poems rely on the same kind of analogical thinking that distinguishes "The Age of Reason": however strenuously they lament the ethical or political repercussions of aesthetic closure, the poems themselves click shut.

In "From the New World" Graham braids together three different narratives: the recent trial of John Demanjuk, known as Ivan the Terrible at Treblinka; the story of a girl who emerged from the gas chamber asking for her mother, only to be raped and sent back in; and the story of Graham's own grandparents, who, after fifty years of marriage, were put into separate nursing homes. When Graham remembers visiting the grandmother who no longer recognized her, the stories begin to line up, making the poem's structure feel more spatial than linear: "I went into the bathroom, locked the door. / Stood in front of the mirrored wall—/ not so much to see in, not looking up at all in fact, / but to be held in it as by a gas, / the thing which was me there in its chamber." Like the "eyemachine," the poem asks us to superimpose the narratives, equating the closed spaces of the bathroom and the gas chamber. And in both cases Graham wants to preserve the moment of possibility that the narrative forecloses; each girl is desperate to save her "thin / young body" from its all but certain end. But by drawing such a broad analogy between such bracingly different realms of human experience, the poem itself seems tightly closed: it focuses our attention so sharply on the similarities of the narratives that it seems oddly unconcerned with their differences. Graham goes so far as to say that "the coiling and uncoiling / billions" were there with her in the bathroom: "the about to be held down, bit clean, shaped, / and the others, too, the ones gone back out, the ending / wrapped round them."

Paraphrasing "What the End is For," Helen Vendler exposes the problem with these analogical poems: "The wish of the speculative mind to halt its drift and take visible shape leads not only to marriage but to atomic piles and B-52's."[6] One wants to know how, precisely, cognitive or aesthetic closure leads to mass destruction. For if what the poem says about narrative closure were true, then it would be easy—just by embracing different formal strategies—to end sexism and stave off nuclear disaster. Writing in defense of the Language poets, Jerome McGann once declared that "narrativity" is an "inherently conservative feature of discourse." But just because our experience of the world is discursive, shaped by narratives, it does not follow that we can change the world by disrupting specific versions of those narratives. Responding to McGann, Charles Altieri rightly pointed out that "there is no one social form—that hypothesis is pure Platonism, not Marxist materialism.''[7] This logic may explain Graham's repeated condemnations of narrative closure: she is—at least in this regard—a kind of Platonist, a poet who sees the same issue of aesthetic form at the root of all social problems. As Graham herself has admitted with characteristic forthrightness, "I'm so much at the outer limits of political action" that the poetry's social dimension is "probably a delusion I create for myself in order to get myself off the hook.''[8]

Graham dismantles this delusion as often as she fosters it. In the early wake of modernism, when Robert Lowell called his first book *Land of Unlikeness* (translating the phrase *regio dissimilitudinis*), he wanted his strictly controlled poems to imply a corresponding spiritual vision—as the chaotic surfaces of Pound's and Eliot's poems did not seem to do. In contrast, the author of *Region of Unlikeness* is interesting because the formal and thematic aspects of her poems are often at odds with each other, undermining accepted notions of openness. Graham has offered the counterintuitive but convincing argument that Whitman is "a very *intellectual* sensibility writing desperately towards his body to recover it," while Stevens is "a poet so fully in the body, in his senses, and moving towards the conceptual and philosophical in order to complete himself." By this same logic, the egregiously fragmentary and digressive poet of *Region of Unlikeness* is preeminently a poet of closure. "We tend to define our poets by that aspect of sensibility they actually most lack and strive towards," continues Graham, and she herself strives most arduously to embrace poems that do not click shut.[9] This is why her poems—unlike the work of contemporaries who champion open-endedness with more consistently doctrinaire fervor—are so moving and unpredictable. In the closing lines of "Soul Says," the last poem in *Region of Unlikeness*, Graham seems desperate to discover a region of "likeness" in which all metaphors are literalized, all stories are the same story: one thing is *likened* to another thing but also *is* that thing.

> Now then, I said, I go to meet that which I liken to
> (even though the wave break and drown me in laughter)
> the wave breaking, the wave drowning me in laughter—

Beautiful as these lines are, they could not serve as the conclusion to *Materialism*. Little of what I've said so far is pertinent to Graham's recent poetry, and neither is it pertinent to most of *The End of Beauty*, the volume that appeared between *Erosion* and *Region of Unlikeness*. Graham once admitted that after publishing *Erosion* she completed and discarded almost an entire book of poems written in the manner of *Erosion*: among the poems included in *The End of Beauty*, "Imperialism" and "What the End Is For" seem like the only remaining evidence of that effort; despite their jittery, disjointed surfaces, they too feel spatial in design (offering stories that we correlate). Other poems in *The End of Beauty* are written in a startlingly different manner—a more resolutely linear manner that, in retrospect, prepares us for the poems of *Materialism*. The title of one of them, "Self-Portrait as Hurry and Delay," may serve to describe them all: although the poems move inexorably and ecstatically forward, Graham slows down the movement, breaking the poem into discrete sections, often line by line. While she tends in the poems of *Materialism* to thicken a single moment of consciousness, Graham imagines in these poems the complexities that lurk between our moments as they pass. In the process, she offers a compelling critique not only of closure but of openness as well.

The End of Beauty* contains five poems called "Self-Portrait." The first of them, "Self-Portrait as the Gesture Between Them," unfolds the story of the first human story: by plucking the forbidden fruit and handing it to Adam, Eve turns her back on the static truth of God, initiating a plot from an error.

27

the feeling of being a digression not the link in the argument,
a new direction, an offshoot, the limb going on elsewhere,

28

and liking that error, a feeling of being capable *because* an error,

29

of being wrong perhaps altogether wrong a piece from another set

30

stripped of position stripped of true function

31

and loving that error, loving that filial form, that break from perfection

32

where the complex mechanism fails, where the stranger appears in the
    clearing,

33

out of nowhere and uncalled for, out of nowhere to share the day.

These breathless final lines, hurrying forward even as Graham delays the end, suggest that human freedom lies in errancy and digression. And inasmuch as the lines seem to describe the poem's movement, Graham expresses her dissatisfaction with the "complex mechanism" of the analogical poems she wrote in *Erosion*. But elsewhere in *The End of Beauty* Graham reveals a deep suspicion of the freedom apparently embodied by this new kind of poem. What seems like the opening of all possibility in "Self-Portrait as the Gesture Between Them" immediately seems like the foreclosure of all possibility in "Self-Portrait as Apollo and Daphne." Pursuing Daphne, Apollo is all closure; he wants "to possess her, to nail the erasures," and all he can offer are the typical lines: "*will you forgive me?* or *say / that you'll love me for / ever and ever.*" Daphne, in contrast, is associated with the aleatory movement of a flock of birds: "the shrill cheeps and screeches of the awakening thousands, / hysterical, for miles, in all the directions." Daphne refuses to "give shape to his hurry by being / its destination," and since Graham is likewise attempting to undo the end (to forge a poetry that resembles the flock of birds more than the single-minded male), she seems to posit a realm of feminine experience that lies outside of narrative—a "given" world untouched by the "made." But Graham skewers this idealism in the final lines of the poem: the random bird calls "marry" in the air, suggesting that the plot of heterosexual desire cannot simply be evaded but must be more resolutely resisted from within.

Part of what makes the sequence of "Self-Portraits" in *The End of Beauty* so exciting is that they are sternly self-critical: each poem not only turns against the one before it but also turns on itself, collapsing the duality posited by its title. In "Self-Portrait as Hurry and Delay [Penelope at Her Loom]," Graham emphasizes more clearly that her own formal strategies of interruption and delay inevitably heighten our desire for closure. Although Odysseus threatens to wrap "himself plot plot and dénouement over the roiling openness," Penelope unweaves her tapestry, delaying the suitors, only to make them "want her more richly"; though Penelope's strategy is delay, her fingers dart over the weaving "like his hurry darts." However compromised, Penelope's power over the suitors is not dispelled. In Elizabeth Bishop's "Brazil, January 1, 1502," the Native American women are "retreating, always retreating" behind the landscape that exists only as a tapestry—an imposed system of European values—for the pursuing men; in "Self-Portrait as Hurry and Delay," Penelope has taken control of the tapestry itself, "beginning always beginning the ending as they go to sleep beneath her."

Even more tellingly critical of Graham's notion of openness is "Self-Portrait as Demeter and Persephone," the last of the five self-portraits.

Once in hell, Persephone discovers a world with no shape, no beginning and, therefore, no end. She wonders how she will recognize anything in the future if she loses all sense of the past.

She watched the smoke where it began what it left off
What will I recognize it to have been she thought
smoke smoke her fingers her eyes like static all over it
Surely I can find it the point of departure she put her hand in
The birds the beaks of the birds the song the heard song
She reached in what is it begins at the end she thought
Where is the skin of the minutes will it ever come off
She reached in there was no underneath what was this coiling over
    her fingers
She reached in she could go no further she was sealed off
It pushed back against her it was hell she could finally lean
It was the given and it was finally given

This and other passages in "Self-Portrait as Demeter and Persephone" offer some of Graham's most virtuosic writing. She eschews all punctuation, suggesting that the poem itself has reached a condition of openness beyond the conventions of grammar and syntax; however, the passage itself maintains that such a condition would be intolerable, even if it were possible. If we really could step outside of narrative, if we could live without any sense of an ending, attaining some sense of the given, of pure being, we would be in hell. And as Graham describes it, this static world of the given resembles the Eden we left behind in "Self-Portrait as the Gesture Between Them." Persephone emerges from hell as gratefully as Eve emerged from Eden, glad to "inhabit a shape," to "suffer completely this wind." Between these two poems, Graham has shown how little may be possible within the human world of narrative; but there is no doubt that this woefully constricted world is the only place in which meaningful resistance is possible at all.

In the penultimate poem of The End of Beauty, "Of Forced Sightes and Trusty Ferefulness," Graham casts her own lot with Persephone, giving herself over to the Shelleyan wind, to relentless forward motion: "through wind, through winter nights, we'll pass, / steering with crumbs, with words, / making of every hour / a thought." This positive argument (the finding of freedom within narrative) is far more complicated and interesting than Graham's negative argument (the unequivocal association of narrative closure with oppression). And one way to explain Graham's development would be to say that the spatial poems of Region of Unlikeness extend the negative argument while the linear poems of Materialism extend the positive argument. The final poem in The End of Beauty is "Imperialism," an analogical poem that, unlike the self-portraits, would not seem out of place in *Region*. But when Graham recently organized her selected poems, she placed "Of Forced Sightes" at the end of *The End of Beauty*, suggesting that it, rather than "Imperialism," prepares us for the more resolutely self-critical poems of *Materialism*. Another way to explain Graham's development would be to say that in *Region of Unlikeness* she recovered from modernism even more of the "big hunger" than she had in *Erosion*; in *Materialism*, she recovered from *The End of Beauty* an equally powerful distrust of "unearned weight."

Just as *The End of Beauty* contains five "Self-Portrait" poems, *Materialism* contains five poems called "Notes on the Reality of the Self." Graham does not return to the freeze-frame structure of the self-portraits, however; like "Recovered from the Storm" (the recent poem with which I began), these "Notes" focus on a deceptively simple action. "I let the dog loose in this stretch," says Graham midway through the first of the "Notes," the opening poem in *Materialism*: the line tells us the poem's entire plot, but our experience of the poem is dominated by Graham's rapidly unfolding drama of consciousness. She watches the river, "each handful of it closing over the next"; leaves are sucked into "the quick throes of another tentative / conclusion"; leaf-matter accrues "round a / pattern, a law"; and the river itself is "Spit forth, licked up, snapped where the force / exceeds the weight, clickings, pockets." *Clickings, pattern, conclusion, closing*: this is the vocabulary of oppression in *Region of Unlikeness*, but here Graham uses the same words to describe the unceasing river of consciousness. Flux is now imagined as a sequence of moments that, however conclusive in themselves, are immediately superseded: "each next right point, inter- / locking, correct, correct again, each rightness snapping loose." As if picking up where her sequence of self-portraits left off, Graham begins *Materialism* by discarding any sense of "roiling openness" that is not patterned, shaped, governed by law.

"What is inwardness?" asked Rainer Maria Rilke in one of his late poetic fragments: "What if not sky intensified, / flung through with birds and deep / with winds of homecoming?"[10] Graham's notion of selfhood throughout *Materialism* is similarly external; she dramatizes consciousness by focusing on the movement of the material world outside the self, ultimately suggesting that the self exists only inasmuch as it is composed of material phenomena. As Helen Vendler has pointed out, Graham can no longer compose self-portraits through mythological figures, as she did in *The End of Beauty*. Once the "instabilities of matter" are assumed by the self, it can no longer assert a "mastery over experience" through myth: the material self, Vendler continues, "is ultimately powerless over fate."[11] Not only has Graham given up the dream of openness, asserting that all experience is governed by patterns or laws; she also admits that the individual self has very little power to impose or disrupt those laws. In the second of the "Notes on the Reality of the Self," Graham makes this point by comparing the self to bushes that are affected in various ways by the evening light, the autumn wind, and the sounds of a marching band practicing in the field beyond the poet's yard. The band, "screeching, rolling, patterning, measuring," is a

> scintillant beast the bushes do not know exists
> as the wind beats them, beats in them, beats round them,
> them in a wind that does not really even now
> > exist,
> in which these knobby reddish limbs that do not sway
> > by so much as an inch
> its arctic course
> > themselves now sway—

Real only inasmuch as it is motion, the self is composed of a world of whose existence it is unaware: the self is swayed but cannot assert itself in return. Yet the sheer verbal mastery of "Notes on the Reality of the Self" belies the notion of a self completely lacking in agency; other poems in *Materialism* will grant greater power to consciousness. And though the poems must be read in dialogue with each other, it is crucial that we see Graham diminishing so severely her sense of her own power, especially since the poems of *Region of Unlikeness* risked the impression of hubris by correlating personal and historical narratives.

Because they also pull together wildly disparate materials, the most ambitious poems of *Materialism* ("Concerning the Right to Life," "The Dream of the Unified Field," "Manifest Destiny") may resemble the longer poems of *Region*. Their narratives do not match up analogically, however, but move steadily if inexplicably forward, linked by the arbitrary repetition of particular words. In "Concerning the Right to Life" the words *spot* and *red* reappear in otherwise unrelated sections of the poem; in "Manifest Destiny" the word *mark* accumulates a penumbra of different associations as it reappears in different contexts. "The Dream of the Unified Field" unfolds in an apparently more simple but ultimately more challenging way: although its six sections are similarly linked by the repetition of the words *white* (referring usually to snow) and *black* (referring to a leotard, starlings, a crow, and skin color), the poem unfolds with narrative ease, each section extending the story of the one before it: "On my way to bringing you the leotard / you forgot to include in your overnight bag, / the snow started coming down harder." This narrative action is not as tersely summarized as it is in

"Recovered from the Storm" or the various "Notes on the Reality of the Self," but it is equally crucial to our experience of the poem. After delivering her daughter's leotard, Graham watches a flock of starlings fly through the snow and settle on a tree (which looks like a head that alternately "explodes" and "recollects"), and then hears a single crow within the swarm of smaller birds ("a voice inside a head, filling a head"). At this point, Graham herself is gripped by the overwhelming sense of emptiness: in contrast to the "head" she imagines in the tree, the pocket that held the leotard (her daughter's "dream") is empty, and so is her own skull.

> See, my pocket is empty now. I let my hand
> open and shut in there. I do it again. Two now, skull and
> > pocket
> with their terrified inhabitants.

Hinging on this moment of crisis, "The Dream of the Unified Field" tells the story of how Graham arrived at the understanding of selfhood she more calmly describes throughout the sequence of "Notes on the Reality of the Self." Feeling that there is nothing inside her, she returns to the window to watch her daughter dancing in the leotard. The scene evokes a memory of the ballet class she took from Madame Sakaroff, a Russian refugee. Changing into her own leotard, she overheard Madame speaking with an unnamed visitor: *"No one must believe in God again."* Graham watched her teacher face herself in the mirror, approaching it until she touched her reflection, and Graham herself now approaches the window, watching her daughter dance, until she touches the glass. Speaking both to her daughter and to herself as a child, she asks, "what should I know / to save you that I do not know, hands on this windowpane?"

In response to the question, Graham undertakes the almost futile but necessary act of recomposing her self from the material world around her: "The storm: I close my eyes and, / standing in it, try to make it *mine*. An inside / thing." The poem breaks from its uncharacteristically placid narrative to one of Graham's most ecstatic flights of consciousness:

> wilderness brought deep into my clearing,
> out of the ooze of night,
> limbed, shouldered, necked, visaged, the white—
> now the clouds coming in (don't look up),
> now the Age behind the clouds, The Great Heights,
> all in there, reclining, eyes closed, huge,
> centuries and centuries long and wide,
> and underneath, barely attached but attached,

like a runner, my body, my tiny piece of
the century—minutes, houses going by—The Great
                                    Heights—
anchored by these footsteps, now and now,
the footstepping—now and now—carrying its vast
white sleeping geography—mapped—
not a lease—*possession*—

In the smallest sense, Graham is describing the act of writing the poem
we are now reading—the act of transforming a sequence of arbitrary
observations and associations (snowstorm, leotard, starlings, crow, ballet class) into a logical narrative. In the largest sense, Graham is attempting to achieve the "dream of the unified field," the dream that all
material phenomena might be described by a single paradigm. Graham's indomitable craving for closure reaches epic proportions in these
lines: pulling The Great Heights into the vacant space of the self, her
hunger has never been bigger.

But it is at exactly this moment that her fear of "unearned weight"
also becomes stronger than ever before. The hubris implied by her metaphors (*colony, new world, wilderness, mapped, possession*) is exposed by a
sudden and apparently unprecedented shift from the poem's narrative
to lines adapted from the diary of Columbus's first voyage to the New
World. Having begun with a domestic chore, ("On my way to bringing
you the leotard"), "The Dream of the Unified Field" ends with one of
the most primal narratives of Western culture.

                    After the cross was set up,
three sailors went into the bush (immediately erased
from sight by the fast snow) to see what kinds of
trees. They captured three very black Indian
women—one who was young and pretty.
The Admiral ordered her clothed and returned her to
                                    her land

courteously. There her people told
that she had not wanted to leave the ship,
but wished to stay on it. The snow was wild.
Inside it, though, you could see
this woman was wearing a little piece of
gold on her nose, which was a sign there was
                                    gold
on that land—

This passage is linked thematically (though tenuously so) to the rest
of the poem; it expresses Graham's fear of allowing her own life—her
own emptiness, her own ambition—to overwhelm her daughter's. But
in contrast to a poem like "From the New World," in which Graham
nearly conflates personal and historical narratives, "The Dream of the

Unified Field" compels us to feel the extraordinary distance the poem has travelled—to interrogate the means by which the poem achieves its leap between different registers of human experience. Because the narrative of "The Dream of the Unified Field" has so far been so apprehensible, we have not needed to pay much attention to Graham's repetitions of the words *black* and *white* in order to link the different sections of the poem. When the narrative falls away, that tissue of repetitions becomes crucial: the passage from Columbus's diary (*white* snow, *black* skin) is drawn into the poem, fulfilling Graham's dream of a "unified field" even as the passage implicitly criticizes the hubris of the dream.

Graham culls material from two entries from the diary, condensing and altering the language. Most dramatically, she adds the word *black* to describe the color of the Native American women; most implausibly, she adds the *white* snowstorm, a meteorological impossibility in the Caribbean.[12] I think Graham wants us to be startled by the utter implausibility of the snow. Although her poem ends in self-critique, a relinquishing of power, Graham cautions us through this blatantly illogical revision of Columbus's diary that she herself remains in control of the poem. If the hubris of the "dream of the unified field" needs to be checked, so does the idealism of the dream of relinquishing all control. As Graham herself has recognized, these complexities, these unresolved tensions, are the driving forces behind her poetry: she recently titled her selected volume—*The Dream of the Unified Field*—after what seems to me her most challenging and beautiful poem.

"What would we really know the meaning of?" asked Emerson: "The meal in the firkin; the milk in the pan; the ballad in the street; the news of the boat; the glance of the eye; the form and the gait of the body;— show me the ultimate reason of these matters; show me the sublime presence of the highest spiritual cause lurking, as always it does lurk, in these suburbs and extremities of nature."[13] Like Stevens before her, Graham makes poetry out of this question, struggling to find the most central knowledge in the most peripheral experience; like Stevens, she not only describes the struggle but makes us feel it in the movement of the poetry. In "The Dream of the Unified Field" the twin exigencies of the "big hunger" and "unearned weight" are made explicit by the poem's startling leap to Columbus, but their dialogue is implicit not only throughout the entire poem but throughout all of *Materialism*. In recent poems like "Recovered from the Storm" (which feels like a coda to "The Dream of the Unified Field"), Graham no longer needs to disempower herself so dramatically. Through the "vivid performance of the present"—delivering the leotard, picking up one fallen limb from the path—Graham discovers the highest spiritual causes in the suburbs.

When she said that American poets needed to recover the "big hunger" of the modernists, Graham did not specify which postmodern poets were responsible for domesticating modernist ambition. If only because so many poets have learned about the enabling virtues of modesty from Bishop, it would make sense if Graham had Bishop in mind; praising the early installments of *The Changing Light at Sandover*, Bishop cautioned (with ominous good humor) that the poem was "much too big" to write about on a "morning when I have to start cleaning house."[14] Graham herself has admitted that Bishop's music does not set her off as Stevens's or Berryman's does, and it's easy to imagine that Bishop would have found Graham's poetry far more unwieldy than Merrill's. But Graham has also emphasized that she feels a deep "temperamental affinity" with Bishop, an affinity that transcends stylistic decorum, and it's arguable that Graham, more than any other poet writing today, has realized Bishop's ideal notion of poetic movement: "not a thought, but a mind thinking" (the phrase Bishop borrowed from the critic Morris Croll). And while it's even easier to imagine that Bishop would have been bemused by the elaborate ambitions of the Language poets, Charles Bernstein has borrowed the same passage from Croll to underwrite his avant-garde project. As Bernstein describes it, his critique of "contemporary expository forms" involves the "attempt 'to portray not a thought, but a mind thinking.' "[15]

In part, this coincidence illustrates Robert Pinsky's belief that an enormous range of American poets are distinguished by a "fluidity of tone," an Emersonian blending of the cosmic and the domestic, the courtly and the vulgar, the ecstatic and the comic. The coincidence also suggests that style never tells the whole story of American poetry: poets who seem, because of their formal choices, to have little to do with one another may share the deepest goals or ambivalences. Remembering the early years of his career, when the academic and beat poets were standing off, John Hollander said that he "felt that there were guys on my team who weren't on my side, and there were guys on the other team who *were* on my side." Hollander is as formidable a stylist as Bernstein, a poet-critic who has invested a great deal of energy in the study of form; but he insists that "what makes a poet is not style alone, but something far deeper."[16] Although he continues to write in the elaborate forms he embraced as a young poet, Hollander insists that his poetry has changed radically—changed in ways that the "breakthrough" narrative, with its essentialized notions of poetic freedom, cannot describe.

If the narrative has been unaccommodating to poets like Hollander or Wilbur, whose styles have remained fairly consistent throughout their careers, it is even more deceptively unkind to poets like Ashbery or Graham, whose styles have changed dramatically. Graham's turn from the slender, controlled poems of *Erosion* to the apparently open-ended poems of *The End of Beauty* looks like one more occurrence of the "breakthrough" that several generations of twentieth-century poets have needed to embrace. But Graham's career is exemplary for different reasons. The poems of *Region of Unlikeness*, so different stylistically from those of *Erosion* and yet so similar in their thematizations of closure, confound the association of formal and ideological freedom. Like any poet writing at the peak of her powers, Graham is many different poets in one; within the parameters of her relatively brief career is a range of positions we all too easily condense into the false opposition of a poet like Wilbur and a poet like Ashbery. Consequently, a vision of American poetry that cannot encompass both Wilbur and Ashbery cannot encompass Jorie Graham alone. Neither can it do justice to Wilbur or to Ashbery. "There are no outsiders in these pages," says Graham in the introduction to her wide-ranging anthology of poetry in English, denying any poet the distinction of standing apart.[17] This is the kind of vision that will carry American poetry beyond postmodernism—whatever it will seem to have been—into the twenty-first century.

# NOTES

ONE  WHAT WAS POSTMODERN POETRY?

1. I adapt a sentence from Jarrell's "The End of the Line" (1942); see *Kipling, Auden & Co.* (New York, 1980), 78. Jarrell first used the word "post-modernist" in his 1947 review of Robert Lowell's *Lord Weary's Castle*; see *Poetry and the Age* (New York, 1953), 216. The first use of the word in a literary context was probably by Federico de Onis in 1934 ("postmodernismo"); other early uses include those by John Crowe Ransom (1941), Dudley Fitts (1942), Charles Olson (1952), and Irving Howe (1959): for a survey of these early and contradictory uses, see Margaret A. Rose, *The Post-modern and the Post-industrial: A Critical Analysis* (New York, 1991).

I use the word *postmodern* to describe any poetry that sees itself self-consciously as coming after modernism—not to refer to any particular style, ideology, or group of writers that is commonly thought of as postmodern. Even conceived this widely, however, the terms of my discussion will not necessarily account for postmodern architecture, film, or critical theory: the most even-handed discussions of postmodernism are sometimes inhibited by a desire to account for many different aspects of culture with a single theoretical paradigm. In *A Poetics of Postmodernism* (New York, 1988), Linda Hutcheon builds her argument from the highly oppositional polemics associated with modern and postmodern architecture; this strategy skews an account of postmodern literature. Although Fredric Jameson points out in his magisterial *Postmodernism, or, The Cultural Logic of Late Capitalism* (Durham, 1991) that critical formulations are often "too rigidly specified and marked by their area of provenance" (xiii), he nonetheless admits that it was "from architectural debates that my own conception of postmodernism . . . initially began to emerge" (2). As Terry Eagleton points out in *The Illusions of Postmodernism* (Cambridge, 1996), "it is difficult to see how any single explanatory scheme could do justice to such a bizarrely heterogeneous entity" (21).

2. Laura Riding and Robert Graves, *A Survey of Modernist Poetry* (New York, 1928), 258. On the relationship of literary and theological modernism, see James Longenbach, *Modernist Poetics of History* (Princeton, 1987), 263–64.

3. Jarrell, *Kipling, Auden & Co.*, 81.

4. See Marjorie Perloff, *The Poetics of Indeterminacy: Rimbaud to Cage* (Princeton, 1981), 251. In "Postmodern Poetics Unfair to Modernist Poetry," in *Painterly Abstraction in Modernist American Poetry* (New York, 1989), 380–85, Charles Altieri discusses the strategic use of oversimplified or old-fashioned ideas of modernism, as does Ronald Bush in "T. S. Eliot and Modernism at the Present Time: A Provocation," in *T. S. Eliot: The Modernist in History*, ed. Ronald Bush (New York, 1991), 191–204.

5. Lowell, *Collected Prose*, ed. Robert Giroux (New York, 1987), 244.

6. Jean Garrigue, "A Mountain on the Landscape," *The New Leader* 7 December 1964: 33. See Irvin Ehrenpreis, "The Age of Lowell," in *Robert Lowell: A Collection of Critical Essays*, ed. Thomas Parkinson (Englewood Cliffs, 1968), 74–98.

7. Berryman, *The Freedom of the Poet* (New York, 1976), 327; David McClelland, "An Interview with John Berryman," *Harvard Advocate* 113 (1969): 5.

8. James E. B. Breslin, *From Modern to Contemporary* (Chicago, 1984), xv. David Perkins also relies on the "breakthrough" narrative in his discussion of postmodern poetry in *A History of Modern Poetry: Modernism and After* (Cambridge, Mass., 1987), as does Walter Kaladjian in *Languages of Liberation: The Social Text in American Poetry* (New York, 1989). Jerome Mazzaro's investment in the narrative is more explicit in *Postmodern American Poetry* (Urbana, 1980), viii: "Rather than T. S. Eliot's belief that poetry 'is not the expression of personality, but an escape from personality,' postmodernists propose the opposite." See also the chapter called "Breakthrough" in Paul Mariani, *Lost Puritan: A Life of Robert Lowell* (New York, 1994), 242–61.

Langdon Hammer offers an excellent critique of Lowell's "break-though" (and James Breslin's version of it) in *Hart Crane and Allen Tate: Janus-Faced Modernism* (Princeton, 1993), 211–32. More deeply suspicious of Lowell is Paul Breslin in *The Psycho-Political Muse: American Poetry since the Fifties* (Chicago, 1987), 59–74. Stephen Cushman usefully places Lowell's "breakthrough" in the larger context of nineteenth- and twentieth-century debates about poetic form in *Fictions of Form in American Poetry* (Princeton, 1993), 3–24. See also Gerald Graff, "The Myth of the Postmodern Breakthrough," in *Literature Against Itself* (Chicago, 1979), 31–62.

9. Kate Daniels, "Interview with Galway Kinnell," in *Poetry and Politics*, ed. Richard Jones (New York, 1985), 297; Frederick Feirstein with Frederick Turner, "Introduction," in *Expansive Poetry: Essays on the New Narrative and the New Formalism*, ed. Frederick Feirstein (Santa Cruz, 1989), xi.

10. Vernon Shetley, *After the Death of Poetry: Poet and Audience in Contemporary America* (Durham, 1993), 16–17.

11. *The Waste Land: A Facsimile and Transcript of the Original Drafts*, ed. Valerie Eliot (New York, 1971), 1. Studies of Eliot that have made this remark meaningful include Lyndall Gordon, *Eliot's Early Years* (New York, 1977) and Ronald Bush, *T. S. Eliot: A Study in Character and Style* (New York, 1984).

12. Alan Filreis, ed., "Voicing the Desert of Silence: Stevens' letters to Alice Corbin Henderson," *Wallace Stevens Journal* 12 (1988): 19.

13. Jarrell, *The Third Book of Criticism* (New York, 1965), 314–15. On Jarrell's plans for a book on Eliot see William Pritchard, *Randall Jarrell: A Literary Life* (New York, 1990), 285.

14. Berryman, "A Peine ma Piste," *Partisan Review* 15 (1948): 826, 828.

15. Joseph M. Conte, *Unending Design: The Forms of Postmodern Poetry* (Ithaca, 1991), 14. Jerome McGann's argument about Language poetry in "Contemporary Poetry, Alternate Routes" presupposes a similarly ahistorical sense of poetic form's relationship to political position; see *Politics and Poetic Value*, ed. Robert von Hallberg (Chicago, 1987), 267: "Narrativity is . . . an inherently conservative feature of discourse." So does Perloff's *Radical Artifice: Writing in the Age of Media* (Chicago, 1991): she rightly criticizes the notion that free verse is a more "natural" or "authentic" mode of poetic discourse, but nonetheless maintains that a postmodern effort to highlight poetry's artificiality necessarily entails the rejection of traditional meters and forms (see 134–39). Just because the heroic couplet bears a "relationship to other phenomena in early eighteenth-century English culture" (136), it does not follow that the couplet is doomed to bear that same relationship in other historical moments.

Shetley points out in "The Return of the Repressed: Language Poetry and New Formalism" (*After the Death of Poetry*, 135–64) that recent New Formalist condemnations of free verse are often as ahistorical as avant-garde condemnations of traditional form. See also Alan Shapiro's subtle discussion of the "connection between political allegiance and aesthetic choice" in "The New Formalism," in *In Praise of the Impure* (Evanston, 1993), 74. As Mutlu Konuk Blasing has argued in *Politics and Form in Postmodern Poetry* (New York, 1995), a static sense of form's social function cannot "account for the fact that, in the postmodern period, closure (metaphysical, moral, or political) can occur within open forms, which have become only one more 'tradition,' and openness is possible within conventional, closed forms" (159). I would only add that, from my point of view, this is true in the "modern" as well as the "postmodern" period.

16. "Richard Wilbur: An Interview by Steve Kronen," *American Poetry Review* 20 (May 1991): 45. On Ashbery's religious background see "John Ashbery: An Interview by Ross Labrie," *American Poetry Review* 13 (May 1984): 29.

17. Jürgen Habermas, "Modernity—An Incomplete Project," in *The Anti-Aesthetic: Essays on Postmodern Culture*, ed. Hal Foster (Port Townsend, Washington, 1983), 11. See also John McGowan's discussion of Habermas and Jean-François Lyotard in *Postmodernism and Its Critics* (Ithaca, 1991), 180–210.

18. See Fredric Jameson, "Postmodernism and Consumer Society," in *The Anti-Aesthetic: Essays on Postmodern Culture*, ed. Hal Foster (Port Townsend, Washington, 1983), 112–13. Jameson says here that postmodernism is not just "another word for the description of a particular style" but also "a periodizing concept whose function is to correlate the emergence of new formal features in culture with the emergence of a new type of social life and a new economic order." This act of correlation becomes more complex once very different styles of poetry (not one particular style) are recognized as legitimately postmodern. In his more recent version of this essay ("The Cultural Logic of Late Capitalism"), Jameson explicitly rejects the notion of postmodernism as a "style," preferring to think of it as a "cultural dominant," a concept that "allows for the presence and coexistence of a range of very different, yet subordinate, features" (*Postmodernism*, 4). But his earlier examples of the particular style (Ashbery, Cage, Godard, Warhol, punk rock) continue to represent postmodernism throughout his work.

19. Lowell to Williams, 3 December 1957 (Beinecke Library, Yale University), in Mariani, *Lost Puritan*, 259.

20. William Meredith, *Poems Are Hard to Read* (Ann Arbor, 1991), 171. Thomas Travisano employs the logic of the "breakthrough" to describe Bishop's career in *Elizabeth Bishop: Her Artistic Development* (Charlottesville, 1988).

21. Jeffrey Meyers, ed., *Robert Lowell: Interviews and Memoirs* (Ann Arbor, 1988), 86. For a version of the Lowell "breakthrough" narrative that emphasizes Williams and slights Bishop, see Steven Gould Axelrod, *Robert Lowell: Life and Art* (Princeton, 1978).

22. Jameson, *Postmodernism*, 4, 302, 303; see also 65–66 and "Postmodernism and Consumer Society," 112, 123. Susan Suleiman has offered a compelling critique of the dualistic tendencies (modernism versus postmodernism) in Jameson's "Postmodernism and Consumer Society" and in work by Leslie Fiedler, Gerald Graff, Ihab Hassan, David Lodge, and William Spanos: see her "Naming and Difference: Reflections on 'Modernism versus Postmodernism,'" in *Approaching Postmodernism*, ed. Douwe Fokkema and Hans Bertens (Philadelphia, 1986), 255–70. See also her *Subversive Intent: Gender, Politics, and the Avant-Garde* (Cambridge, 1990), 183–91. Hutcheon surveys the variety of postmodern stances toward modernism in *The Poetics of Postmodernism*, 48–53, as does Jameson himself in *Postmodernism*, 55–66.

23. Stevens, *Opus Posthumous*, ed. Milton Bates (New York, 1989), 213.

24. Moore to Stevens, 11 July 1935 (Huntington Library).

25. Jarrell, *Kipling, Auden & Co.*, 48, 81.

26. Jarrell, *Kipling, Auden & Co.*, 36.

27. Jarrell, *Kipling, Auden & Co.*, 51.

28. John Crowe Ransom, "Constellation of Five Young Poets," *Kenyon Review* 3 (1941): 378.

29. Jarrell, *Poetry and the Age*, 216.

30. Berryman, *The Freedom of the Poet*, 297.

31. Jarrell, *Poetry and the Age*, 216.

32. Lowell to Williams, 3 December 1957 (Beinecke Library, Yale University), in Mariani, *Lost Puritan*, 259.

33. Lowell, *Collected Prose*, 38.

34. Pound, "Harold Monro," *Criterion* 9 (1932): 590.

35. Eliot, "Reflections on Contemporary Poetry [IV]," *Egoist* 4 (1919): 39. See *The Letters of Hart Crane*, ed. Brom Weber (Berkeley, 1965), 90–91. For matters of chronology I am indebted to Edward Brunner, *Splendid Failure: Hart Crane and the Making of "The Bridge"* (Urbana, 1985). For a more detailed version of my argument, see "Hart Crane and T. S. Eliot: Poets in the Sacred Grove," *Denver Quarterly* 23 (1988): 82–103.

36. Hammer, *Hart Crane and Allen Tate*, 230.

37. Lowell, *Collected Prose*, 244. In *Five Temperaments* (New York, 1977), David Kalstone rightly maintains that *"Life Studies* presents only one aspect of a career which has changed directions several times and whose appetites are complicated and contradictory" (43–44). Describing Lowell's "seesaw" development, Stephen Yenser suggests that after *Life Studies*, in which "form itself seems almost to be viewed as a deity . . . that needs to be challenged," the poetry was in danger of losing "its identity" as poetry. Lowell's subsequent return to formal verse in *Near the Ocean* suggests that he needed to reassert "the integrity of poetry" (*Circle to Circle: The Poetry of Robert Lowell* [Berkeley, 1975], 5, 8).

38. Robert Hass, *Twentieth Century Pleasures* (New York, 1984), 8. Richard Tillinghast's recent attempt to rehabilitate Lowell's reputation

fails because he continues to judge Lowell according to the values of the "age of Lowell"; see *Robert Lowell's Life and Death: Damaged Grandeur* (Ann Arbor, 1995). More helpful (since it avoids the now dated sense of the "breakthrough") is Helen Vendler's discussion of Lowell's stylistic development in *The Given and the Made* (Cambridge, 1995), 1–28.

39. Bishop, *One Art: Letters*, ed. Robert Giroux (New York, 1994), 562.

40. Jarrell, *Poetry and the Age*, 213, 235.

41. Lowell to Bishop, 3 December 1957 (Special Collections, Vassar College Library), in Travisano, *Elizabeth Bishop*, 153.

42. Meyers, ed., *Robert Lowell*, 77

43. Seamus Heaney, *The Government of the Tongue* (London, 1988), 141, 146. See also Christopher Ricks's discussion of Lowell's "attempt to create a positive non-violence" in the "more gentle forms and words" of *Day by Day* (*The Force of Poetry* [New York, 1984], 272).

44. Lowell to Jarrell, 7 November 1961 (Berg Collection, New York Public Library), in Ian Hamilton, *Robert Lowell: A Biography* (New York, 1982), 296.

45. *The Letters of John Keats*, 2 vols., ed. H. E. Rollins (Cambridge, 1958), 2: 213.

46. Berryman, *Freedom of the Poet*, 286.

47. Theodore Weiss, *The Man from Porlock* (Princeton, 1982), 135.

TWO  ELIZABETH BISHOP'S BRAMBLE BUSHES

Quotations from Bishop's poetry are from *The Complete Poems: 1927–1979* (New York, 1983).

1. "T. S. Eliot Reads and Comments on His Poetry," *Vassar Miscellany News* 10 May 1933: 4. Bishop remembered interviewing Eliot in Ashley Brown, "An Interview with Elizabeth Bishop," in *Elizabeth Bishop and Her Art*, ed. Lloyd Schwartz and Sybil P. Estess (Ann Arbor, 1983), 293. William Logan, in "The Unbearable Lightness of Elizabeth Bishop," *Southwest Review* 79 (1994), has suggested provocatively that Eliot "was the author of much of Bishop's imaginative circumstance, and his influence was more deeply absorbed and is therefore more difficult to trace than an influence on style like Moore or an alter ego and negative example like Lowell" (132). On Bishop's first meeting with Moore, see Bishop's own memoir, "Efforts of Affection: A Memoir of Marianne Moore," in *Collected Prose*, ed. Robert Giroux (New York, 1984), 121–56. See also David Kalstone, *Becoming a Poet: Elizabeth Bishop with Marianne Moore and Robert Lowell* (New York, 1989), *passim*; Bonnie Costello, "Marianne Moore and Elizabeth Bishop: Friendship and Influence," *Twentieth Century Literature* 30 (1984): 130–49; Betsy Erkkila, *The Wicked Sisters: Women Poets, Literary History, and Discord* (New York, 1992), 99–151; and Lynn Keller, *Re-making It New: Contemporary American Poetry and the Modernist Tradition* (New York, 1987), 79–136.

2. Gary Fountain and Peter Brazeau, *Remembering Elizabeth Bishop: An Oral Biography* (Amherst, 1994), 153.

3. Eliot, *The Sacred Wood* (New York, 1960), 50. Among Eliot's more recent critics, see especially Louis Menand, *Discovering Modernism: T. S. Eliot and His Context* (New York, 1987).

4. Bishop, "Dimensions for a Novel," *Vassar Journal of Undergraduate Studies* 8 (1934): 97, 100, 99. This essay grows out of an earlier one in which Stein and Richardson are discussed at length: "Time's Andromedas," *Vassar Journal of Undergraduate Studies* 7 (1933): 102–20.

5. Bishop, "Seven-Days Monologue," *Con Spirito* 1 (1933): 4.

6. Bishop made this comment as a junior in high school in a review of Edna St. Vincent Millay's *The Buck in the Snow*, in *The Blue Pencil* 12 (December 1928): 30.

7. *The Letters of Gerard Manley Hopkins to Robert Bridges*, ed. C. C. Abbott (London, 1935), 46; see Kalstone, *Becoming a Poet*, 36–39.

8. Bishop, "Gerard Manley Hopkins: Notes on Timing in His Poetry," *Vassar Review* 23 (1934): 6–7.

9. Morris W. Croll, "The Baroque Style in Prose," in *Studies in English Philology in Honor of Frederick Klaeber*, ed. Kemp Malone and Martin Ruud (Minneapolis, 1929), 430. Bishop also quotes from this essay in a 1933 letter: see *One Art: Letters*, ed. Robert Giroux (New York, 1994), 12.

10. Jarrell, *Kipling, Auden & Co.* (New York, 1980), 127–28.

11. Moore to Bishop, 1 March 1937 (Special Collections, Vassar College Library), in Kalstone, *Becoming a Poet*, 77.


THREE   ELIZABETH BISHOP'S SOCIAL CONSCIENCE

Quotations from Bishop's poetry are from *The Complete Poems: 1927–1979* (New York, 1983).

1. Rich, *Blood, Bread, and Poetry: Selected Prose 1979–1985* (New York, 1986), 124, 125.

2. Lowell, *Collected Prose*, ed. Robert Giroux (New York, 1987), 78.

3. George Starbuck, " 'The Work!': A Conversation with Elizabeth Bishop," in *Elizabeth Bishop and Her Art*, ed. Lloyd Schwartz and Sybil P. Estess (Ann Arbor, 1983), 324, 321. Elsewhere Bishop dated her feminism from the age of six; see Brett C. Millier, *Elizabeth Bishop: Life and the Memory of It* (Berkeley, 1993), 23.

4. Ashley Brown, "An Interview with Elizabeth Bishop," in *Elizabeth Bishop and Her Art*, ed. Schwartz and Estess, 294. "Suicide of a Moderate Dictator" has been published in the *Georgia Review* 46 (1992): 611; in Lorrie Goldensohn, *Elizabeth Bishop: A Biography of a Poetry* (New York, 1992), 237; and in Victoria Harrison, *Elizabeth Bishop's Poetics of Intimacy* (New York, 1993), 166.

5. See Millier, *Elizabeth Bishop*, 138.

6. Rich, *Blood, Bread, and Poetry*, 130–31. This statement is a modification of Rich's earlier view that Bishop simply "kept sexuality at a measured and chiseled distance in her poems" (*On Lies, Secrets, and Silence* [New York, 1979], 36). Margaret Dickie responds to Rich's ar-

gument by pointing out that Bishop's poems "about mistress and servant, landowner and tenant, white woman and black woman, are really about the intimacy of such contacts across race and class boundaries" ("Race and Class in Elizabeth Bishop's Poetry," *Yearbook of English Studies* 24 [1994]: 45). See also Betsy Erkkila, "Elizabeth Bishop, Modernism, and the Left," *American Literary History* 8 (1996): 284–310.

7. Brown, "An Interview with Elizabeth Bishop," 293–94.

8. Mary McCarthy, *On the Contrary* (New York, 1961), 199. See also McCarthy's recollections of Bishop at Vassar in Gary Fountain and Peter Brazeau, *Remembering Elizabeth Bishop: An Oral Biography* (Amherst, 1994): "I was very, very much to the right. . . . Discussions with her sort of opened my eyes to the socialist argument." Because Bishop's political positions were not typical, she could seem to another Vassar classmate to be "wildly unpolitical in a completely political time" (48). Yet another classmate recalled provocatively that it "was a strength, really, that all the people [Bishop] played with were politically oriented, and she never *seemed* to be" (48; my emphasis).

9. Brown, "An Interview with Elizabeth Bishop," 293.

10. Granville Hicks, "The Crisis in American Criticism," *New Masses* 8 (February 1933): 5; William Phillips and Philip Rahv, "Editorial Statement," *Partisan Review* 1 (1934): 2.

11. I quote from the slightly expanded version of "Then Came the Poor" that appeared in *The Magazine* 1 (1934): 105–10; an earlier version appeared in *Con Spirito* 1 (1933): 2–4.

12. Bishop, *One Art: Letters*, ed. Robert Giroux (New York, 1994), 55–56, 73, 48.

13. Bishop, *One Art: Letters*, 48. See Barbara Page, "Off-Beat Claves, Oblique Realities: The Key West Notebooks of Elizabeth Bishop," in *Elizabeth Bishop: The Geography of Gender*, ed. Marilyn May Lombardi (Charlottesville, 1993), 202.

14. Brown, "An Interview with Elizabeth Bishop," 297.

15. Bishop, *One Art: Letters*, 96. On gender and World War II, see Susan Hartman, *The Home Front and Beyond: American Women in the 1940s* (Boston, 1982) and Susan Gubar, " 'This Is My Rifle, This Is My Gun': World War II and the Blitz on Women," in *Behind the Lines: Gender and the Two World Wars*, ed. Margaret Randolph Higonet et al. (New Haven, 1987), 227–59. My reading of "Roosters" responds more specifically to Alicia Ostriker, *Stealing the Language: The Emergence of Women's Poetry in America* (Boston, 1986), 54 and Susan Schweik, *A Gulf So Deeply Cut: American Women Poets and the Second World War* (Madison, 1991), 213–41.

16. An unpublished poem linked to "Faustina," "Vague Poem (Vaguely Love Poem)," offers a clearer glimpse of the ideal same-sex relationship that the terms of class and race dominate in both "Cootchie" and "Faustina"; it has been published in Bonnie Costello, *Elizabeth Bishop: Questions of Mastery* (Cambridge, 1991), 73; in Golden-

sohn, *Elizabeth Bishop*, 71–72; in Harrison, *Elizabeth Bishop's Poetics*, 204; and in Millier, *Elizabeth Bishop*, 437. Like Rich, Goldensohn laments the fact that Bishop's published work (in contrast to "Vague Poem") often "projects the problems of trust within love and intimacy onto the more remote arena of the world of servants" (75). This is true in the sense that Bishop could publish more comfortably her poems testing the boundaries of race and class than those challenging the terms of gender and sexuality; but when those terms are present in Bishop's published work (even subtly, as in "Faustina") they are not isolated from those of race or class. In "The New Elizabeth Bishop" (*Yale Review* 82 [1994]: 135–49), Langdon Hammer offers a subtle critique of the way in which many of Bishop's admirers demand autobiographical explicitness from her poems.

17. Bishop and the Editors of Life, *Brazil* (New York, 1962), 114.

18. Bishop, *Brazil*, 114, 116.

19. Barbara Page, "Nature, History, and Art in Elizabeth Bishop's 'Brazil, January 1, 1502,'" *Perspectives on Contemporary Literature* 14 (1988): 42. Page is responding to David Bromwich's reading of the poem in "Elizabeth Bishop's Dream-Houses," *Raritan* 4 (1984): 77–94.

20. Costello, *Elizabeth Bishop*, 119. Lee Edelman offers the most comprehensive account of these important ambiguities in "The Geography of Gender: Elizabeth Bishop's 'In the Waiting Room,'" *Contemporary Literature* 26 (1985): 179–96.

21. Lowell, *Collected Prose*, 287.

22. Rich, *On Lies, Secrets, and Silence*, 40–41. Rich has subsequently softened this position, maintaining that poetic form as such is not necessarily the problem; see *What Is Found There: Notebooks on Poetry and Politics* (New York, 1993), 219: "It's a struggle not to let the form take over, lapse into format."

23. Rich, *The Fact of a Doorframe: Poems Selected and New, 1950–1984* (New York, 1984), 151. In *Woman Writers and Poetic Identity* (Princeton, 1980), 222–36, Margaret Homans shows how Rich both endorses and undermines "a poetics of literal truth" (223). For an analysis of the rhetorical self-consciousness of all of Rich's poetry, early and late, see Willard Spiegelman, *The Didactic Muse: Scenes of Instruction in Contemporary American Poetry* (Princeton, 1989), 147–91.

24. Bishop, "On the Railroad Named Delight," *New York Times Magazine* 7 March 1965:86. Millier describes the attack on this article in *Elizabeth Bishop*, 362–65.

FOUR   RANDALL JARRELL'S SEMIFEMININE MIND

Quotations from Jarrell's poems are from *The Complete Poems* (New York, 1969).

1. *Randall Jarrell, 1914–1965*, ed. Robert Lowell et al. (New York, 1967), 15, 102.

2. *Randall Jarrell, 1914-1965*, 71.

3. Jarrell, *Letters*, ed. Mary Jarrell (Boston, 1985), 399.

4. Bishop to Lowell, 20 March 1973, in David Kalstone, *Becoming a Poet: Elizabeth Bishop with Marianne Moore and Robert Lowell* (New York, 1989), 226.

5. Christopher Benfy, "The Woman in the Mirror: John Berryman and Randall Jarrell," in *Recovering Berryman*, ed. Richard Kelly and Alan Lathrop (Ann Arbor, 1993), 160.

6. Bishop to Lowell, 20 March 1973, in Kalstone, *Becoming a Poet*, 226.

7. Langdon Hammer, "Who Was Randall Jarrell?" *Yale Review* 79 (1990): 403. See also Wendy Lesser, "Through the Looking-Glass," *Threepenny Review* (Spring 1984), 10: "if these contradictions are to blame for what is disturbing about Jarrell, they are also responsible for what is powerful and compelling in him." Lesser is responding to James Dickey's conflicted account of Jarrell in *Babel to Byzantium* (New York, 1981), 13–25.

8. Jarrell, *Letters*, 420. Mary Kinzie shows the similarity of Bishop's and Jarrell's styles in *The Cure of Poetry in an Age of Prose* (Chicago, 1993), 93-94.

9. Jarrell, *Letters*, 4.

10. Jarrell, *Kipling, Auden & Co.* (New York, 1980), 58, 48.

11. Jarrell, *Letters*, 153.

12. Jarrell, *Poetry and the Age* (New York, 1953),108.

13. Jarrell, *Letters*, 133, 117.

14. Helen Vendler, "The Inconsolable," *New Republic* 23 July 1990: 34.

15. Jarrell, *Letters*, 19.

16. Jarrell, *Letters*, 30.

17. William Pritchard, *Randall Jarrell: A Literary Life* (New York, 1990), 80; Jarrell, *Letters*, 38.

18. Mary Jarrell, "Ideas and Poems," *Parnassus* 5 (1976): 218–19. Richard Flynn discusses Jarrell's fascination with childhood in *Randall Jarrell and the Lost World of Childhood* (Athens, 1990).

19. Jarrell, *Poetry and the Age*, 98; *Letters*, 26.

20. Jarrell, *Kipling, Auden & Co.*, 80.

21. Jarrell, *Letters*, 131.

22. See Bruce Michaelson, "Randall Jarrell and Robert Lowell: The Making of *Lord Weary's Castle*," *Contemporary Literature* 26 (1985): 402–25.

23. Seamus Heaney, *The Government of the Tongue* (London, 1988), 141.

24. Jarrell, *Poetry and the Age*, 259. In fact, as Ian Hamilton has shown, Lowell constructed his heroine quite explicitly from Jean Stafford's letters, much as he would adapt Elizabeth Hardwick's letters in *The Dolphin*. See *Robert Lowell: A Biography* (New York, 1982), 178–86.

25. Jarrell, *Poetry and the Age*, 234–35.

26. Jarrell, *Letters*, 422.

27. Jarrell, "Levels and Opposites: Structure in Poetry," *Georgia Review* 50 (1996): 697. This lecture was recently discovered by Thomas Travisano.

28. Jarrell, *Letters*, 420.

29. Lowell, *Collected Prose*, ed. Robert Giroux (New York, 1987), 89.

30. Jarrell, *Poetry and the Age*, 258.

31. Suzanne Ferguson explicates the many allusions in "Night before the Night" in *The Poetry of Randall Jarrell* (Baton Rouge, 1971), 143-48.

32. Jarrell, *Letters*, 217.

33. Lowell, *Collected Prose*, 89.

34. Bishop, *One Art: Letters*, ed. Robert Giroux (New York, 1994), 319, 432.

35. Hammer, "Who Was Randall Jarrell?" 402.

36. Mary Jarrell, "Ideas and Poems," 229; Jarrell, *Letters*, 191.

37. The review is reprinted in Jarrell's *Letters*, 509.

38. Judith Butler, *Gender Trouble: Feminism and the Subversion of Identity* (New York, 1990), 137.

## FIVE  RICHARD WILBUR'S SMALL WORLD

Unless noted otherwise, quotations from Wilbur's poetry are from *New and Collected Poems* (New York, 1988).

1. Wilbur, "Seven Poets," *Sewanee Review* 88 (1950): 141.

2. Jarrell, *Letters*, ed. Mary Jarrell (Boston, 1985), 413.

3. Robert Bly, "the first ten issues of kayak," *kayak* 12 (1967): 47.

4. Wendy Salinger, ed., *Richard Wilbur's Creation* (Ann Arbor, 1983), 130.

5. Wilbur, "A Postcard for Bob Bly," *kayak* 13 (1968): 15.

6. Cited in Ted Solotaroff, "Captain Bly," *Nation* 9 September 1991: 270–71. On Wilbur's Harvard years see Peter Davison, *The Fading Smile: Poets in Boston, from Robert Frost to Robert Lowell to Sylvia Plath, 1955–1960* (New York, 1994).

7. Louise Bogan, "The Pleasures of Formal Poetry," *Quarterly Review of Literature* 7 (1953): 176. The conference itself took place in 1948.

8. Wilbur, "The Bottles Become New, Too," *Quarterly Review of Literature* 7 (1953): 190, 187, 188. This essay is reprinted in Wilbur's *Responses* (New York, 1976), 215–23.

9. Nathan A. Scott, Jr., *Visions of Presence in Modern American Poetry* (Baltimore, 1993), 194.

10. See Bruce Michaelson, *Wilbur's Poetry: Music in a Scattering Time* (Amherst, 1991), 40.

11. Helen Gardner, *The Composition of Four Quartets* (London, 1978), 67.

12. William Butts, ed. *Conversations with Richard Wilbur* (Jackson,

Mississippi, 1990), 43. In *American Poetry and Culture, 1945–1980* (Cambridge, 1985), Robert von Hallberg points out that the notion of "protest" poetry limited the scope of political poetry during the 1960s (see 117ff).

13. Along with two others, this poem appeared in *Touchstone* 4 (December 1938): 9. I am deeply grateful to John Lancaster, Curator of Special Collections at the Amherst College Library, for helping me to locate Wilbur's early writings.

14. Wilbur, "The Debate Continues," *Amherst Student* 6 April 1939: 2.

15. Wilbur, "Strange Setting for Intolerance," *Amherst Student* 7 March 1940: 2.

16. Butts, *Conversations*, 117.

17. Wilbur, "Fight, Fight, Fight," *Amherst Student* 2 May 1940: 2; "Consequences of the War to Public Morals," *Amherst Student* 16 December 1940: 2; "For the Record," *Amherst Student* 22 May 1941: 2; "Reply to the Editor of the *Williams Record*," *Amherst Student* 10 November 1941: 2.

18. James E. B. Breslin, *From Modern to Contemporary* (Chicago, 1984), 25.

19. Wilbur, "Short Laments for Some Poets," *Amherst Student* 25 September 1941: 2; "Now that We Are in It," *Amherst Student* 8 December 1941: 1; "Decency, Honesty, Guts," *Amherst Student* 15 December 1941: 2.

20. Wilbur, *Responses*, 118.

21. Wilbur, "Italy: Maine," *Saturday Evening Post* 23 September 1944: 37.

22. Wilbur, "The Mock Turtle," *Amherst Student* 13 May 1940: 2.

23. Wilbur, "Robert Graves' New Volume," *Poetry* 87 (1955): 176–77.

24. James Dickey, *Babel to Byzantium* (New York, 1981), 172.

25. Wilbur, "The Day After the War," *Foreground* 1 (Spring–Summer 1946): 112.

26. Wilbur, "The Genie in the Bottle," in *Mid-Century American Poets*, ed. John Ciardi (New York, 1950), 6.

27. Betsy Erkkila, *The Wicked Sisters: Women Poets, Literary History, and Discord* (New York, 1992), 125. See also David Bromwich, " 'That Weapon, Self-Protectiveness,' " in *Marianne Moore: The Art of a Modernist*, ed. Joseph Parisi (Ann Arbor, 1990), 67–80.

28. See *A Critical Supplement to Poetry*, ed. John Frederick Nims (December 1948): 2–7.

29. Wilbur, "We," *Poetry* 73 (1948): 127–28.

30. Wilbur, *Responses*, 101. In "On Richard Wilbur," *Southern Review* 9 (1973): 626, William Heyen deftly points out that Wilbur's style (in contrast to Lowell's) has not changed much simply because it has not needed to.

31. Wilbur, "Poetry and the Landscape," in *The New Landscape in Art*

*and Science*, ed. Gyorgy Kepes (Chicago, 1956), 89, 90. See also Peter Sacks's discussion of this issue in "Richard Wilbur," in *American Writers: A Collection of Literary Biographies*, suppl. 3, part 2, ed. Lea Baechler and A. Walton Litz (New York, 1991), 541-65.

32. Wilbur, *Responses*, 218, 220.

33. Frost, *Collected Poems, Prose, and Plays*, ed. Richard Poirier and Mark Richardson (New York, 1995), 739.

34. Wilbur, *Responses*, 107.

35. Wilbur, "Between Visits," *Poetry* 74 (1949): 116.

36. Butts, *Conversations*, 49.

37. Wilbur, "Robert Graves' New Volume," 175.

38. Wilbur, *Responses*, 122, 123.

## SIX JOHN ASHBERY'S INDIVIDUAL TALENT

Quotations from Ashbery's poems are from *Some Trees* (New Haven, 1956); *The Tennis Court Oath* (Middletown, 1962); *Rivers and Mountains* (New York, 1966); *The Double Dream of Spring* (New York, 1970); *Three Poems* (New York, 1972); *Self-Portrait in a Convex Mirror* (New York, 1975); *Houseboat Days* (New York, 1977); *Flow Chart* (New York, 1991); *Can You Hear, Bird* (New York, 1995).

1. Ashbery, *Reported Sightings: Art Chronicles, 1957–1987*, ed. David Bergman (New York, 1989), 99.

2. Ashbery, "Frank O'Hara's Question," *Book Week* 25 September 1966: 6.

3. Louis Simpson, "Dead Horses and Live Issues," *Nation* 24 April 1967: 521. Five years prior to this exchange, Ashbery criticized Simpson for his superficial sense of what it would mean to move beyond Eliot in American poetry: see "Reverdy en Amérique," *Mercure de France* 344 (January 1962): 110.

4. Ashbery submitted his letter twice, since the *Nation* first published a cut version of it: see the *Nation* 8 and 29 May 1967: 578, 674, 692. Ashbery has continued to maintain this position throughout his career: see Piotr Sommer, "An Interview in Warsaw," in *Code of Signals*, ed. Michael Palmer (Berkeley, 1983), 307–308. See also Mutlu Konuk Blasing's discussion of O'Hara's similar position in *Politics and Form in Postmodern Poetry* (New York, 1995), 40–41.

5. Ashbery, "A Game With Shifting Mirrors," *New York Times Book Review* 16 April 1967: 4.

6. Marjorie Perloff, "Ashbery," in *Contemporary Poets*, 5th ed. (Chicago, 1991), 25; " 'Transparent Selves': The Poetry of John Ashbery and Frank O'Hara," *Yearbook of English Studies* 8 (1978): 183. These comments depend on a strategically weak reading of modernism, as does Jonathan Monroe's "Idiom and Cliché in T. S. Eliot and John Ashbery," *Contemporary Literature* 31 (1990): 17–36. In "Reverdy en Amérique" Ashbery did explain that in 1962 most American poetry languished in

the shadow of a tamed version of Eliot (110). But in his undergraduate thesis, written at Harvard several years after his first poems appeared in *Poetry* magazine, Ashbery credited Eliot with introducing "the idea that the everyday world is part of the province of poetry," though he cautioned that Eliot's poetry "remains allusive and refined, lacking in the immediacy and concreteness which Auden gives to all that he touches" (quoted in John Shoptaw, *On the Outside Looking Out: John Ashbery's Poetry* [Cambridge, 1994], 132). Auden's work does not stand opposed to Eliot's in this formulation; Auden capitalizes on an aspect of Eliot's work just as Ashbery extends both Auden's and Eliot's in turn.

More sensitive to the complex nature of Ashbery's Eliotic inheritance are Fred Moramarco, who in "The Lonesomeness of Words: A Revaluation of *The Tennis Court Oath*," points out the many Eliotic aspects of "Our Youth" (*Beyond Amazement: New Essays on John Ashbery*, ed. David Lehman [Ithaca, 1980], 150-62); and Mary Kinzie, who suggests in *The Cure of Poetry in an Age of Prose* (Chicago, 1993) that however similar Ashbery's and Eliot's use of disjunction may be, Eliot's lines are held together by a consistent tone (243).

7. Robert von Hallberg, ed., *Politics and Poetic Value* (Chicago, 1987), 256-57. Vernon Shetley offers a perceptive analysis of this and other critiques in *After the Death of Poetry: Poet and Audience in Contemporary America* (Durham, 1993), 146.

8. Ashbery, "Tradition and Talent," *Book Week* 4 September 1966: 14.

9. Ashbery, *Reported Sightings*, 393.

10. Eliot, "Modern Tendencies in Poetry," *Shama'a* 1 (April 1920): 12.

11. Stephen Koch, "Performance Without a Net," *Nation* 24 April 1967: 526.

12. Ashbery, "The Impossible," *Poetry* 90 (1957): 252; "Second Presentation of Elizabeth Bishop," *World Literature Today* 51 (1977): 10.

13. Peter Stitt, "The Art of Poetry XXXIII: John Ashbery," *Paris Review* 90 (1983): 58; A. Poulin, "The Experience of Experience: A Conversation with John Ashbery," *Michigan Quarterly Review* 20 (1981): 245; Janet Bloom and Robert Losada, "Craft Interview with John Ashbery," in *The Craft of Poetry: Interviews from The New York Quarterly*, ed. William Packard (Garden City, 1974), 124; Ashbery, "In the American Grain," *New York Review of Books* 22 February 1973: 4. A similarly mimetic logic is often used to justify the most elaborately disjunctive poetry: see Fredric Jameson's reading of Bob Perelman's "China" (*Postmodernism, or, The Cultural Logic of Late Capitalism* [Durham, 1991], 30).

14. Kenneth Koch, "A Note on This Issue," *Locus Solus* 2 (Summer 1961): 196.

15. O'Hara to Ashbery, 7 January 1960, in Shoptaw, *On the Outside Looking Out*, 55.

16. Shoptaw, *On the Outside Looking Out*, 43.

17. Richard Kostelanetz, "How to Be a Difficult Poet," *New York Times Magazine* 23 May 1976: 24. "Clepsydra," collected in *Rivers and Mountains*, was actually written after "Fragment," the long poem later collected in *The Double Dream of Spring*.

18. Ashbery, "Reverdy en Amérique," 111 (my translation). Perloff has argued in favor of this effort; see *The Poetics of Indeterminacy*, 255, and *Frank O'Hara: Poet Among Painters* (Austin, 1977), 124.

19. Ashbery, "The Decline of the Verbs," *Book Week* 18 December 1966: 5.

20. Ashbery, *Reported Sightings*, 302.

21. Ross Labrie, "John Ashbery: An Interview," *American Poetry Review* 13 (May 1984): 33.

22. Charles Altieri, *Self and Sensibility in Contemporary American Poetry* (New York, 1984), 132. Altieri recognizes that the self-conscious rhetoric he admires in Ashbery might be found in all poems, but he maintains that Ashbery (in contrast to Yeats) is distinguished by his *intention* to display the slippage of metaphor (150).

23. John Koethe, *The Late Wisconsin Spring* (Princeton, 1984), 30. Koethe also addresses this question in his excellent critique of Language poetry: "Contrary Impulses: The Tension between Poetry and Theory," *Critical Inquiry* 18 (1991): 64–75.

24. Ashbery, "In the American Grain," 4.

SEVEN   AMY CLAMPITT'S UNITED STATES

Quotations from Clampitt's poems are from *Multitudes, Multitudes* (New York, 1973); *The Isthmus* (New York, 1981); *The Kingfisher* (New York, 1983); *What the Light Was Like* (New York, 1985); *Archaic Figure* (New York, 1987); *Westward* (New York, 1990); *A Silence Opens* (New York, 1994).

1. Moore, *Complete Prose*, ed. Patricia Willis (New York, 1986), 321–22. Moore quotes from James's *Notes of a Son and Brother* (New York, 1914), 366–68.

2. Clampitt, *Predecessors, Et Cetera* (Ann Arbor, 1991), 70.

3. Eliot, "In Memory of Henry James," *Egoist* 5 (1918): 2.

4. Clampitt, *Predecessors*, 5.

5. Louis Simpson, "Dead Horses and Live Issues," *Nation* 24 April 1967: 520.

6. Clampitt, *Predecessors*, 17.

7. Auden, "Address on Henry James," *Gazette of the Grolier Club* 7 (1947): 224.

8. Frank T. Clampitt, *Some Incidents in My Life: A Saga of the "Unknown" Citizen* (Ann Arbor, 1936), 122. In "Lasting the Night," in *Where We Stand: Women Poets on Literary Tradition*, ed. Sharon Bryan (New York, 1973), Clampitt said that her grandfather "left a poignant record,

whose importance to me can scarcely be exaggerated, of anxiety amounting almost to terror" (28).

9. Henry James, *Hawthorne* (New York, 1879), 42–43. See Richard Poirier's discussion of this passage in *A World Elsewhere* (New York, 1966), 101–106. Even more skeptical of the logic of modernist exile is James Buzard in "Eliot, Pound, and Expatriate Authority," *Raritan* 13 (1994): 106–22.

10. Laura Fairchild, "Amy Clampitt: An Interview," *American Poetry Review* 16 (July 1987): 19.

11. Judson Brown, "Out of Iowa: A Literary Nomad Encamps Here," *Daily Hampshire Gazette* 17 June 1987: 25.

12. See J. D. McClatchy, *White Paper: On Contemporary American Poetry* (New York, 1989), 318. Clampitt discusses her first memory (and many other aspects of her Iowa upbringing) in "Providence," in *Townships*, ed. Michael Martone (Iowa City, 1992), 31–37.

13. Clampitt, *Predecessors*, 164.

14. See Walter Jackson Bate, *John Keats* (Cambridge, 1963), 383, 617.

15. Robert von Hallberg, *American Poetry and Culture, 1945–1980* (Cambridge, 1985), 91.

16. Clampitt, *Predecessors*, 164. Bonnie Costello also discusses the implications of these remarks in "Amy Clampitt: Nomad Exquisite," *Verse* 10 (1993): 34–46.

17. Pound, "Pastiche: The Regional VIII," *New Age* 25 (1919): 300.

EIGHT   RICHARD HOWARD'S MODERN WORLD

Quotations from Howard's poems are from *Quantities* (Middletown, 1962); *The Damages* (Middletown, 1967); *Untitled Subjects* (New York, 1969); *Two-Part Inventions* (New York, 1974); *Fellow Feelings* (New York, 1976); *Lining Up* (New York, 1983); *No Traveller* (New York, 1989); *Like Most Revelations* (New York, 1994).

1. Howard, "Reflections on a Strange Solitude," *Prose* 1 (1970): 90–91.

2. James Wright, *Collected Prose*, ed. Anne Wright (Ann Arbor, 1983), 174.

3. Howard, "Dear Allen," *New York Times Book Review* 4 April 1971: 18.

4. Howard, *Alone With America*, enlarged ed. (New York, 1980), 548.

5. Peter Sacks, "The Divine Translation: Elegiac Aspects of *The Changing Light at Sandover*," in *James Merrill: Essays in Criticism*, ed. David Lehman and Charles Berger (Ithaca, 1983), 160. This essay offers a useful summary of Sacks's argument in *The English Elegy: Studies in the Genre from Spenser to Yeats* (Baltimore, 1985). See also Jahan Ramazani, *Poetry of Mourning: The Modern Elegy from Hardy to Heaney* (Chicago, 1994).

6. Sanford Friedman, "An Interview with Richard Howard," *Shen-*

*andoah* 24 (1972): 22. In an excellent survey of Howard's career, "The Master of Voices," *New Republic* 27 March 1995, Robert Boyers points out that the difference between monologue and lyric is, in Howard's case, "a difference in strategy rather than a difference in motive"; even when the poems "are written in what we take to be the first-person voice of the poet, we are apt to hear a range of voices, swelling, complicating and informing the music" (40, 39).

7. Howard, "A Career in Consciousness," *Nation* 18 January 1965: 63–64.

8. Howard, "Marianne Moore and the Monkey Business of Modernism," in Joseph Parisi, ed., *Marianne Moore: The Art of a Modernist* (Ann Arbor, 1990), 3.

9. David Bergman, *Gaiety Transfigured: Gay Self-Representation in American Literature* (Madison, 1991), 46. More productively, Bergman recognizes Howard's anti-Oedipal relationship to his precursors (especially Crane). See also Robert Martin, *The Homosexual Tradition in American Poetry* (Austin, 1979), 196–202.

10. Judith Butler, *Gender Trouble: Feminism and the Subversion of Identity* (New York, 1990), 31.

11. Howard, "An Outward Movement," *The New Leader* 6 December 1965: 27. In "Five Poets," *Poetry* 101 (1963), Howard commended Sexton for having "in Mr. Lowell's choppy wake, restored to our poetry . . . the lyric of self-dramatization that had hidden out in the novel" (413).

12. Howard, "Fragments of a 'Rodin,'" *Shenandoah* 22 (Autumn 1971): 3–6.

13. See Richard Ellmann, *Oscar Wilde* (New York, 1988), 170–72.

14. Robert Richman, "A Chronicle of Vanishings," *New Criterion* 8 (1989): 77.

### NINE   ROBERT PINSKY'S SOCIAL NATURE

Unless noted otherwise, quotations from Pinsky's poems are from *The Figured Wheel: New and Collected Poems, 1966–1996* (New York, 1996).

1. Pinsky, *Poetry and the World* (New York, 1988), 78–79.

2. Howard, "Art or Knack?" *Poetry* 129 (1977): 228.

3. Pinsky, *Poetry and the World*, 98.

4. Pinsky in *Contemporary Authors Autobiography Series*, ed. Adele Sarkissian (Detroit, 1986), 4: 245.

5. Pinsky, *Poetry and the World*, 137–38.

6. Pinsky, "The Idiom of the Self: Elizabeth Bishop and Wordsworth," in *Elizabeth Bishop and Her Art*, ed. Lloyd Schwartz and Sybil P. Estess (Ann Arbor, 1983), 49, 57.

7. Pinsky, "Said, and Unsaid," *Poetry* 122 (1973): 168.

8. Pinsky, "Far From Prose," *Poetry* 123 (1974): 241–42. This review was recast as pp. 162–69 of *The Situation of Poetry* (Princeton, 1976).

9. J. D. McClatchy, "Shapes of Desire," *New Republic* 24 Sept.

1990: 47. See also Willard Spiegelman, *The Didactic Muse: Scenes of Instruction in Contemporary American Poetry* (Princeton, 1989), 99–109.

10. Pinsky, *Poetry and the World*, 192.

11. Pinsky, *Poetry and the World*, 44. See also his remarks on movement in the "Translator's Note" to *The Inferno of Dante* (New York, 1994), xxiii.

12. Pinsky, *Poetry and the World*, 133.

13. Pinsky, *Poetry and the World*, 155-56.

14. Pound, *Literary Essays* (New York, 1968), 23.

## TEN   JORIE GRAHAM'S BIG HUNGER

Quotations from Graham's poems are from *Erosion* (Princeton, 1983); *The End of Beauty* (New York, 1987); *Region of Unlikeness* (Hopewell, New Jersey, 1991); *Materialism* (Hopewell, New Jersey, 1993); *The Errancy* (Hopewell, New Jersey, 1997).

1. Thomas Gardner, "An Interview with Jorie Graham," *Denver Quarterly* 26 (1992): 81.

2. Merrill, *Recitative*, ed. J. D. McClatchy (San Francisco, 1986), 162, 161; *A Scattering of Salts* (New York, 1995), 88. See also Allen Grossman and Mark Halliday's fascinating remarks on the rise and fall of modernist ambition in *The Sighted Singer* (Baltimore, 1992), 28–57.

3. Gardner, "Interview," 81.

4. Bonnie Costello, "Jorie Graham: Art and Erosion," *Contemporary Literature* 33 (1992): 374.

5. Costello, "The Big Hunger," *New Republic* 27 January 1992: 36.

6. Helen Vendler, *Soul Says: On Recent Poetry* (Cambridge, 1995), 237. See also Mark Jarman, "The Grammar of Glamour: The Poetry of Jorie Graham," *New England Review* 14 (1992): 252-61.

7. Robert von Hallberg, ed., *Politics and Poetic Value* (Chicago, 1987), 267, 305. See also Terry Eagleton, *The Illusions of Postmodernism* (Cambridge, 1996): "It is not a question of denouncing closure as such, a universalist gesture if ever there was one, but of discriminating between its more enabling and more disabling varieties" (67).

8. Gardner, "Interview," 89.

9. Gardner, "Interview," 90.

10. Rilke, *Uncollected Poems*, trans. Edward Snow (New York, 1996), 219.

11. Vendler, *The Given and the Made* (Cambridge, 1995), 128–29.

12. See *The* Diario *of Christopher Columbus's First Voyage to America*, trans. Oliver Dunn and James E. Kelley, Jr. (Norman, Oklahoma, 1989), 203–207, 219–21 (entries for 6 and 12 December 1492). As Tzvetan Todorov suggests in *The Conquest of America*, trans. Richard Howard (New York, 1984), 34–50, Columbus usually takes every opportunity to comment on the natives' skin color; however, in these entries he does not. The only time snow is mentioned (14 November 1492) is when Colum-

bus notes that high mountains are *not* snow-covered. Graham also concludes "Concerning the Right to Life" with a passage derived from Columbus's *Diario* (23 October 1492), and she offers suggestive comments about the linguistic ramifications of the discovery of the New World in her introduction to *Earth Took of Earth: 100 Great Poems of the English Language* (New York, 1996).

13. Emerson, *Complete Works*, 12 vols. (Boston, 1903), 1: 111.

14. Bishop, *One Art: Letters*, ed. Robert Giroux (New York, 1994), 597.

15. Charles Bernstein, *Content's Dream: Essays 1975–1985* (Los Angeles, 1986), 222. John Palattella points out this connection between Bishop and Bernstein in "After Such Knowledge, Knowledge Is What You Know," *Contemporary Literature* 35 (1994): 791. See Graham's remarks on Bishop in Gardner, "Interview," 97–98.

16. Langdon Hammer, "Working Through Poems: An Interview with John Hollander," *Southwest Review* 80 (1995): 427–28.

17. Graham, *Earth Took of Earth*, xvii.

# INDEX

197

*Weary's Castle*, 11–13, 17–18, 56–58, 177n1; "The Mills of the Kavanaughs," 58, 60; *Near the Ocean*, 181n37; "The Quaker Graveyard in Nantucket," 12; "Skunk Hour," 9, 19; "Where the Rainbow Ends," 57; "Words for Hart Crane," 16–17
Lyotard, Jean-François, 180n17

McCarthy, Mary, 23, 37, 39, 184n8
McClatchy, J. D., 111, 149
McGann, Jerome, 87, 165, 179n15
McGowan, John, 180n17
MacNeice, Louis, 39
Maeterlinck, Maurice 132–33
Mann, Thomas, 23
Mariani, Paul, 178n8
Marshall, Margaret, 52
Martin, Robert, 193n9
Marx and Marxism, 37, 51, 61, 69. *See also* Communism, American
Matthiessen, F. O., 7
Mazzaro, Jerome, 178n8
Menand, Louis, 183n3
Meredith, William, 9
Merrill, James, 122–23, 156, 160–61, 175; "Overdue Pilgrimage to Nova Scotia," 161; *The Changing Light at Sandover*, 161, 175
Merwin, W. S., 6, 86
Michaelson, Bruce, 56
Millay, Edna St. Vincent, 183n6
Millier, Brett, 183n3
Milton, John, 71, 79–80, 113
modernism, 3–6, 8–14, 20–21, 175–76; Bishop and, 22–24, 33–34; Eliot and, 3, 5–10, 33–34, 65, 87; Graham and, 160–62, 166,

170, 175–76; Howard and, 130–31, 135, 138–39; Jarrell and, 3–4, 10–13, 20–21, 55–56, 62, 139; Lowell and, 5–7, 11–13, 17; New Critics and, 4–6, 14, 51; Pinsky and, 142–43; politics of, 8–10, 33–34, 87–88; postmodernism and, 3–5, 20–21, 33–34, 87–88, 141–42, 160–62; romanticism and, 3, 10–11; varieties of, 3, 177–78n1; Wilbur and, 65–66, 83–84. *See also* antimodernism, breakthrough narrative, postmodernism
Monet, Claude, 137
Monroe, Jonathan, 189n6
Moore, Marianne, 3, 10, 156, 161; Ashbery and, 92, 104; Bishop and, 22, 25–27, 36, 39–40, 73–74, 182n1; Clampitt and, 102–103, 105, 107, 120; First World War and, 73–74; "Henry James as a Characteristic American," 102; Howard and, 124, 131–32; Jarrell and, 25–26, 51, 59; "The Octopus," 104; *Poems*, 73; "Reinforcements," 73–74; Wilbur and, 66–67, 72–74, 76, 82
Moramarco, Fred, 190n6
Morgan, Robin, 36
Morris, Jane, 129–30, 132
Moss, Stanley, 88

*Nation* (New York), 52, 86–87, 90, 97
New Criticism, 66, 67, 88; Ashbery and, 7, 86, 94; breakthrough narrative and, 5–6, 9–10, 12–13; Crane and, 13–16, 23, 54, 143; Eliot and, 7–8, 14–16, 34, 130, 160–61;